The New Brooklyn

The New Brooklyn

What It Takes to Bring a City Back

Kay S. Hymowitz

ROWMAN & LITTLEFIELD
Lanham • Boulder • New York • London

Published by Rowman & Littlefield
A wholly owned subsidiary of The Rowman & Littlefield Publishing Group, Inc.
4501 Forbes Boulevard, Suite 200, Lanham, Maryland 20706
www.rowman.com

Unit A, Whitacre Mews, 26-34 Stannary Street, London SE11 4AB

Distributed by NATIONAL BOOK NETWORK

British Library Cataloguing in Publication Information Available

Library of Congress Cataloging-in-Publication Data

Names: Hymowitz, Kay S., 1948- author.
Title: The new Brooklyn : what it takes to bring a city back / Kay S. Hymowitz.
Description: Lanham : Rowman & Littlefield, [2017] | Includes bibliographical references and index.
Identifiers: LCCN 2016040320 (print) | LCCN 2016045386 (ebook) | 9781442266575 (cloth) | ISBN 9781442266582 (ebook)
Subjects: LCSH: Brooklyn (New York, N.Y.)—History. | Brooklyn (New York, N.Y.)—Social conditions. | Brooklyn (New York, N.Y.)—Economic conditions. | Community development—New York—New Yok (State) | Urban policy—New York—New Yok (State) | Urban renewal—New York—New York (State)
Classification: LCC HN80.B856 H96 2017 (print) | LCC HN80.B856 (ebook) | DDC 306.09747/23—dc23
LC record available at https://lccn.loc.gov/2016040320

Printed in the United States of America

Contents

Acknowledgments

$\mathscr{F}$or the past decade I've been the lucky beneficiary of the generosity of the William E. Simon Foundation. My deepest gratitude to Janice Riddell, Amy Allred, and most of all to Sara Fay Snider, Peter and Bill Simon, and the whole wonderful clan. It must be a rare thing for a donor to offer not only financial support but warmth, spiritedness, and humor.

At the Manhattan Institute, thanks to both Larry Mone and Vanessa Mendoza for allowing me to pursue what might have struck them initially— but hopefully no longer—as a dubious project. Bernadette Serton was an indispensible guide and advisor for the past several years. Brian Anderson, my editor at *City Journal*, has always been thoughtful, even-tempered, and gracious. He significantly improved several articles that eventually made their way into this book, just as he did my previous books. Thanks also to Paul Beston, Matthew Hennessy, Karen Marston, Dan Cleary, Howard Husock, Dean Ball, Alex Armlovich, Stephen Eide, Aaron Renn, Robert Sherwood, Michele Jacob, Leigh Harrington, Pete Pappas, Mike Dotsikas, and that Houdini of copy editors, Janice Myerson. Finally, Jonathan Sisk at Rowman & Littlefield gave *The New Brooklyn* a felicitous publishing home for which I will always be grateful.

Many friends, contacts of friends, and assorted strangers helped guide me to sources and flesh out my understanding of a place that was so much bigger and more varied than I realized when I started this book. I want to thank—in no particular order—Bob Begleiter, Diana Lopez, Jim Rutenberg, Paul Mak, Bernie Graham, Frank Seddio, Fred Siegel, Jan Rosenberg, Steven Raphael, Chris Vecchione, Norm Oder, Nicole Gelinas, Robert Cherry, Angela Rachidi, Jennifer Senior, Anne Heller, Erasma Monticciolo, Phil Kasinitz, Nancy Foner, Yang Chen, Tucker Reed, Jon Askin and Paul Gangseii, Naomi Schaeffer Riley, Kathleen Vance, Ron Shiffman, Orly Clerge, Peter Cove, Lee

Bowes, Dan Berner, Lenore Berner, Tom Mariano, and Marc Rosenbaum. Note to the overlooked: please take it as a sign of less-than-perfect notes taken over many years, not ingratitude.

Thanks as always to my husband Paul Hymowitz for his love, endurance, and indispensible sense of humor.

Introduction

$\mathcal{I}$n 1982, I moved with my husband and our two young children into a partially renovated brownstone in the Park Slope neighborhood of Brooklyn. We were part of a small but growing group of young college-educated parents arriving in the zip code just thirty minutes by subway from Manhattan, stripping the graying varnish from mahogany woodwork, replacing linoleum kitchen counters with butcher block (before granite was vogue), gossiping with neighbors about local schools while our children raced up and down the scarred sidewalks and climbed the century-old stoops.

Living in the fraying house next door to us was an elderly Irish couple, a retired postal worker and his wife, who had served meals to a revolving population of boarders during the 1960s and 1970s while raising their children, who were now grown and living on Long Island. Immigrants like these had given Brooklyn its stolid working-class identity and its onetime nickname, the "Borough of Homes and Churches."

We newcomers knew of Saint Xavier only because it sponsored our children's little-league teams, but it remained the religious and community center to our white working-class neighbors who celebrated Saint Patrick's Day with dancing and corned beef, in smoke-filled pubs like Mooney's on Seventh Avenue. Little did I know at the time that I was a harbinger of a New Brooklyn, about to all but swallow up our neighbors' old version.

In truth, Old Brooklyn was in big trouble way before we moved there. Near Park Slope was a more notorious Brooklyn—and it was too close for comfort for some newcomers, who packed their belongings into the family Volvo for a one-way trip to New Jersey or Westchester. When my children went to overnight camp in Maine in the late 1980s and revealed where they were from, suburban bunkmates would respond, "Brooklyn?! Have you ever been shot?" They hadn't, I'm relieved to say, but they had to learn "street smarts" to spy the punks intent on pushing them to the concrete in order to relieve them of their backpacks or simply to impress their friends.

Though it was only five blocks away, we rarely took the R train because it meant crossing Fifth Avenue, where the cashiers in liquor and secondhand stores sat inside bulletproof cages for protection against drug-fueled thugs. Less than a mile to the northwest was Myrtle Avenue (aka "Murder Avenue"), winding ominously through crime-ridden Fort Greene, Clinton Hill, and the legendary black ghetto Bedford-Stuyvesant ("Do or Die" Bed-Stuy). Along the waterfront of the East River from the Brooklyn Bridge, past Williamsburg, lay the abandoned hulks of industry uninhabited except by a few squatters and the occasional dead body dumped by henchmen of the Gambino or Genovese crime families. Unless they were the discarded artifacts of an exotic past, there were no lattes or café mochas, no sushi bars or Thai restaurants, no retro Edison bulbs, ironic Buddy Holly eyeglasses, or rooftop bars in the vicinity. There sure wasn't any "Brooklyn Brewery," now one of the largest craft-beer companies in the country. Why would any company want to associate its products with a place so forlorn, so forgotten, so *not* aspirational?

And then, at the risk of understatement, Brooklyn changed. The older immigrant population moved or passed away, and the criminals either altered their professions or "went upstate." Liquor-store owners dismantled the Plexiglas, added picture windows, and held weekly tastings of their Italian and French wine selections. Mooney's Pub became a boutique selling skinny distressed jeans for $175. The house next door to me belonging to the Irish couple, vacant for nearly a decade after a terrible fire, was purchased, divided, and turned into condominium apartments, which, over subsequent years, would house an architect and his furniture-designer wife, an editor for *Real Simple* and her music-journalist husband, and a Wall Street trader whose wife was a freelance writer staying home with their three children.

Now bankers and celebrities seek out Park Slope and nearby neighborhoods and pay millions for brownstones that a previous generation saw as rubble from a lost era. Developers can't build residential towers fast enough to keep up with the crush of people wanting Brooklyn apartments. As of 2015, the Census Bureau estimated the borough's population at 2,637,735,[1] an increase of over 400,000, or 20 percent, since 1980.[2] Private-sector employment grew by almost 20 percent between 2003 and 2012, nearly two times as fast as the rest of New York City.[3] Many of those jobs have been created by entrepreneurs who have proudly branded themselves with the name Brooklyn: Brooklyn Winery, Brooklyn Gin, Brooklyn Brine, Brooklyn Cured, Brooklyn Roasting Company, Brooklyn Industries. All over the country, Americans are drinking Brooklyn Brewery beer, wearing Brooklyn T-shirts and baseball caps; they're even naming their babies "Brooklyn."

Bizarre as it seems to veterans of the crack-and-mugging "Crooklyn" era, Brooklyn has taken on the aura of an internationally shared urban fantasy.

Condé Nast spreads promise glorious travel weekends in Bed-Stuy and Green-point.[4] Tour buses the size of ocean liners glide down the streets of brownstone neighborhoods. There's a Brooklyn Brewery in Stockholm and one planned for Trondheim, Norway, and the brew itself is sold in just about every city meriting a *Lonely Planet* guide. There's a Brooklyn Bowl (a combined bowling alley, restaurant, and concert venue) in London and Las Vegas. Brooklyn Industries has outposts in Philadelphia, Chicago, and Portland, Oregon; São Paolo has a Brooklyn Restaurant; Tokyo, a Brooklyn Parlor jazz club; Dubai, a Brooklyn Diner; Helsinki and Ljubljana (Slovenia), a Brooklyn Café. The number of places with a "Brooklyn Bar" could make up a hipster geography game: Toronto, Reykjavik, Madrid, Copenhagen, Oslo, Budapest, Buenos Aires, Istanbul, Hamburg, and Berlin. The fabled Parisian department store Bon Marché celebrated "Brooklyn Mania" in the fall of 2015 with an exhibit called "Brooklyn: Rive Gauche" (Brooklyn: Left Bank), selling products either made in Brooklyn or seeming as though they could be worn or eaten by a Brooklynite . . . at least, a Parisian's idea of a Brooklynite.

This book will explore how, against all odds and predictions, a seventy-one-square-mile flatland wedged between the East River, the New York harbor, and the Atlantic Ocean, a left-for-dead city marinated in more than a century of industrial soot, a cultural and economic peasant enviously eyeing the seigneur just across the East River, became just about the coolest place on earth and the paragon of the postindustrial, creative city. It's a story that contains plenty of New York gumption, innovation, and aspiration. Brooklyn now boasts a splendid population of postindustrial and creative-class winners. But in the east and south of the borough, where nary a hipster or celebrity can be found, it is home to a much larger population of immigrants and minority poor whose futures are far less promising and, in many cases, outright bleak.

Like all cities, Brooklyn has a unique history, demography, and geography that have defined its present. Yet the changes it has undergone over the past three decades or so are reshaping cities and ways of life all over the developed world. From London to Copenhagen, Sydney to Philadelphia, Vancouver to Washington, D.C., Stockholm to Paris, college-educated young singles and professionals have decided that they want to ride their bikes, sip their espressos, stare at their laptops, and raise their children in cities. To house them, these cities have repurposed old buildings and built new ones. Condos and rental apartments are sprouting up everywhere—in razed or vacant lots in Brixton in the southern section of London, in renovated factories in Amsterdam-Noord, in warehouses in Toronto's "Little Portugal," and in churches in the Wicker Park section of Chicago. To feed and entertain them, young entrepreneurs are opening up farm-to-table and fusion restaurants in Atlanta, music clubs in the Tenderloin area of San Francisco, art galleries in Melbourne's Fitzroy district, and creating a global coffee culture of proportions that must bewilder the Folgers generation.

Any serious reckoning with the metamorphosis of Brooklyn and its fellow prospering cities has to begin with this elemental fact: over the past thirty years, advanced nations have been in the grip of a profound economic shift from an industrial to a knowledge economy. The transformation provides a textbook example of the Austrian economist Joseph Schumpeter's idea of "creative destruction." Economies evolve, Schumpeter proposed, only as industry and technology upend a preexisting order. Creative destruction has led to higher living standards, better health, and new, safer, and more interesting ways of working. But it has also destroyed whole industries—in the process, ruining companies, damaging lives, and sometimes, though the economist didn't dwell on it, fracturing communities.

Looking at cities like Brooklyn, the destruction part of creative destruction is easy enough to grasp. One by one, the paint and shoe factories, the slaughterhouses, meatpacking companies, sugar refineries, breweries, and dockworks that had added to the congestion, dirt, and harshness of city living have closed their doors and moved to cheaper, more spacious (and less highly taxed) industrial parks—and eventually, overseas to cheaper Third World countries. Jobs moved as well—at least, those that weren't already disappearing altogether into the claws of robots.

The effect on the urban industrial economy that had sustained and grown both cities and their working-class population for more than a century was calamitous. Deindustrialization came earlier to New York than to other American cities.[5] The city's blue-collar workforce reached its peak in 1950, when Brooklyn boasted a major share of New York City's 1 million manufacturing jobs. By 2000, those jobs had dwindled to 43,000. Ten years later, a mere 20,000 were left. Brooklyn's experience was repeated in industrial cities all over. Between 1970 and 1987, Chicago, the "Windy City" where immigrants once toiled in the stockyards and steel mills, lost a quarter of its million manufacturing jobs. Many European cities have suffered the same fate: Copenhagen lost almost half[6] of its manufacturing jobs in the 1970s as shipping's container revolution decimated its traditional port business. Since the 1970s, Amsterdam has watched its Amstel and Heineken breweries, a large Ford plant, all of its toy factories, and many other industries shut their doors.

That low-skilled workers were losing their livelihoods in once-vibrant manufacturing cities was bad enough; worse was that anyone with any money or hope was scared off from living or investing in many neighborhoods. Populations fled from urban centers that seemed on the verge of collapse. In both Brooklyn and the Bronx, things were so bleak that there was talk about letting some areas revert to farmland. "Will the Last One Leaving Seattle Turn Out the Lights?" a 1971 airport billboard read. It was a stunt that would have had people nodding in recognition, especially in cities in North America where the suburbs had become the highly preferred middle-class destination.

Less well understood is the creative part of Schumpeter's useful paradox, for, as it happened, the lights not only stayed on; they brightened. At the same time that manufacturing companies were fleeing urban areas, new life was percolating in the "knowledge" and (later) "creative" sectors. Knowledge jobs are those that rely on abstract information rather than physical labor or low-skill, often rote, activity. The knowledge economy also appeared earlier to New York than in other cities. By the 1960s, jobs in finance, law, management, media, and government were all in growth mode; by the 1990s, the nonprofit, design, and technology sectors were also expanding. Just as the industrial labor market was aging out, a postindustrial job sector was being born.

The high-paying urban knowledge economy produced dramatic changes in domestic life that also helped reverse the decline of many cities. First, as the name suggests, the knowledge economy demands higher levels of education from its workers, as well as early career training in the form of internships and associate positions. Years of grad school and early career apprenticeships were leading men and women to delay marriage and parenthood until they were well into their twenties and thirties. These educated singles, who don't need much living space and don't much care about their school district's test scores, gravitated to center cities that had everything that they needed: a dense labor market, bars, clubs, art galleries, and similarly educated peers.

Second, knowledge-economy jobs in media, design, law, education, and health services were proving especially appealing to educated women—even after they became mothers. While a lot of young knowledge-economy workers are drawn back to the suburbs once they start families and begin to take notice of their local public school's performance, others are unwilling to tolerate the hour-long commute that worked well enough for their own fathers, who were often the single breadwinning parent. They want to live where they work—if they can afford it.

The result is "gentrification," a form of creative destruction that is as hated as it is misunderstood. It's a word that will appear frequently in the following pages. This book tries to disentangle it from the many related ideas with which it is sometimes confused: displacement, foreign investment capital, rezoning, inequality, racial animus, development, and renewal.

Strictly speaking, gentrification is the movement to lower-income urban neighborhoods of the large young educated class who used to settle in America's suburbs. In Brooklyn, the number of residents between the ages of twenty-five and thirty-four grew significantly faster between 2000 and 2012 than elsewhere in New York City; 43.8 percent of the residents within this age group had at least a bachelor's degree, second only to Manhattan. Between 2000 and 2005 alone, the number of college educated Brooklynites grew by 24 percent.[7] Most of those college grads gravitated to neighborhoods like Park Slope and Williamsburg in Brooklyn. Brooklyn was not the only attractive destination for this crowd, of course. In Seattle, 57.4 percent of the population over twenty-five now has a BA or higher; San Francisco comes in just a little lower, at 52.4 percent. Washington, D.C., has 52.4 percent.[8] Yet in the United States as a whole, only 30 percent of the population has a college degree.

It's easy enough to poke fun at the new class of urban folk, with their endless number of stock signifiers: bike lanes, artisanal pickles, pour-over coffee, slouchy wool caps, and statement facial hair. The industrial buildings retrofitted into workplaces, homes, restaurants, bars, and hotels are now the lingua franca of a new global aesthetic that is well on its way to becoming a cliché. Brooklyn has plenty of examples: the Liberty Warehouse on the Red Hook piers, once ringing with the shouts of longshoremen and stevedores, is now a $200-a-head event space for Brooklyn's martini-tippling yuppies and hipsters. The glossy brochure for a new residential building in Williamsburg promises "authentic [the money word among Brooklyn marketers] industrial loft living in this former rocket and plane parts factory." The same architectural design and earnest public-relations pitch permeates the early-twenty-first-century culture of Berlin, Copenhagen, and Amsterdam, not to mention Chicago, San Francisco, and Boston.

Still, the caricature misses something important. In the best tradition of American entrepreneurialism, the borough's educated newcomers are re-creating the city's identity as a postindustrial center. In the nineteenth century especially, Brooklyn buzzed with innovation: in its factories, the borough gave birth to products ranging from the significant to the convenient to the whimsical: the steel-wire suspension cables that gave us the Brooklyn Bridge and many bridges that followed, insulated wiring, the electric sign, packaged coffee, Sweet'n Low sweetener, the teddy bear, the hot dog. These entrepreneurs provided jobs for millions of poor Irish, German, Italian, Polish, and Jewish immigrants—whose children or grandchildren went on to become members of America's twentieth-century mass middle class.

Today's educated newcomers have brought with them the sort of creative dynamism that had largely disappeared from Brooklyn by the 1930s. The borough's industrial past endows their novel undertakings with a sense of possibility; they are, after all, standing on the shoulders of the borough's giants. Some of the new companies have moved into the very spaces built by the earlier generation of entrepreneurs. Greenpoint's Eberhard Faber Pencil Factory, for instance, has been tastefully (and sustainably) transformed into the headquarters of the crowdsourcing website Kickstarter. In Brooklyn's Navy Yard, where carpenters and welders built some of the U.S. Navy's biggest battleships, they have launched high-tech manufacturing ventures. In other abandoned and underused warehouses, especially along Brooklyn's "creative crescent" (the waterfront stretching from Sunset Park north through Dumbo, all the way up to Greenpoint on the Queens border) are 3-D printer, biotech, robotics, and digital design companies.

Suneris, to take just one of many examples, was founded by two NYU grads who rehabbed an old wood shop where they now manufacture their own discovery called Vetigel, a gel that stops bleeding in seconds. In 2015, the product was chosen by *Tech Insider*[9] as one of the forty most exciting innovations of the year. In shared offices in Williamsburg, in communal writers' spaces in Park Slope, or in cafés with Wi-Fi, other educated and cosmopolitan young urban arrivistes, alert to the changing economic realities and tastes spurred by globalization, have seized upon the possibilities opened up by the digital revolution.

Many of these young businesspeople are what I call "artist-entrepreneurs," artists of all kinds who, with the help of computers, have found a way to "pursue their passion projects" while making a decent living. There are boutique businesses selling clothing, jewelry, shoes, soap, and stationery, or making maps, shoes, knives, slate cutting boards, and so on. A stunning number of new businesses are centered on food: restaurants, wine bars, beer halls, tea shops, small-batch—or artisanal—chocolates, granola, pickles, mustards, syrups, and takeout dinners to service an educated, well-traveled population with an adventurous palate—and little time to cook.

Cities like Brooklyn now promise a lifestyle that would have seemed beyond the reach of all but a tiny 1 percent in previous generations. This is not to say that the gentrifiers don't work hard or that they are all getting rich designing websites or canning kimchi. Far from it. But the economy that they are helping to build gives them opportunities to make their cupcakes and eat them, too. Not so long ago, dining out was a treat reserved for birthdays and anniversaries; Sunday mornings were for going to church. Now, long Bloody Mary brunches, gallery openings, live music bars, and tête-à-têtes with friends or lovers over coffee and pastries are the right and ritual of every red-blooded educated twenty- and thirtysomething.

That's the good news, as they say. The transformation from an old to a new Brooklyn, from an industrial to a knowledge economy, and the attendant gentrification have not been nearly so kind to the urban working class and poor. Though you would never know it from the glossy spreads on farm-to-table restaurants and quirky fashion boutiques, almost a quarter of Brooklyn's population lives below the poverty line.[10] A similar number are on food stamps, while 32 percent have an income low enough to qualify for Medicaid.[11]

Travel south and east from the tourist-packed Williamsburg, and you'll find yourself in neighborhoods like Brownsville and East New York, where jobless men, decaying city housing projects, and gang shootings remain Situation Normal. Go hard to the south, and find newly arrived Chinese, living four to a room and working in near-feudal conditions. Along the major avenues traversing east from brownstone Brooklyn toward the Atlantic Ocean is a new generation of struggling immigrants from Pakistan, Afghanistan, Bangladesh, Haiti, Trinidad, and Jamaica, to name only a few departure points. Some 39 percent of Brooklyn's population is foreign-born, a number that continues to rise. Like most of Brooklyn's immigrants from long ago, they arrive dirt-poor.

In the past, an industrial city like Brooklyn could absorb the unschooled into a large network of manufacturing and port-related companies. These were dirty, tedious, and sometimes dangerous jobs, but you didn't need an education to get one. In places like Brooklyn, you didn't even need to speak the local language, and, well, these jobs were better than the ox-and-plow farming endured by their parents and grandparents.

The New Brooklyn's manufacturing sector is unlikely to perform the same service for the borough's less educated population. Traditional smokestack, assembly-line companies required workers by the hundreds or more; at its peak during World War II, the Navy Yard employed 17,000. Today's technologically sophisticated companies need only a small fraction of that number. Those jobs that do appear in the want ads tend to require skills that are not in the repertoire of the people most in need of work. Low-wage service jobs with few benefits and unpredictable hours—wait staff, food preparers, hospital orderlies, and janitors—are what's available now.

The plight of today's poor and low-skilled service class in urban centers, especially in American cities like Brooklyn, then, is the flip side of the prosperity of a new, well-fed educated class in a knowledge-based, high-tech economy. The latter has the education, networks, and "soft skills" to adapt to a turbulent, labyrinthine global knowledge economy; the former, without skills and, in many cases, without the English language, get the jobs at the bottom.

Gentrifying cities are likely to have an "hourglass economy," and the phenomenon is especially pronounced in the United States for a variety of reasons. Between 1970 and today, the share of low-income Americans has grown, and so has the share of upper-income Americans;[12] Stephen Rose of the Urban Institute estimates that in the past forty years, the upper middle class has grown from 13 percent to 29 percent of the population.[13] That's consistent with Brooklyn's transformation: in 2000, the borough had no census tracts that were considered rich. By 2010, it had two: Dumbo (the abbreviation for the neighborhood located "Down Under the Manhattan Bridge Overpass") and Brooklyn Heights. During the same decade, Brooklyn went from being a home to the four poorest tracts in New York to having five of them.[14]

The working class and poor are not only dealing with deteriorating job options but also with soaring rents and disorienting changes in their neighborhoods. Gentrification creates a seemingly unquenchable demand for housing in space already limited by rivers, oceans, or mountains; in metropolitan centers with a well-deserved fondness for history, like New York, Paris, and London, policymakers are even more confined by untouchable landmarks and historic districts. Brooklyn is far from alone in finding that the rising middle-class demand has led to the displacement of less affluent, longtime residents, to neighborhoods in flux, and to opportunities for real-estate developers, their political friends, and unscrupulous speculators that often provoke angry protests.

In Brooklyn, some of those who can no longer afford their old neighborhoods move to poorer areas in the East. Others move to inner suburbs around New York or to the American South. They are part of a much bigger shift that *Governing* editor Alan Ehrenhalt calls "the great inversion." Instead of the suburbs, center cities are now the aspirational home of an educated middle class, while lower-income residents, particularly immigrants, take their place in the suburbs.

All these trends have intensified economic and racial inequality and helped to revive concerns about immigration. In Brooklyn, they have also deepened worries of a particularly American cast: the endurance of black inner-city poverty and the fragile promise of upward mobility. Since the 1930s, Brooklyn has had a large population of poor African Americans. A majority of them first settled in formerly white middle-class brownstone neighborhoods of central Brooklyn. In the mid-twentieth century, they moved into the very different East New York and Brownsville, sections that had been called "slums" since the swampy areas of central and east Brooklyn were first developed in the mid-nineteenth century. Bedford-Stuyvesant has begun to see some gentrification—a striking amount of it fueled by the arrival of young, college-educated African Americans; but in their own way, all three neighborhoods provide a stark contrast to places like Park Slope and Williamsburg. They are also an illustration of the failure of policy, government, business and community leaders, and communities themselves to rise above America's racial history to produce the sort of upward mobility that benefited so many other poor Brooklynites in the past.

"Cities don't lure the middle class. They create it," Jane Jacobs once wrote. Jacobs was not prescient here; cities today *do* lure the middle class. But her assumption that cities incubated the middle class remains true at the beginning of the twenty-first century for some groups. New York City's current mayor, Bill de Blasio, famously lamented this "tale of two cities," one prosperous and one struggling. One lesson of Brooklyn's multifarious neighborhoods is that poverty is not one thing. In a number of the neighborhoods that have been missing in all the Brooklyn hype, the borough continues to create a middle class, as Jacobs put it. They are every bit as poor—and unskilled—as the African Americans in the housing projects of Brownsville; yet their social networks and traditions put the middle class within reach of their children.

No single book can give a comprehensive picture of the New Brooklyn, with its 2.6 million people—more than Boston, San Francisco, and Detroit combined. By necessity, the seven areas that I've chosen to study leave out some fascinating tales. Rezoning has made the sky the limit, literally, for downtown Brooklyn, radically transforming it from a mildly shabby, daytime retail district with courthouses and law offices into a twenty-four-hour business and commercial skyscraper district. The historically rich Coney Island, as well as many middle-class neighborhoods like Bay Ridge, the Victorian Ditmas Park, and immigrant Bensonhurst are also going through changes worth exploring. I focus on the fortunes of two immigrant groups—the Chinese of Sunset Park and the Jamaicans of Canarsie—in part because they are the two largest in Brooklyn but also because they offer insight into the possibility of social and economic mobility today. That doesn't mean that there aren't other groups and neighborhoods with a great deal to teach: the Russian immigrants of Brighton Beach, the Mexicans of Sunset Park, the Hasidim of East Williamsburg, the West Indians of Crown Heights, and the Bangladeshis, now the borough's fastest-growing immigrant group, of Kensington.

Still, the parts of Brooklyn you'll read about in the following pages capture in microcosm the economic, demographic, and social forces behind the perplexing creative destruction of the more successful urban centers in today's advanced economies.

The Old Brooklyn, Part One

$\mathcal{H}$istory is not for the tenderhearted or the naïve. That's one lesson you learn from studying the past of any great city, and Brooklyn is no exception. From its first recorded years, Brooklyn's history has mirrored the "worst and best of times" moniker that we could apply to almost any period of American—indeed, to all human—history. Slavery, small-pox-infected natives, bigotry, violent gangs, ghettos, drug epidemics, inequality, dark Satanic mills, cholera, yellow fever, toxic land and waterways, greed—and harmful creative destruction: all have been part of the contradiction that is Brooklyn today.

But so, too, is Brooklyn a product of brilliant, even heroic, engineering feats, entrepreneurial verve and innovation, multiethnic tolerance, abolitionist fervor, philanthropic generosity, rags-to-riches striving, civic passion, opportunities for the poor unparalleled anywhere on earth—and thrilling creative destruction. Perhaps Rome is an Eternal City, but most places dense with human activity are always in flux—especially when a stream of migrants and new technologies churn up traditional ways of doing things. Like many other cities—American cities, in particular—Brooklyn has had plenty of the worst and the best.

BROOKLYN'S AGRICULTURAL AGE

Change first arrived quietly in the primeval, heavily forested, western tip of Long Island in the mid-seventeenth century, when several nondescript skiffs appeared on the western shore facing what we now call the East River. The boats were carrying a few adventurous Dutch families venturing out from New Amsterdam, a small settlement at the southern tip of today's Manhattan. The fertile land that they found was—inconveniently, from their point of view—occupied by the Canarsee Indians, a small tribe that was part of the larger

Lenape. In the face of the more worldly and crafty Dutch arrivals, "the wild people," as the settlers called them, didn't stand a chance. For "eight fathoms of duffle cloth, eight fathoms of wampum . . . twelve kettles," and a variety of tools,[1] the Dutch traded the land where the Canarsee had gathered berries, hunted game, and grown corn for untold generations. The transaction seemed peaceable enough, but the calm proved short-lived. Some Indians died in the inevitable skirmishes with the newcomers; others succumbed to diseases resulting from the sudden exposure to alien European microbes. The lucky ones made their way to the less disturbed land of eastern Long Island. Within fifty years after the Dutch arrival, the Brooklyn Canarsee, at least as a cohesive tribe, were no more.

The Dutch had good reason to covet the land that we now know as Brooklyn. With the rolling hills and lush forests between the East River and the Atlantic Ocean, as well as the Edenic bounty of game, fish, oysters, dolphins, and whales in the local waters, the area promised a thriving future for whoever was lucky enough to use it. By the mid-1600s, the small band of Dutch settlers had grown and spread widely enough to create five villages. The name Breuckelen, a town near Amsterdam, was bestowed on the hills and woods nearest the East River that would become Brooklyn Heights. Boswijck, meaning "little town in the woods," at the time encompassed the land we now call Bushwick, Williamsburg, and Greenpoint; Midwout, which would soon be renamed Flatbush; New Utrecht, at the very southwestern tip of Long Island that eventually became Bay Ridge; and Flatlands, the district along today's Jamaica Bay. A sixth village, Gravesend—including today's neighborhoods of Coney Island and Bensonhurst—had a different provenance. It was established in 1643 by Lady Deborah Moody, an English aristocrat and Anabaptist fleeing the persecution that she had encountered, ironically enough, among the religious freedom–seekers of the Massachusetts Bay Colony. She was not the only pilgrim to find the New York Dutch more tolerant than the Massachusetts colonists, as Russell Shorto notes in *The Island at the Center of the World*; but she was the first woman to do so and, as a result, the first woman to found a New World settlement.[2]

The Dutch presence also lives on in a few remaining farmhouses in Flatbush and Gravesend, one of them owned by the Lott family and another, legend has it, by Lady Moody herself. The ghosts of that Dutch era are also alive in names that still mark Brooklyn's street signs—Wyckoff, Schermerhorn, Boerum, Remsen, Bergen, Ditmas (originally Ditmars), and Cortelyou—as well as in the Dutch Reform churches in Park Slope, Flatbush, and Flatlands.

Still, actual Dutch rule turned out to have a short life span. By 1664, the New York Dutch ceded control to a more determined—and now larger—band of English colonists. New Amsterdam became New York, named for the

Duke of York (though its Indian name of Manhatta remained part of the local lexicon); the six original Dutch towns were brought under one jurisdiction called Kings County, in honor of the duke's brother, King Charles II. Its boundaries, just southwest of the congruently named Queens County, remain synonymous with the borough of Brooklyn today. Otherwise, the change of regime was remarkable for being a nonevent. The Dutch continued to go about their business, speaking their own language, following their own customs, and introducing a habit of live-and-let-live that has ever since defined Brooklyn at its best. It's fair to note, however, that this habit was made easier by the fact that Brooklyn remained sparsely inhabited for the next two centuries. Odd as it might seem to the contemporary mind, Brooklyn, one of the most renowned urban districts of the past century, was a quiet farm district for more years than it has been a city.

When they arrived in Brooklyn, the Dutch had faced a superhuman task. Clearing the hundreds of square miles of oaks, hemlocks, birches, the thick brush and bramble, and the numerous streams and marshes required muscle power far beyond that possessed by their motley crew. Some Dutch settlers pressed Indians into service to clear land and till fields, but soon the possibility of cheap, abundant labor presented itself to both the Dutch and English in the person of enslaved Africans.

It's worth lingering over this jarring fact: when you walk past the fine townhouses and churches of Brooklyn Heights, eat at a pizza joint in Bensonhurst, or wander through the art galleries of Bushwick, you are traversing land once tilled by African slaves—and a substantial number of them, given the small size of the white population. Flatbush and New Utrecht, the most rural of Brooklyn's towns, had a larger concentration of slaves than Virginia and the Carolinas. By the late 1600s, the population of Brooklyn was about two thousand people; about half of them were Dutch, and 15 percent of them slaves. One hundred years later, the percentage of the slave population had doubled, to 30 percent. In 1790, the first census survey found that 59 percent of white Brooklyn households had slaves; the more prominent the landowner, the more slaves he had.[3]

Memoirists and early historians have tried to soften these facts, assuring us that Brooklyn slavery was nowhere near as bad as the brutal institution then taking shape in Virginia.[4] Some have insisted that the Dutch were kinder than the English, that their households were smaller and more intimate;[5] others opine that no, the Dutch were far worse than the English. It may well be true that the Dutch interest in slaves remained strictly pragmatic—they simply needed more hands to clear and plant the land—than the southern version, where an entire economic base and aristocratic culture would evolve. Still, there is little doubt that Brooklyn's earliest civilization was built on the backs of enslaved Africans, many of them bought and sold by the Dutch India Company.

Heavy irony that it is, slavery was at its height in Brooklyn at the same time that locals were caught in the middle of the colonists' battle for freedom against King George III. Abandoning their outpost in Boston, the British set out to conquer New York, "the key to the whole continent."[6] As it happened, after camping on Staten Island, the British landed in Brooklyn—not, as expected, in New York. There, they fought the Continental Army in the first battle since the signing of the Declaration of Independence. Though well fortified, the colonists were outnumbered and, in the end, commanded by a young and inexperienced George Washington, who led them under cover of fog across the river to New York. In a further irony, the British forces included slave recruits from the West Indies who had been promised freedom for their service; they may have also had help from local slaves, though it's unlikely that would have affected the royal victory. Slavery certainly was not a major concern of the British; the entire area, including slave-owning households, remained under British occupation for the remainder of the war.

ON THE EARLY WATERFRONT

The next momentous turn in Brooklyn's story came after 1825, with the opening of the awesome (the overused contemporary word is appropriate here) Erie Canal. Though 200 miles away, the canal was one of the first of many examples of American technology and engineering—and the ridiculed visionaries who believed in them—to alter Brooklyn's path. Even the ingenious Thomas Jefferson laughed at the idea of a canal when it was first proposed, not that you could blame him. Building it, as historian Suzanne Spellen has written, meant excavating "363 miles, across wilderness, forests, swamps, mountains and valleys" and negotiating the 600-foot rise between Buffalo and Albany.[7] Its construction was one of the most important turning points in pre–Civil War America, second only to the Louisiana Purchase, and remains one of the great catalysts of creative destruction in U.S. history.

Understanding why the canal was so momentous means recalling a time before planes, trains, and automobiles, when water travel was the cheapest, most efficient means of transporting people, raw materials, and goods over long distances. By connecting the Hudson River and Lake Erie, it vastly eased transportation and communication between the middle of the United States and the East Coast and, by extension, Europe, the southern states, and the Caribbean. New York and Brooklyn couldn't have been better positioned, offering a final stop before the Atlantic Ocean and the wide world beyond.

Until that time, New York was an also-ran town, compared with its more sophisticated sisters to the south and north, Philadelphia and Boston; it was only the fifth-largest city in the young country. Within thirty years, thanks in large part to upstate's magnificent engineering feat, Manhattan, New York, was the kingpin of the expanding United States, and Brooklyn became its successful half-sibling.

The canal woke up the sleepy, rural Brooklyn of the seventeenth and eighteenth centuries in two ways. First, it brought cheap midwestern grain to the East Coast—grain prices plummeted by 90 percent within a year after the canal came online.[8] The falling prices destroyed the market for the wheat, barley, and corn that Kings County farmers had been growing until that time, but locals quickly adapted. Soon the fields of Gravesend, Utrecht, and Flatbush were full of cabbages, turnips, potatoes, and other fruits and vegetables to grace the tables of the populace in the thriving commercial city across the river, many of whom were themselves prospering because the canal had exploded opportunities for trade and finance, which, in turn, helped fund Brooklyn's coming industrialization.

Contemporary Brooklynites might be charmed by what appears to be a precursor to their own locavore preferences, but mid-nineteenth-century Brooklyn's agricultural economy was of a different order entirely. As late as the 1880s, Kings County was the second-largest provider of produce in the entire country; first, amazingly enough, was its immediate neighbor to the northeast, Queens County. At that time, in Brooklyn more than 400 farms covered 12,359 acres and produced $1.2 million a year in farm products.[9] You can still find old-timers who remember small farms near the East New York tenements where they spent their childhoods. It was only in 1949 that the *Brooklyn Eagle* reported the retirement of Brooklyn's "last farmer."[10]

The opening of the canal also changed Brooklyn's economic and geographic center of gravity. Even as the Erie Canal increased Brooklyn's stature as New York's breadbasket and created new markets and wealth, it also foretold its rural demise. Up until then, Brooklyn had largely faced inland toward its farms. Not that the waterfront didn't matter: in 1801, the U.S. Navy purchased and opened a shipyard that would eventually play a large role in the county's fortunes. But it had little impact on Brooklyn's economy during these early decades. And the Dutch farmers driving their cabbage- and potato-laden wagons up an Indian path known as "Ferry Road" had long depended on the sailboats and rowboats bound for Manhattan markets.

The interdependence of Manhattan and Brooklyn took a big step in 1814, when an engineer and inventor by the name of Robert Fulton started the first regular steam-ferry service in the nation. By surmounting some of the effects of the wind and currents, Fulton's ferry brought a new level of modern predictability to commuting by water. One result of his reliable, twelve-minute ferry ride across the East River to the Wall Street area of Manhattan was to transform Brooklyn Heights, as the area around the landing would come to be known, into one of the world's first suburbs as English merchants, financiers, professionals, and ship captains built homes away from the clamor of New York commerce. Another was to change Ferry Road into Fulton Street, thereby turning an ancient Indian path into what remains one of the primary east–west arteries in Brooklyn today.[11]

With the Erie Canal, activity at Brooklyn's port along the East River and south around New York Harbor expanded to include far more than Gravesend farmers and Brooklyn Heights burghers. Between the two, Manhattan and Brooklyn now had, in historian David McCullough's words, "one of the greatest concentrations of shipbuilding anywhere on earth."[12] By the mid-nineteenth century, there were "ships everywhere"; looking out from the Heights, you could see barges, tugs, schooners, pleasure yachts, and the South Ferry traveling between Brooklyn Heights and the southern tip of Manhattan.

If there was competition between the two cities for port prominence, as there surely was, Brooklyn had a chance of coming out on top. Brooklyn had a longer coastline to dock ships and far more space for storage. In Brooklyn, warehouses could be built right smack at the edge of the water, easing the movement of goods from ship to shore; the teeming Manhattan piers made such a convenience impossible. Warehouses for goods arriving from upstate before going abroad and vice versa sprouted up along the shoreline like so many Brooklyn cabbages. The area we now call Dumbo was so thick with the hulking buildings that it soon became known as "the walled city."

Another early Brooklyn creative destroyer, Daniel Richards, built the enormous Atlantic Basin and Docks in Red Hook. It had thirty-two granite storehouses and the area's first steam-powered grain elevator. Now instead of ropes and pulleys and backbreaking manpower, engines and a lift system could unload the grain from incoming ships.[13] It was mercifully efficient. Soon, small factories to service the boats and process the raw materials they carried in their holds appeared on Brooklyn's shores. Wheat arrived in Brooklyn and left as flour; cotton and wool became textiles; sealskins were cured and shaped into leather goods; coffee beans were ground into coffee. The new enterprises needed loans, means of exchange, and insurance; that meant more banks, finance companies, and law offices. One thing was clear: along the East River, at least, it wasn't your Dutch grandfather's Brooklyn anymore.

The ship traffic set loose by the Erie Canal didn't just bring raw materials to Brooklyn. It also brought people—floods of them. The swelling numbers of would-be Brooklynites inevitably challenged the district's rural identity—especially since industrial wages would prove to be higher than those paid for tilling and harvesting fields. In 1834, Kings County officially became a chartered city. (Twenty years later, the town of Williamsburgh would merge with the City of Brooklyn, though for unknown reasons, it lost the final *h* during the transition.) Brooklyn had started the nineteenth century with a mere 6,000 souls. By 1850, it had nearly 150,000.[14] Almost half the residents had been born overseas—half of them from Ireland and the rest mostly from Germany and England. The canal did not just change the economy of Brooklyn; it made it grow dramatically.

Brooklyn's Dutch and English culture changed with its growth. While the elite promenaded the emerging grid of streets in genteel Brooklyn Heights, the newly arrived Irish created the rough atmosphere of the commercial waterfront. "If the port made New York, the Irish made the port," writes James T. Fisher in *On the Irish Waterfront*.[15] Many of the dockworkers were refugees from the Great Hunger that immiserated the island between 1845 and 1849, a famine so cataclysmic that nearly 1.5 million people were willing to risk voyage to America on the too aptly named "coffin ships."[16] Most of the workers were desperately poor and more than willing to take the dangerous, miserably paid, erratic jobs on the piers of Red Hook and near the Navy Yard. Some of the earliest arrivals had dug the Erie Canal; nearly 500 of those following them built the Atlantic Docks, and many more simply did the more forgettable work of unloading cargo, repairing masts, and braiding ropes.[17]

Like urban migrants everywhere, the Brooklyn Irish huddled into enclaves. Theirs became informally known as "Irishtown," first near Red Hook and then in Vinegar Hill, conveniently close to the Navy Yard, where many of them worked.[18] Vinegar Hill might be thought of as Brooklyn's first urban ghetto, bearing all the familiar troubles that would infect East New York, Brownsville, and Bedford-Stuyvesant in later decades. The residents were "the most destitute people on earth at the time," according to one student of the period. Their clothes were filthy rags; shoes were an unknown luxury.[19] They lived in squalid shanties made of tarps and brush; there were no toilets, not even running water. Disease, especially cholera, was a frequent visitor, and so was virulent discrimination.[20] The newcomers were met with "No Irish Need Apply" signs at establishments looking for workers; there were frequent attacks on Catholic property and violent brawls with hostile locals.

Irishtown also suffered with its own version of a drug epidemic, complete with gangs, street murders, kingpins, and even military raids. The Irish had brought with them a thirst for both work and drink. At the neighborhood's peak in 1885, according to the Brooklyn researcher Rachel Dozell, 110 of its 666 retail outlets were liquor establishments. Most of them were saloons. Irish distilleries were one of Brooklyn's most productive early industries, some of them providing 100 gallons of whiskey a day. One by the name of Whiteford's was said to make 45,000 gallons of whiskey a week. The proximity of the waterfront gave the "industrialists" of Irishtown access to markets for whiskey up and down the eastern seaboard.

The problem that came to face the distillers was not the legality of producing whiskey but another legal requirement. The immigrant distillers, unfamiliar with, or perhaps indifferent to, the power of a modernizing central government—the United States had first introduced income taxes in 1862 to raise funds for the Civil War—were not especially interested in paying the heavy taxes on liquor. The scofflaws soon met the ire of the new Bureau of Internal Revenue, the precursor of the IRS, whose G-men might well have been peeved as much by the jewels and finery flaunted by the whiskey kingpins and their wives as they were by their lawbreaking. The "Whiskey Wars" between the Irish bootleggers and their local supporters, on the one hand, and the Brooklyn police and the U.S. military, on the other hand, soon commenced; it took two years to settle. In one predawn raid in 1869, 500 artillerymen stormed the area from the East River tugboat. The *New York Times* wrote on December 4, 1869: "The quantity of whiskey poured in the streets in its pure state will surly [*sic*] go a great way toward disinfecting the Fifth Ward even if it fails in reducing the rate if [*sic*] mortality. The general opinion relative to the streams of whiskey is that pouring it was the quickest way to settle disputes."[21]

THE INDUSTRIAL AGE

The Irish were not the only immigrants in the mid-nineteenth century to escape the hunger and dead-end lives of the Old Country by landing at Brooklyn's piers (the famous landing spot of Ellis Island was not in use until 1892). Nor were they the only immigrants to seek New World profits in chemical substances. In the early nineteenth century, a few Germans and Scandinavians had joined the Irish in Red Hook to work on the piers and warehouses. But the Germans really made their mark in the growing northern districts of Williamsburg, Greenpoint, and, most especially, Bushwick, where they became the prototype of contemporary Brooklyn's creative class.

Before the Germans arrived, Bushwick was still a largely rural village set on the banks of Newtown Creek, a tidal estuary dividing Queens County and Kings County. The first hint of its industrial future arrived when the famous Dutch inventor and Cooper Institute founder Peter Cooper founded the Cooper Glue Factory. Demonstrating the thrift and ingenuity of his Dutch ancestors, he made the glue out of the "waste of slaughter horses" according to a frank article in the *Brooklyn Eagle*.[22] Another Dutch descendant, Martin Kalbfleisch, who had studied chemistry as a boy in the Netherlands, started the

Brooklyn Chemical Works in nearby Greenpoint. Later, he would become mayor of Brooklyn and later still, a U.S. congressman. He is now buried in Brooklyn's landmark Greenwood Cemetery. When Kalbfleisch became dissatisfied with the glass containers holding his acids, he started the Bushwick Glass Works, later renamed Brookfield. Nearby in Williamsburg and a little later in 1849, two cousins, one named Charles Pfizer, became the first of a long line of German entrepreneurs to put their mark on the area. In 1849, they opened an even more successful chemical works, which became one of the largest pharmaceutical companies in the world—inventor of Zoloft, Lipitor, and Viagra, among other essential chemicals of modern life.

As important as these chemicals and factories were to North Brooklyn's emerging industrial identity, it's only a slight exaggeration to say that it was German beer that really made Bushwick famous. (It should be mentioned that with respect to beer making, Brooklyn's early creative class anticipated—and, in some ways, outperformed—today's artisanal masters.) German "lager" has a different fermentation process and a lighter texture than English ales familiar to most New Yorkers before then. From the moment that Samuel Liebman, a German Jew fleeing the displeasure of the king, and his three sons first began producing the unfamiliar brew in the 1850s, New Yorkers were ready to change their brand. Rheingold would reign as the queen of New York beers until the 1960s, though it was hardly the only one. By 1898, a twelve-block-long stretch of Bushwick had twelve breweries, hence the name "Brewer's Row." By 1898, the area was teeming with close to fifty.[23]

Another member of Brooklyn's nineteenth-century creative class, from a different background, had a hand in bringing one other addictive drink to the American people. In 1871, Scottish-born, Pennsylvania-raised John Arbuckle and his brother opened a plant near the Dumbo docks, where coffee beans arriving from South America were roasted, ground, and, in a brand-new process, packaged. Arbuckle's special roasting and packaging method—involving "[o]ne ounce of Irish moss; half an ounce of isinglass; half an ounce of gelatine; one ounce of white sugar; and twenty-four eggs"[24]—kept the coffee fresher and for far longer than the beans sold in the barrels customary at the time. His Ariosa—later called Yuban—was an immense success. By 1876, 75 percent of the coffee coming into the United States first arrived in Manhattan and Brooklyn. Even with plenty of competition, Arbuckle earned the name the "Coffee King," with eventual satellite offices in Kansas City, Chicago, Brazil, and Mexico, as well as ownership of sugar plantations and a fleet of boats to transport the beans. He even built a railroad track through Dumbo to transport his product to the piers.[25]

Between the raw materials arriving on ships from so many corners of the world, the Manhattan companies moving into Brooklyn for its cheaper, undeveloped land, and the pent–up entrepreneurial energy of immigrants from foreign shores as well as from less dynamic parts of New England and Pennsylvania, Brooklyn was leaving its agricultural past behind and becoming one of the country's premier industrial cities. Its factories were producing such a wide variety of goods that they would give archaeologists from a distant future considerable insight into the state of American material civilization at that time. In its North Brooklyn factories, Brooklyn's first-generation creative class developed new methods for manufacturing sugar, kerosene, packaged groceries, shoes, metal springs, soap, handkerchiefs, kitchenware, and steel wool, in addition to the coffee, beer, glue, and chemicals that we've already seen.

As the century came to a close, growing national affluence expanded the output of Brooklyn's industries well beyond basic domestic and maritime necessities. The city's industrialists adapted quickly to changing consumer tastes. Once a center of shipbuilding, Greenpoint was now fashioning items such as porcelain tea sets, doorknobs, pitchers, bowls, and glassware. A surprising number of the products manufactured at the time became enduring national consumer brands. In the 1870s, Robert Gair developed machines for manufacturing corrugated paper and folding boxes that became enormously popular for packaging dry goods such as flour, biscuits, and cereal. He needed so many buildings for his operation that part of Dumbo became known as "Gairville." In the 1880s, two brothers launched the brand that we know as Benjamin Moore, though—inexplicably, given the Brooklyn buzz—the brothers moved the factory to New Jersey before the turn of the century. The Eberhard Faber Pencil Factory started its industrial life in Greenpoint and went on to become one of the largest pencil manufacturers in the world. Vaseline was invented in Red Hook, Chiclets and the vending machine to sell them in Dumbo. Nearby, just west of Dumbo, was the home of the Drake factory, producer of Ring Dings, Devil Dogs, and Yodels (now part of Hostess Foods). Given what we'll see in later chapters, something in the Brooklyn water seems to nurture a sweet and savory tooth.

With jobs as plentiful as whiskey and coffee, an even larger crowd of immigrants made their way into Brooklyn in the 1880s and the decades following: Russian Jews, Italians, Poles, Hungarians, Swedes, Norwegians, Danes, and Finns. Unfortunately, industrial and waterfront jobs were often as dangerous as they were copious, though most immigrant job seekers were not in a position to be picky. Perhaps the most precarious and Dickensian positions were in sugar refineries, fast becoming one of Brooklyn's most vibrant sectors. Brooklyn had nearly twenty refineries, and by 1900, New York had become one of the biggest providers of refined sugar to the United States and, indeed, the world. The temperature of the boiling sugar regularly reached 140 degrees.

Skin and lung ailments were common, and so were boiler and dust explosions.[26]

The biggest refinery—in fact, for a while the largest in the world—was founded by the German-born Havemeyer brothers, one of whose sons, H. O. Havemeyer, became what architectural historian Francis Morrone called the "John D. Rockefeller of Sugar."[27] Despite the fortune that they made in Brooklyn and the thousands of local workers whose meager salaries they paid, the Havemeyers built their homes in Manhattan and Greenwich, Connecticut, and don't appear to have had much allegiance to Brooklyn or its laboring masses—notwithstanding the family's twenty plots in Greenwood Cemetery. Fortunately, they were not typical. Brooklyn's nineteenth-century industrialists used some of their great fortunes to bring the city charitable works as well as enduring beauty. They helped create Brooklyn's superb architectural legacy— notably, in Park Slope's Eighth Avenue and in Clinton Hill, just far enough up a hill from the Navy Yard to bring healthful breezes. By the 1840s, Clinton Hill had already become a fashionable "suburb" for well-to-do Manhattan commuters. Now Brooklyn's growing crowd of self-made millionaires turned it into the late-nineteenth-century version of Silicon Valley moguls' Atherton or Los Altos Hills. Though the offices of Underwood Typewriter were in Manhattan, the owner John Underwood's mansion was in Clinton Hill. Joining him were the Liebmans of the Rheingold Brewery, the Coffee King John Arbuckle, and the daughter of Pfizer cofounder Charles Erhart.

At a time when there was no such thing as welfare, reformed or otherwise, no such thing as public housing or food stamps or Social Security, Brooklyn's 1 percenters also played a role in making early industrial Brooklyn a more forgiving place for the poor and working class. John Jackson, a prosperous Vinegar Hill landowner and shipbuilder, may have been the first Brooklyn business owner to build housing for his workers on his property, which he did as early as the 1820s. Other business owners followed. City tenements like those in Brooklyn were often horrid places: overcrowded, windowless, airless, and waterless. Philanthropist Alfred Tredway White built large apartment complexes for the poor in Brooklyn Heights and Cobble Hill.[28] The units were so unusually sanitary and airy that they earned the title "the beau ideal" from Jacob Riis in his landmark *How the Other Half Lives*.[29] A bit later, at the turn of the century, John Thatcher, a contractor who had built several apartments for White—he also helmed the company that gave us the Brooklyn Academy of Music and many of Brooklyn's schools—joined his friend on his mission and constructed tenement buildings in Clinton Hill, with many of the most modern amenities.

The Bill Gates of Brooklyn at this time was Boston-born Charles Pratt. Pratt began his career in the whale-oil business, but quickly came to believe that the future was in petroleum. He built a successful company, the Astral Oil Works, on the Greenpoint waterfront. Astral made him a wealthy man, and with some of his money he built the block-long, elaborately Romanesque Astral Apartments. They were well-ventilated, fireproofed units with modern plumbing, a communal library, an outdoor playground, and onsite kindergarten. Fortunately for lovers of fine architecture, Pratt still had enough money left to build a Clinton Hill home for himself and four villas for his grown children, as well as the ornate Emmanuel Baptist Church. Three of the homes and the church still grace the area today.[30]

After selling Astral to John D. Rockefeller, Pratt vaulted into tycoon category. He used some of his great wealth to establish the Pratt Institute in 1887. The Institute's early mission was to provide engineering and mechanical training for unskilled, mostly immigrant, workers. Andrew Carnegie was inspired enough by Pratt's school that he used it as a model for his Carnegie Mellon University. Though he himself was not a Brooklynite, Carnegie also bestowed his largesse on the city. He built twenty-one new libraries there, each bringing much-needed construction jobs, books, and architectural refinement to their communities.

Brooklyn moguls helped create a city that was a vortex of Tocquevillian energy. The Liebmans, the Rheingold beer family, built housing and drainage systems. "Coffee King" John Arbuckle retrofitted aging ships into floating recreational centers for the poor and established a vacation resort upstate in New Paltz for his workers. Brooklyn elites, including many immigrants-made-good, helped support orphanages, day nurseries, settlement houses, and boys' clubs. Almost all the do-gooders were religious people—Pratt, a Baptist; Thatcher, a Methodist—who helped build the edifices that gave Brooklyn the nickname "Borough of Homes and Churches." The churches were a mainstay of immigrant religious and social life. They also helped to support much-needed almshouses and hospitals: Methodist Hospital in Park Slope, Lutheran Hospital in Sunset Park, Maimonides in Borough Park, Saint Mary's in Crown Heights, and Baptist Medical Center in East New York—all were founded during this period. Brooklynites continue to find medical care in some of those same hospitals today.

· 2 ·

The Old Brooklyn, Part Two

THE MIDDLE CLASS AND
BROOKLYN'S "SUBURBS"

*F*or all the activity at Brooklyn's port, industrial, and nearby residential districts, it would be a mistake to think of the city as having one particular identity. Always in flux, always absorbing great masses of newcomers with unique histories, traditions, and languages, Brooklyn would be difficult to define as a single place even in the late nineteenth century. In economic and demographic terms, it might be imagined—very roughly speaking—as three Brooklyns. First, there was the just-mentioned industrial and port corridor to the west, which included residential sections for workers and their bosses. Second, and to the south in Flatbush, New Utrecht, and Gravesend, was the still-green Dutch farmland, now also enjoyed by some nouveau riche country squires. And between the two lay the formerly rural sections that we now know as Cobble Hill, Fort Greene, Bedford-Stuyvesant, Crown Heights, Park Slope, and Prospect Heights, on their way toward intensive development in the final decades of the nineteenth century.

Today, these brownstone neighborhoods epitomize Jane Jacobs's idea of the urban village, beloved by the educated class. At the time, however, they were the ambiguous artifacts of Brooklyn's unceasing creative destruction. Brooklyn's old farm families looked with suspicion at the noisy goings-on just to their west. They feared, in the words of a local newspaper, that "the quiet and exclusiveness of their communal life which they had maintained for centuries . . . would be forever destroyed."[1] Contemporary city dwellers seeing the cranes and construction fences near their familiarly settled neighborhoods should recognize the sentiment while also appreciating the irony: their contemporary urban idyll was once also a source of anti-gentrification-style heartache.

Like the noises of today, the construction sounds heralded an economic and social shift far greater than a few new housing tracts might suggest. Brooklyn's industrialization not only offered new opportunities to poor immigrants near the waterfront. It also expanded and reshaped the middle class of professionals, small merchants, brokers, and engineers providing services and goods for the new industries and their owners. Like later suburbanites, these upwardly mobile folks wanted quiet, spacious, private homes, perhaps with a bit of green space—homes befitting their new status. But they also needed to be near downtown Brooklyn and Manhattan to get to their places of work; as of 1860, 40 percent of Brooklyn's wage earners worked in Manhattan, and ferries carried more than 32 million passengers a year.[2]

Today, we think of the suburbs as a post–World War II invention, a product of government policies such as the GI Bill and the interstate highway system and fueled by white hostility and fear of the increasingly black inner city. Brooklyn's nineteenth- and twentieth-century expansion reveals this story to be incomplete. The urge for private domestic space far from the frenetic noise and dirt of downtown is as old as industrialization itself. As early as the nineteenth century, an upwardly middle class was leaving the poor neighborhoods of London and Manchester for the suburbs.[3] Around that time, a number of popular American writers—the educator Catherine Beecher and the landscape designers Andrew Dowling Jackson and Calvert Vaux—were offering a vision of a different style of life from the dense city or the countryside. "By romanticizing the benefits of private space and by combining the imagery of the New England village with the notion of Thomas Jefferson's 'gentleman farmer,'" Kenneth Jackson writes about this threesome in *Crabgrass Frontier*, they "created a new image of the city as an urban-rural continuum."[4]

And so it was that New York City's industrialization began turning Brooklyn's rural areas into Manhattan's and downtown Brooklyn's bedroom. By the early 1800s, affluent Manhattan workers built their homes in Brooklyn Heights, which, as we've seen, was often described as the "first suburb." More intrepid well-to-do commuters built villas in central Brooklyn by the middle of the century. The creative destruction caused by improved railroads and ice cooling increased competition from the Hudson Valley and the post-reconstruction South, reducing the local demand for Brooklyn produce. Understandably, Dutch landowners in central Brooklyn became more interested in speculators now offering large sums of cash for their properties. Developers began to develop, as is their wont, imposing planned, grid-like streets on the rich fields and pastures that not long before had been farmed by the early Dutch and English settlers. They tore down the wooden homes that remained, flattening pastures and fields, in order to create blocks of brownstone homes for the new burghers.[5] As demand grew, so did the size of the buildings; by the

1890s, the single-family brownstones were followed by low-rise multifamily apartment houses.

The middle-class march into rural Brooklyn could not have happened if homeowners had had to rely on actual horsepower for getting to their workplaces. New technologies creating faster, safer, and more reliable transportation are a primary source of creative destruction and a crucial part of any city's growth. Such was the case with Brooklyn. In the early nineteenth century, the city's "suburbanization" remained modest partly because the only way to get to the ferry was by an urban version of the stagecoach. These "omnibuses," as they were called, held only fifteen passengers—or perhaps more, if people were willing to hang on to the sides or ride on top of the vehicles. Soon came the larger and more efficient horse trolleys. Just two years before Brooklyn became a city, the Brooklyn and Jamaica Railroad was incorporated to travel from the "village of Brooklyn" to the "village of Jamaica." The horse trolleys could make it from Fulton Ferry to Bedford, Crown Heights near Atlantic Avenue and Franklin, in thirty minutes—not bad, by the standards of contemporary commuting times.[6]

More transportation advances quickly followed. By 1853, another outfit, the Brooklyn City Railroad, was also improving commuting times. A little later in the century, twelve railroad lines covered thirty-seven miles and extended northwest along Myrtle Avenue to Greenpoint and east to Flatbush, adding up to 22 million passenger rides a year.[7] By that time, horsepower had given way to faster, cleaner steam. Horses were slow; they had to be fed and rested, and, most uncharmingly, they left great piles of manure in their wake. Steam-driven cable cars arriving in the mid-1880s solved many of these problems, though they came with their own difficulties; they were hard to control, especially around corners and down the hills leading to the ferries. Not for long, though; they quickly disappeared, to be replaced by more efficient electric trolleys and, eventually, elevated trains. By 1890, an electric streetcar went all the way to the beaches of Coney Island, giving Brooklynites a welcome glimpse at the possibilities for leisure that would also become an unforeseen benefit of the affluence accompanying industrialization. The trolleys and streetcars and the swift darting that they demanded of pedestrians were such a ubiquitous part of the Brooklyn experience that they eventually inspired the name for the city's baseball team: "the Trolley Dodgers," later shortened to "the Dodgers."

THE GREAT MISTAKE

Of all the inventions in engineering and transportation propelling Brooklyn's head-spinning growth, none was more important than the great bridge connecting Brooklyn and Manhattan finished in 1883. People all over the world still delight in the bridge's aesthetic and iconic power; it remains one of New York City's premier tourist attractions. Less appreciated, perhaps, is the bridge's immense practical value for a growing city.

The ferries—by the time the Brooklyn Bridge was first being constructed, fourteen of them were carrying 30,000 passengers a day[8]—had some serious limitations. During severe winters, they were iced in, leading workaholics to skate across the East River and stranding everyone else. Brooklyn's business and political elites had long wanted a bridge. But how to span such a wide, current-buffeted body of water? The technology of suspension bridges was only in its infancy. Skeptics could easily remind boosters that in 1845, seventy-nine people drowned when the cables of a bridge in Yarmouth, England, snapped after a crowd gathered to watch a clown roll down the Bure River in a barrel. Now people were talking about spanning a river with a bridge 50 percent longer than any tried before—and in a city legendary for its Tammany Hall corruption, no less.

As in the case of the Erie Canal, the creative visionaries had their way, thanks in large measure to the genius of a German engineer named John Augustus Roebling. Roebling devised several innovations. First, he used steel instead of iron for the suspension cables. Second, he designed "cassions," huge wooden boxes to be set on the river floor from which workers could excavate the soil to anchor the two 276-foot-high towers that would hold the cables. Pressurized air was pumped into the boxes, though they didn't protect workers—known as "sandhogs"—from "cassion disease," a miserable disablement that could mean speech impediments, excruciating joint pain, convulsions, and even death.[9]

Just as in the case of the Erie Canal, people were aghast at the costs of the bridge; the *New York Times* noted that with the money spent, the ferries could have operated free of charge for decades.[10] It took fourteen years to finish, employed 600 workers, and had a price tag of $15 million (more than $320 million in today's dollars). Altogether, at least two dozen people died during construction because of accidents, including Roebling himself. It's an amusing footnote, though one that would probably be of little comfort to the bridge's victims, that the builders tried to allay some of its costs by building an underground wine cellar between the two pillars on the Manhattan side. Known as the "Blue Grotto," in honor of the statue of the Virgin Mary standing at its entrance, it was painted with elaborate Old World frescoes and the words "Who Loveth Not Wine, Women, and Song, He Remaineth a Fool His Whole Life Long." Sadly, it is inaccessible today.[11]

More than a few New Yorkers were suspicious of the huge foreign contraption that was this colossal bridge. On several occasions, rumors of imminent collapse caused stampedes. In May 1884, P. T. Barnum led twenty-one elephants across the span to reassure a nervous public. Soon enough, nerves were settled, and New Yorkers became as proud as new parents of this "Eighth Wonder of the World." For several years after its construction, it remained the tallest structure in the Western Hemisphere. It inspired poems, paintings, photographs, and con men: a particularly gifted one named George C. Parker made such convincing forged documents showing that he was the bridge's owner that several duped "buyers" erected toll booths on the entrance to the new roadway before being chased away by the police.[12]

Most of all, the Brooklyn Bridge made it easier to move people, goods, and ideas between two of the most innovative cities in the world. Cable cars regularly traversed the span, from the Brooklyn trolley yards to the Manhattan business district and back again. A few Brooklyn Heights blue bloods kept the ferry in business; they didn't care for hoi polloi crowds and squeals of the cable cars. But like so many favored and familiar things in Brooklyn, the ferry was eventually done in by technology's creative destruction—this time, when the subway tunnel underneath the East River crossing was built in 1908.

Perhaps it was inevitable that the Brooklyn Bridge would result in the "consolidation" of Manhattan and Brooklyn into the governmental entity that the world now knows as New York City. Perhaps Brooklyn should have been left to make its way as the independent city it was. Regardless, in 1898, the deed was done, celebrated with fireworks, parades, and floats—at least on the west side of the East River. For many, however, the decision was no consolidation; it was an "annexation" or the "Great Mistake," resented for decades, and a sore point even today among a few stalwarts.

The ire was understandable.[13] The consolidation also brought the Bronx, Queens, and Richmond, aka Staten Island, into the fold, but unlike the other boroughs-to-be, Brooklyn was a large, successfully integrated city in its own right. In many respects, it was the equal of Manhattan and, in fact, within two decades would surpass it in population. Brooklyn had its own mayor, its own fire and police departments, its own commissioners of water and sewage, and its own comptroller. The practical challenges of unraveling all these agencies were immense, not to mention a blow to the dignity of their workers and managers. Equally galling to civic pride was Manhattan's control over seemingly small decisions: Brooklyn now had to buy new police uniforms to match Manhattan's finest. Brooklyn's cops had always had their choice of what guns to carry; now they would have to adopt Manhattan's Colt revolvers. Brooklyn's precinct numbers had to change as well, since many Manhattan and Brooklyn precincts had the same numbers. It was Manhattan's way or the highway, and that was all there was to it.

New York Republicans supported the deal; they hoped to find enough new party members in the city across the river to seize power from Tammany Hall. But a lot of Brooklynites weren't biting. Only a few years before the Great Mistake, a referendum on the idea passed in Brooklyn by fewer than 300 votes out of 29,000. They feared the corruption of New York's city hall, and presumed, with some prescience, that the chief beneficiaries of consolidation would be Manhattan banks, insurers, property owners, and markets. More mythically, they imagined their city as the more virtuous counterpart to the shady place across the river; the *Brooklyn Eagle* contrasted "a city of homes and churches" to Manhattan, "a city of Tammany Hall and crime government."[14]

Still, there were some powerful reasons to get behind the radical move. Supporters argued, very reasonably, that it could unify transportation and harbor operations. The Brooklyn Bridge was already at capacity, and the city would be hard-pressed to build another span on its own dime. Brooklyn had some scary debt and financial obligations; now it could dig into deeper pockets to keep the books balanced.

Perhaps more important, the future seemed to be on the side of The Big—big cities, big bridges, big plans. New York's elites were looking nervously over their shoulders at the rising fortunes of Chicago. The largest city in the Midwest was now growing faster than New York, voraciously annexing nearby land only a few decades after a devastating fire burned much of the town to the ground. In 1893, it held a world's fair that gave it global stature; millions of visitors to the Windy City gasped at such futuristic amenities as dishwashers, fluorescent lightbulbs, and Ferris wheels. A consolidated New York had the potential not only to outclass Chicago but to be as great as—or even greater than—Europe's finest cities.

WORKING-CLASS BROOKLYN

By the first decade of the new century, it was already becoming clear that consolidation's naysayers had one thing right: making New York into a single metropolis would lower Brooklyn's position in the eyes of the world. Manhattan became the big-shot sophisticate, the capital of wealth and glamour, "the city," as Brooklynites even today sometimes find themselves referring to it, as in, "Do you work in the city?"

Brooklyn became the outer-borough bumpkin, the poor cousin in grease-stained overalls, the home of greenhorns who couldn't even speak English and, even if they could, were too lazy to enunciate properly. Fuhgettaboutit, shaddup, whaddya mean: that was Brooklyn. Charles Pratt and family, like other people of wealth, traded in their mansions in Clinton Hill for ritzier addresses in Manhattan.[15] No one would have realized it at the time, but the elegant Clinton Hill's decline following the Great Mistake was an ominous forecast into the future of many Brooklyn neighborhoods in the next century.

Still, for the time being, Brooklyn grew and prospered in its own patois-rich, scrappy way. In addition to chemicals, coffee, spices, ironworks, and ships, of course, Brooklyn factories were now producing new kinds of candy, boots, and, for a time, so many shoes that it could almost be called the national cobbler.

Even more than before the consolidation, the factories would not go wanting for eager employees. With the Williamsburg Bridge completed in 1903, the first subway line under the East River in 1908, and the Manhattan Bridge in 1909, distances shrank between the two boroughs (how lowly a word, boroughs, compared with cities!).

Poles, already a growing presence in Greenpoint, created "Little Poland," building churches and opening butcher shops and bakeries. Around the same time, poor Jews who had traveled from their native Russia and Galicia to the packed tenements of the Lower East Side of Manhattan made their way to cheaper quarters in Williamsburg, Brownsville, and farther south in Borough Park. These Jews were nothing like the refined, bourgeois German Jews who had arrived earlier in the nineteenth century and were spreading into the brownstone suburbs of Brooklyn. These immigrants spoke Yiddish, and their education was largely limited to the "needle trades." They would make their way as furriers, tailors, dressmakers, and seamstresses. Their German Jewish forerunners may not have wanted to live with their poor cousins, but they did help establish orphanages, training schools, and YMHAs. The Hebrew Benevolent Society was established in Williamsburg in 1868; in 1909, the name was changed to the Brooklyn Federation of Jewish Philanthropies.

Italians may have made the biggest mark on the borough. Fast earning their place as the third-largest immigrant group in the United States—after the Irish and Germans—Italians, mostly from poorer southern parts of Italy, settled in North Williamsburg, Brownsville, and near the Navy Yard, though they became most strongly identified with Carroll Gardens, simply known as South Brooklyn at the time, and later with Bensonhurst to the southwest. The Italians were poor and even more unskilled than their Jewish counterparts; "Guidos" were also sorely tested by discrimination. Lucky for them, the hordes of new arrivals in need of housing, schools, hospitals, and workplaces meant plenty of work in the trades at which they excelled: ditchdigging, bricklaying, and stonecutting. The Italians brought other traditions with them, building churches and social clubs, and enjoying saints' feast days that spilled into the streets. To this day, each July hipsters and old-timers celebrate "Giglio" in the streets near Our Lady of Mount Carmel in Williamsburg with a seventy-two-foot-high flower-bedecked tower. Most of all, Italians gave Brooklyn their food: spaghetti and meatballs, Sunday red-sauce "gravy," and, of course, to New Yorkers' everlasting gratitude, pizza.

Partly thanks to the new arrivals—Italians and Jews, in particular—Brooklyn truly earned its tough-guy reputation in the early decades of the twentieth century. Irish gangs had roamed the docks since the 1830s. Now there were new guys in town, ready to compete for turf and jobs. The Irish and Italians were both clannish and suspicious of the law, which, in the Old Country, had looked like a rich man's con game. They were used to settling disputes on their own, a habit that made street violence a fact of life in many neighborhoods, though it was generally targeted at other wiseguys. Willie Sutton, born in Greenpoint to Irish-American parents—a wily, chain-smoking, squirt—cut his teeth among the gamblers, loan sharks, and thugs hanging out along the waterfront. He went on to become "Slick Willie," one of the most successful bank robbers in the nation's history and the source of the answer to the question: Why rob banks? "Because that's where the money is."

The most legendary of all Brooklyn gangsters was surely Al Capone. Generally thought of as Chicago's problem, Capone was actually born near the Navy Yard to parents who had moved there from Naples—the family name was Caponi—at the end of the nineteenth century. He cut his criminal teeth hanging out near the Navy Yard while playing hooky from school. There, he befriended a gangster named Johnny Torrio, who got young Al a job at a hangout as a bouncer. Capone offended a customer who gave him the slash that gave him his nickname "Scarface." Eventually, partly because of the numerous enemies he had made in Brooklyn, Capone left for the Windy City. Brooklyn was so tough that even Al Capone had to get out of town.

Jewish immigrants added their own *landsmen* to Brooklyn's gang of thieves and hit men. The Manhattan-based Bugs and Meyer Club, founded by Meyer Lansky and Bugsy Siegel, disbanded and regrouped as Murder, Inc., with operations in the Jewish ghetto of Brownsville. The Kosher Nostra, as some wag dubbed it, included the Amberg brothers (Hyman, who committed suicide after unsuccessfully trying to escape the Tombs prison; and Joseph and Louis, who were both murdered by Murder, Inc. in Brownsville in 1935). More successful was the dapper lothario Harry "Pittsburgh Phil"—or "Pep"—Strauss, who was a real connoisseur of murder, varying his preferred weapons among ropes, knives, axes, revolvers, and ice picks. Pep was said to have assassinated 100 souls, though there are those who believe this to be a gross understatement. Certainly, he did not limit his talents to Brooklyn. His reputation was great enough to make capos in Detroit and Florida, among other places, call for his services. Pittsburgh never made the list of his targets, and the origin of his nom de guerre remains a mystery.[16]

Aside from organized crime, the 1930s brought two other challenges to Brooklyn that collided in unfortunate ways. First was the Depression. Perhaps in the spirit of "the harder they come, the harder they fall," New York was probably about the worst hit of any American city. By 1932, half of New York's manufacturing plants were closed, and one in every three New Yorkers was unemployed. Brooklyn's seemingly endless line of construction projects halted. The borough became thick with Salvation Army outposts and soup kitchens.

This was the same decade in which Brooklyn began to see an influx of African Americans as part of the Great Migration northward from the Jim Crow South. After their agricultural era, New Yorkers had an uneven history in their treatment of the black race. Shortly after the Revolutionary War, future chief justice John Jay brought together a group of New York worthies, including Alexander Hamilton, to create the New York Manumission Society, whose purpose was to bring an end to slavery in their state. Brooklyn slaveholders were already showing some queasiness about their status. Public auctions were banned in 1790. Still, slavery was officially banned only in 1827, though some masters freed their own slaves well before the official date.

Antebellum Brooklyn would reject its own complicity in the "peculiar institution" to become a hotbed of antislavery sentiment. Locals hid slaves in underground railway "stations" around the city. In 1847, Henry Ward Beecher, brother of *Uncle Tom's Cabin* author Harriet Beecher Stowe, became the preacher at the Plymouth Church of the Pilgrims in Brooklyn Heights and turned it into the nation's center of abolitionism. His sermons lured so many people from Brooklyn and Manhattan that on Sunday, the ferries were referred to as "Beecher's Boats." After riots in Manhattan protesting the Civil War draft, blacks fled to the apparent safety of Brooklyn. Brooklyn was also home to Weeksville, one of the first free black communities in the country. Established in 1838, Weeksville's eventual 500 residents supported several newspapers, churches, an orphan asylum, and a home for the aged.

Though better than many places in the country, life was hardly easy for Brooklyn's blacks. Brooklynites referred to the area near Weeksville as Crow Hill, a term that was very possibly a derogatory name for the black residents. According to historian Craig Wilder, segregation was commonplace in hospitals and schools. White churches were also known to reject black members. Until the 1930s, blacks were a tiny percentage of the population, making up less than 1.4 percent of the 2.5 million people living in the borough.[17] Their small numbers probably kept hostility toward them in check. Natives had plenty of other, far larger, groups to dislike; as we've seen, the Irish had been a despised minority for almost a century. Not that native New Yorkers much liked poor Poles, Jews, or Italians, or the few Chinese who found their way to Brooklyn, either.[18]

But as the numbers and percentage of very poor blacks from the South mounted after 1930, blacks' lowly position became unique. A large number of the Southern migrants moved to an area in central Brooklyn called Bedford-Stuyvesant, a Dutch settlement that turned German and then became a Jewish middle-class enclave. With the opening of the A train that stopped at both Harlem and Bed-Stuy in 1936, many blacks left Manhattan for Brooklyn. During the 1940s, the population of blacks in Bed-Stuy more than doubled. As in the case of other oppressed groups, there was a sizable black middle class whose civic organizations and sports clubs serviced their poorer brethren.[19] But the numbers of impoverished soon swamped their capacity to be of much help. The future of Bedford-Stuyvesant and some neighboring communities was looking increasingly fragile.

Even as the black ghettos in the center of the borough were forming, white working-class Brooklyn was in its heyday, or so one would have to conclude from its place in popular culture in the 1940s and 1950s. In 1945, *A Tree Grows in Brooklyn*, a film directed by a young Elia Kazan based on the novel by Brooklynite Betty Smith, gave a bittersweet depiction of the borough in its portrayal of a poetic and ambitious young girl growing up in a troubled, destitute Irish family in Williamsburg. *The Jackie Gleason Show*, imagined to take place in a sparsely furnished apartment in Bensonhurst, came to American television screens in 1951 and turned a Brooklyn bus driver with a world-weary wife into an American Everyman. The egg cream, stickball, Coney Island's Cyclone: Brooklyn's mid-twentieth-century Americana became every bit as resonant as the drive-in movie theater or the small-town, Capraesque soda fountain.

Helping Brooklyn's mid-century reputation have been the dozens of reminiscing celebrities who grew up there during that period: Lauren Bacall (née Betty Joan Perske), Woody Allen (né Allen Stewart Konigsberg), Mel Brooks (Melvin Kaminsky), Danny Kaye (David Daniel Kaminsky, though probably no relation to Melvin), Larry King (Lawrence Harvey Zeiger), and Barbra Streisand, to name but a few. True, many had to change their names before they could become national personages. But not only did they keep their feisty Brooklyn sensibility; they were able to use it to broaden the taste of a white-bread America. Brooklyn's staggering number of successful scientists, artists, writers, actors, ballplayers, singers, and producers during the twentieth century represented a powerful advertisement for the borough as a staging ground for the American dream. These were people who grew up in circumstances somewhere between shabby and poor; yet through their own gumption and smarts—both nourished on the streets and in the schools of working-class Brooklyn—they grew up to dine with presidents and, in a few cases, to live like Hollywood sultans.

The reminiscences of Brooklyn at this time can be laced with nostalgia, but there is something to the schmaltz. It would be an exaggeration, but only a moderate one, to say that during these decades, the borough's disparate ethnic and racial groups—always with the exception of African Americans—melted into a single Brooklyn working-class identity. The docks mixed Italians, Jews, Scandinavians, Irish, Hungarians, Poles, and blacks—though the latter were few in number—into a daily, viable blue-collar brew. Ethnic enclaves were not entirely segregated; Jews and Italians often lived next door to each other in places like Bensonhurst; Irish and Italians inhabited nearby blocks in South Brooklyn. Joshua Freeman, author of *Working-Class New York*, argues that labor unions also had the effect of intensifying class consciousness over tribal identity. "The complex demography of neighborhoods and occupations spurred New Yorkers to embrace and transcend ethnic racial and religious loyalties," he writes.[20]

The motley crew of working-class Brooklynites played ball together. They went to dance halls and movies together. They were drafted and fought in Germany and the Pacific together. Outsiders made fun of them. In the 1930s, *The New Yorker* published a famous story by Thomas Wolfe called "Only the Dead Know Brooklyn." Its first sentence: "Dere's no guy livin' dat knows Brooklyn t'roo an' t'roo, because it'd take a guy a lifetime just to find his way aroun' duh goddam town."[21] But by the 1940s, with television and movies paying attention, Brooklyn's working class was wearing its quirks proudly.

Most of all, Brooklynites rooted for the Dodgers together. Sports teams add to the esprit de corps of any city, town, or school, but the Dodgers took the axiom to another plane entirely. Walter O'Malley's legendary team didn't just play in Brooklyn; it wasn't just followed by Brooklyn fans; in some profound sense, it *was* Brooklyn. The beloved Ebbets Field sat almost in the dead center in this borough of 2.5 million. The seats were so close to the field that fans could, and did, banter with the team. Though they weren't native to the area, famous players like Pee Wee Reese, Duke Snider, Gil Hodges, Roy Campanella, and, of course, Jackie Robinson often lived among, and shared a beer with, regular Brooklyn folks. Freeman notes that the 1949 team included three blacks, one Jew, one Hispanic, two Poles, a Slovak, two Italians, two Scandinavians, and, for good measure, an Italian-Hungarian. There was nothing more Brooklyn than that. Robinson's addition to the team and his friendship with Pee Wee Reese and other white team members allowed Brooklynites to pretend briefly that they were better than other people. At the very least, the team's multicultural camaraderie modeled Brooklynites' own civic affection and self-effacing goodwill.

The Dodgers also inspired the sort of shared storytelling so essential to any cohesive group. The Dodgers "provided common ground: Italians, Irish, blacks, Jews, Poles, all went to the games," as Pete Hamill has written. They also "provided something to talk about that did not involve religion, politics or race." Fans would pour in to Prospect Park on summer evenings to walk to Ebbets Field. When the Dodgers won the pennant in 1941, schools closed, and the streets were lined with cheering, crying fans waving to the adored motorcade. "The Dodgers were called 'Dem Bums,' and the laughter came in part from knowing that they were not."[22]

But let's not take the sweet memories too far. All rapidly changing cities tempt those putting up with the hypocrisies and corruption of their own day to imagine a more "authentic" time, an era when their city had a "soul" and an honest heart. Working-class New York, at its height in Brooklyn's Ebbets Field era, presents that temptation for many New Yorkers today. But there was a dark side to proletarian life that shouldn't be forgotten. Brooklyn had suffered its share of thugs and gangsters for at least a century by the time the Dodgers helped define the borough's golden age, and the bad guys were not about to disappear now. "Gangsters and petty criminals were a daily presence in working-class life," writes Freeman.[23] Numbers running and illegal drug dealing pervaded the streets of South Brooklyn. Kickbacks and stolen merchandise were so common on the Brooklyn waterfront that some shipping companies were thinking of taking their business elsewhere. The Academy Award–winning Elia Kazan–Marlon Brando film *On the Waterfront* (actually filmed in Hoboken) exposed the mob-controlled union violence, racketeering, and general corruption at the piers in South Brooklyn. The complex ambience of the time and place was rich enough to inspire other literary works, including Arthur Miller's 1955 *A View from the Bridge* and, retrospectively, Hubert Selby Jr.'s 1964 book *Last Exit to Brooklyn.*

INDUSTRIAL DECLINE

"I coulda been a contender, instead of a bum, which is what I am," mourns Marlon Brando, speaking as the longshoreman and once-promising boxer Terry Malloy in *On the Waterfront*. Were the Brooklyn of the 1960s and 1970s a character in a movie, she could have mused something in that vein.[24] Even as Brooklyn was enjoying its multicultural, proletarian success, by the 1950s signs of loss hovered over the borough. Those signs went far beyond the usual gangs and lowlifes. The landscape itself was undergoing massive changes, some of them ordered from on high with the best of intentions, some of them the product of forces no one completely understood.

In the first category was the now-despised "urban renewal." The master planner for this massive undertaking in New York was Robert Moses, the city's legendary parks commissioner. Moses was condemned by the urban theorist Jane Jacobs and her many followers. But it's worth recalling that Moses also brought to New York City generally, and Brooklyn more specifically, many treasures. With the assistance of federal Works Progress Administration funds, Moses was a Houdini of construction. He built 658 playgrounds in New York, many dozens of them in Brooklyn. In a mere two years, Moses, a superb swimmer himself, built eleven swimming pools in New York City, including four beauties in Brooklyn: Williamsburg's McCarren Park pool; the Sunset pool; Brownsville's Betsy Head pool; and the Red Hook recreational center and pool designed by Gilmore D. Clarke, one of the nation's most prominent landscape designers. The four opened just in time to cool off the public in the sizzling summer of 1936 and remain part of the fabric of Brooklyn's summer life and a reminder of a seemingly more civic-minded past.

In other Brooklyn projects, Moses confirmed the worst of Jacobs's criticisms. Wielding the right of eminent domain, the backing of city hall, and a vigorous, often bullying, belief in his own vision of the public good, Moses pronounced assorted tenement neighborhoods "slums" and proceeded to flatten, bisect, or pave them over. The 1937 federal Housing Act and the 1949 Title I of the Housing Act gave Moses the money and power to replace poor but vibrant tenement neighborhoods with huge complexes in the current fashion of "towers in the park." The arrangement isolated residents from surrounding neighborhoods and distanced them from all-important street life, leading Jacobs to formulate a theory about a community's need for "eyes on the street." Eventually, many of Moses's Brooklyn projects would help bring their own blight to Williamsburg, Brownsville, Coney Island, East New York, and Red Hook.

Moses's most reviled Brooklyn venture was the Brooklyn-Queens Expressway, particularly the extension running across the Gowanus Canal and through the working-class neighborhood of Sunset Park. With no thoroughfares in the borough, cars and trucks trying to get to the East River crossings crawled along local streets of South Brooklyn. The traffic could be a misery for residents, blocking their neighborhoods and businesses, polluting their homes, and endangering pedestrians.[25]

Moses had good reason to believe that a highway was called for, but common sense stopped there. He decided that his expressway should be elevated atop Third Avenue, a bustling, if modest, shopping district for the mostly Scandinavian immigrants living nearby. Locals pleaded with Moses not to enshroud their favored street in steel supports and a roof made of heavily trafficked pavement, but, as was generally the case, Moses and his project could not be moved. He built his highway, thereby helping turn a lively neighborhood commercial avenue with numerous well-used businesses and its cross streets into a loitering ground for drunks, junkies, and hookers. His highway also managed to sever the waterfront area of Red Hook from the rest of South Brooklyn, ensuring this already-rough neighborhood of further decline.[26]

Robert Moses was not the only reason Brooklyn's urban landscape was changing. The borough's industrial base was dwindling, first gradually, and then, it seemed, suddenly. Over the many decades of Brooklyn's deindustrialization, some companies went bankrupt or simply expired after a good run. Others fled for more space and cheaper land. Just as industries had come to Brooklyn from Manhattan looking for more space, so many of them were to leave Brooklyn for open lots in upstate New York, Pennsylvania, and the Midwest.

For the most part, what was happening was yet another chapter in our old story: new technologies were creating new ways of doing things and thereby destroying Brooklyn's past.[27] The first industry to teeter was, fittingly, the beer business. The same generation of German immigrants who had made Brooklyn a center of lager production was also finding eager customers in midwestern states like Wisconsin and Minnesota, where they opened saloons and beer gardens of the sort they knew from the Old Country; breweries were soon to follow. As brewers learned how to increase their products' shelf life through pasteurization and refrigerated railcars, Brooklyn beer manufacturers were looking at some serious competition. Midwestern companies like Anhesuer-Bush and Schlitz were setting new records in bottling brew and broadening their distribution networks. At the beginning of the twentieth century, Brooklyn had forty-five breweries, enough to keep many locals employed and the entire borough and a significant part of the nation well lubricated. As early as 1910, the number had shrunk to thirty-one. Prohibition brought another blow; before the Twenty-First Amendment, Brooklyn was still staggering along, with twenty-three breweries. The amendment left only nine. Rheingold was the biggest of those still standing, and it stuck around in Bushwick for a good thirty years longer. By 1976, however, both Rheingold and Schaefer, two once-favorite local sons, surrendered to the more efficient behemoths of the Midwest.[28]

There were many other Brooklyn casualties of the disruptive innovations of the twentieth century. Sugar refineries laid off workers with improvements in refining procedures. In 1920 it took 23,000 workers to produce Domino's 3 million pounds of sugar a day. Fifty years later, it took only 240. By 1945, the Dumbo Arbuckle sugar refinery was shuttered and turned into warehouses.[29] Meanwhile, transportation advances offered new opportunities for businesses to grow and prosper. In the 1950s, the Eberhard Faber pencil company moved from Greenpoint, where it had employed thousands over the years since it opened its doors in 1872, to Wilkes-Barre, Pennsylvania. The Gair box factory left Dumbo for the Rockland County town of Piermont. As of 1913, three out of ten industrial companies in Brooklyn that employed more than a thousand people in 1913 were located in Dumbo. Now, like the abandoned mining towns of America's West, Dumbo was fast turning into an industrial ghost town.

Equally disastrous for Brooklyn's old economy was the 1960s arrival of containerization. Even before then, widespread corruption on the Brooklyn waterfront and larger ships needing bigger quarters had led some companies to look beyond the Kings County piers. Between 1924 and 1953, one-third fewer boats were going through the Gowanus Canal, and businesses there slumped by half. Containers would become the final blow to Brooklyn's waterfront.[30]

In one sense, packing goods into huge metal containers that were then lifted by crane off ships and into trucks and trains was good for longshoremen; it saved hours, bones, and backs. But over time—the move to containerization was spread out over years—it also meant the virtual end of a traditional way of life in Brooklyn. Red Hook didn't have the space or railroad connections that would allow it to keep shippers interested in its services. The Port Authority put its energies and money into developing the deeper waters and less densely settled New Jersey waterfront. "The ships chandlers, rope works, and saloons that had lined the shores of Brooklyn and Manhattan since the days of Melville disappeared," Freeman writes. The waterfront workforce in New York City went from 35,000 in 1954, to 21,600 in 1970, to a mere 8,000 in the late 1980s, and even some of those were a gift to a weakening union. All in all, manufacturing employment dropped by half between 1954 and 1990, and the decline has continued to the present day.[31]

More heartbreaking still were three departures that forecast the end of Brooklyn's golden age as clearly as any tabloid headline. In its reporting of local news, professional and high school sports, and gossip, the *Brooklyn Eagle* newspaper had helped unify residents since its founding in 1841. By 1955, after a prolonged newspaper strike, it was gone, leaving Brooklynites dependent on Manhattan dailies' second-class coverage of their local doings. And in a move that brought forth enough tears to cleanse the Gowanus Canal, in 1957 Walter O'Malley moved the Dodgers to Los Angeles. Fans damned O'Malley to hell, but the truth was that Ebbets Field was getting shabby. The team was losing its audience, who now balked at having no place to park their cars; no one needed reminding that Yankee Stadium had plenty of parking. At any rate, fans no longer had just radio to follow games; they could watch games on their brand-new black-and-white televisions. In 1960, Ebbets Field fell to a wrecking ball, which, in a nice touch, had been painted to look like a baseball. The final blow to Brooklyn's working-class identity came in 1966, when, despite demonstrations at Madison Square Garden and a personal visit from Robert Kennedy, the great 300-acre Navy Yard, a Brooklyn fixture since 1801, shut its gates, leaving behind only the ghosts of shouting longshoremen, pipe fitters, welders, engineers, and their history-making ships.

Departing industries left Brooklyn with the wreckage of abandoned buildings and piers and Stygian waterways. The Gowanus Canal holds centuries of industrial and human waste so foul, so odorous that even to this day, the best engineering minds have been stymied by how to clean it. Newtown Creek, dividing Brooklyn and Queens, once a vital passageway to factories in Greenpoint and Bushwick, was said to be so polluted that it could blister the paint off tugboats. It "strikes me as the most awful stretch of water I have ever seen," the prolific travel writer James (now Jan) Morris wrote. "You couldn't put a fire out with it, there was too much oil. No fish could live in it: only germs and water rats."[32]

Another ominous sign came in the form of migration. After centuries in which Irish, German, Italian, Jewish, Polish, and Scandinavian immigrants clamored for a chance to start their new lives in Kings County, Brooklyn's population was shrinking. Brooklyn's aspiring middle class had always pushed farther east and south from the hyperactive and now-decaying areas in the north and center of the borough. Now taking advantage of expanded subway lines, Italians, Jews, and Irish left South Brooklyn, Williamsburg, Brownsville, and East New York for Bensonhurst and the suburban-like detached homes of Gravesend and Canarsie. Though their departure meant abandoned buildings and shuttered movie theaters and retail businesses, at least they continued to be part of the city. Far worse for Brooklyn was the massive white flight to the suburbs. With the easy availability of government-sponsored mortgages and the convenience of new highways, they left the enfeebled county altogether for Long Island, New Jersey, and Westchester, or maybe even someplace farther. "It wasn't a matter of moving from one neighborhood to the next; the transportation system was too good for all that," wrote Hamill. "It was out 'to the island' or to California or Rockland County. The idea was to get out." Brooklyn lost 135,000 people in the 1950s. In the 1960s and 1970s, another 290,000 Brooklynites bid good-bye. " 'We gotta get outta Brooklyn.' You heard it over and over in those days."[33]

By the 1960s, Brooklyn was increasingly populated by poor blacks and Puerto Ricans, the newest generation of immigrants escaping dead-end lives in their home country. Almost all of them were uneducated and unskilled; tens of thousands lived in one of the over 200 public housing buildings that by then were spread all over the borough. The welfare rolls soared, as did the numbers of single mothers. Next came heroin and, inevitably, violent crime, leading the few middle-class stubborn hangers-on to shake their heads in disgust and finally put up for-sale signs. Where Ebbets Field, the symbol of peak Old Brooklyn, had stood was a housing project. In 2007, the place that once rang with the jubilant shouts of proud Brooklynites was described by one local: "The cold months, seemed like every Monday morning you'd find a body. The roof was blacktop, and, since heat rises, junkies'd go up there to sleep. They'd get sick or mugged or thrown off the top. Monday morning, you call the police station up at 6:10, 6:15. 'We have one break-in, a window on the south side. There's a drunk on the corner—please send a patrol car, the kids are coming to school soon. I think there's a body, someone was screaming.' Every Monday, routine."[34]

By the 1970s, like Detroit, Cleveland, Buffalo, Chicago, Portland, St. Louis, Philadelphia, Baltimore, and so many other once-proud industrial cities, Brooklyn was in a race to the bottom.

· 3 ·

Park Slope

The New Brooklyn Takes Shape

$\mathcal{N}$amed after the hill that slopes gently west from Prospect Park toward, but comfortably distanced from, the toxic Gowanus Canal, Park Slope has all the assets that would seem to immunize it from urban blight: block after block of charming three- to five-story nineteenth-century townhouses, said to include some of the finest Romanesque revival and Queen Anne homes in the United States, tree-lined residential streets, excellent transportation lines to central business districts, and that magnificent Olmstead and Vaux–designed 526-acre park. Today its two commercial avenues are lined with attractive shops and enough varied food establishments to keep residents' palates endlessly stimulated: sushi, ramen, burritos, (brick oven) pizza, wine bars, Indian, Chinese, Japanese, Thai, and, for the undecided, Asian fusion, French and Italian cheeses and charcuterie, hamburgers, typically advertising hormone- and antibiotic-free meat. In 2007 the American Planning Association named it one of the top ten "great neighborhoods" of America.[1] Three years later, in New York magazine, the statistician Nate Silver ranked the best neighborhoods in New York City. Contemporary Slope dwellers were hardly surprised when their nabe topped the list at number one.[2]

Yet, as of the 1930s, the great neighborhood was a "slum"—at least, according to planners and, presumably, the upwardly mobile middle class who had recently tired of the area. The decline continued into the dark days of the 1960s, 1970s, and 1980s, when toddlers began to wave around crack vials that they had dug up in park sandboxes, and their parents waited to see doctors in local emergency rooms after being mugged (or worse) on the way home from work or going to the supermarket. Homeowners spent a good part of a week's salary on the toughest deadbolt locks and iron bars for their windows. No one dared put even a heavy planter on the stoop; no way it wouldn't be gone by the next morning.

What makes a prosperous urban neighborhood crash and burn? And, more relevant to today's debates, what makes it become desirable again? Park Slope's zigzagging trajectory over the past century or more is not so different from that of dozens of other neighborhoods in cities in the United States, Europe, and Australia. Its story can give some insight into the neighborhood transformation that we call gentrification, clarifying a few myths and exaggerations about a subject rife with many of them.

A MIDDLE CLASS GROWS IN BROOKLYN

Park Slope, like other urban townhouse neighborhoods, was the product of America's expanding industrial wealth. By the mid-nineteenth century, Brooklyn's busy immigrant-inventors were beginning to make fortunes; they needed homes befitting their new status. As we saw in the previous chapter, the 1 percent built their mansions in Clinton Hill, just far enough from the industrial waterfront to offer salubrious surroundings and easy access to their offices and factories. Brooklyn's prosperity, city elders and state officials had decided, called for a grand park on the order of Manhattan's recently completed Central Park. And so Brooklyn's industrialists set their sights on the undeveloped areas just west of a large plot of farmland, much of it owned by the prescient landowner Edwin Lichfield, ready to be groomed as the city's grand Prospect Park.

By the 1880s, another group of industrialists began to see the potential for the area just to the west of the park, the side closer to Manhattan. Their buildings were impressive enough that the district came to be known as "the Gold Coast." A sprawling Romanesque mansion of paper mogul Henry Hulbert now occupied by Poly Prep School occupied a large lot on what we now call Prospect Park West. A few blocks away on Eighth Avenue, Thomas Adams, Jr., inventor of the world-famous Adams Chiclets and its automatic vending machine, built another Romanesque pile, frequently described as the finest private home in that style in New York City. Across the street was a huge structure (since demolished) belonging to Charles L. Feltman, a former German peddler who became an ultra-successful Coney Island restaurateur after inventing the sausage on a bun, aka the hot dog. And so on.

When the Gold Coast avenues first began to fill in, the narrower east-to-west blocks remained largely empty swaths of fallow farmland. Brooklyn Heights, nearest to downtown Manhattan, long a bedroom community for affluent Manhattan workers, was full. Developers had already purchased parcels of the planned street grid in other parts of South Brooklyn and created neighborhoods that would eventually come to be known as Cobble Hill, Boerum Hill, and Carroll Gardens. The fields abutting the Gold Coast were the logical domino to fall next.

Developers knew that to build on the streets of these neighborhoods profitably, they needed to satisfy two requirements: they had to appeal to the pride and tastes of the upwardly mobile middle class; and they had to do so as cheaply and efficiently as possible. That meant that they couldn't afford to use the expensive marble and stone of the Gold Coast homes; nor could they please the new class of buyers by building structures in working-class brick or shantytown wood. They found their answer in brownstone.

Actually, it isn't quite accurate to call most of the buildings on the side streets "brownstones." They have brownstone fronts, a four- to six-inch veneer of stone. The veneer was meant to give the impression of grandeur, though it covered only the plebeian brick apparent in the outer back walls. That didn't seem to matter to the new middle class: excavated from conveniently located Connecticut and Pennsylvania quarries, brownstone was first and foremost a stone, the material that contemporaries associated with important buildings. After the 1870s, decorative details could be cut by "pneumatic drills" (Americans today refer to them as jackhammers), a new invention that made decoration much cheaper and much faster than hand carving, allowing mass-produced wood details outside and inside. To enhance the sense of opulence, entrances were adorned with columns, wreaths, and garlands, as well as large carved wooden doors.[3]

To the modern eye, the high stoops and majestic doors, not to mention the interiors with their parquet floors and tall ceilings, can make the brownstone seem almost aristocratic. That's not the way aesthetes of the time saw them. For them, these were the nineteenth-century tract houses, and Park Slope might as well have been Levittown. Edith Wharton scorned the brownstone dominating the blocks of this part of Brooklyn, calling it "the most hideous stone ever quarried."[4] At a time when the trees that now soften the streetscape had yet to be planted, her assessment might have seemed less severe, especially given the monotony of some brownstone blocks. Developers typically used the same plans for a group of houses, ordering the same tile, mahogany or oak trim, stairways, and mantels from catalogs. "When one has seen one house, he has seen them all," another contemporary critic scowled.[5] Fortunately for the developers, Brooklyn's Victorian middle class was sold on the "hideous stone" and eagerly filled the houses with their families and servants.

But not for very long. In the early twentieth century, just as today, technology's creative destruction and America's demographic churn were transforming middle-class lifestyles. A slowing of immigration and the continuing growth in manufacturing jobs made it harder to find servants to tend the coal furnaces and dust the elaborately decorated parlors of the maturing brownstones. By the 1920s, new subway lines helped lure the Slope's middle class to the newer, leafier "suburbs" farther east in Ditmas Park, Flatbush, and Gravesend. Gradually, Park Slope and other brownstone neighborhoods began to lose their cachet. When the Depression came, the areas descended into "slum" category. The smaller townhouses and apartments on blocks farther away from Prospect Park and in the area nearer Sunset Park known as the South Slope had long been home to Irish and Italian immigrant servants, dockworkers, shop owners, and salarymen at the Ansonia Clock Factory, said to be one of the largest clock manufacturers in the world and one of the few sizable industries abutting the brownstone neighborhood. When Park Slope's original homeowners put up for-sale signs, it was working-class immigrants who moved into these once-proudly bourgeois brownstones.

Few of those immigrants could afford to buy these homes, and those who could frequently were speculators who had no interest in actually living in them. Trying to make it through tough times, absentee landlords and resident owners turned their brownstones into boardinghouses, destroying moldings, decorative plaster, mantels, and parquet floors and installing dropped ceilings in the process.[6] During the Depression, the Home Owners' Loan Corporation (HOLC) rated most of brownstone Brooklyn outside Brooklyn Heights and a few blocks closest to Prospect Park as third- or fourth-grade—third-grade being modestly risky, fourth being the worst, the equivalent to what is commonly called redlined. The HOLC's rankings were based in part on widespread contemporary assumptions about the limited appeal of older, urban, and ethnic neighborhoods as well as on racial and ethnic suspicion.[7] It's worth noting, however, that when the ratings were determined and for several decades following, Park Slope was almost entirely white; as of 1960, the neighborhood was still only 10 percent non-Caucasian.[8] The original redliners were no more eager to lend money to lower-class Irish, Italians, or Jews than they were to blacks and Puerto Ricans.

With the exit of the middle class, crime and other urban ills started to rise. The gangs who had always roughed up the dock areas and the Gowanus were taking their rumbles to the lower blocks of the Slope, as well as to the elegant Prospect Park and John Jay High School on Seventh Avenue. Now they had battles to fight with new Puerto Rican gangs staking out turf in the northern part of the lower Slope. In 1973, one Fifth Avenue dispute between Italians and Puerto Ricans escalated into a forty-eight-hour riot. Five people were shot.[9] That same year, a neighbor threw acid in the face of a four-year-old boy, blinding and horribly disfiguring him for life; the incident occurred on the very block I would move to a decade later.[10] Shopkeepers closed early out of fear of attacks.[11] Landlords around those parts began to realize that they could make more money by renting to welfare recipients, whose numbers soared throughout the 1960s in New York, just as the taxpaying white middle and working class was making its escape. Other landlords simply abandoned properties that they believed were hopeless.[12] In the 1960s and 1970s, Park Slope—in fact, much of Brooklyn—was looking as though it was on its way to becoming Detroit.

HOW PARK SLOPE GENTRIFIED

It's safe to say that a suburban and small-town America didn't much care what was happening in places like Brooklyn; in truth, those who did care didn't have a clue as to what to do. But across the Atlantic Ocean were signs of a way to reverse the decline of former middle-class urban neighborhoods. In the early 1960s, Ruth Glass, a young British sociologist, noticed something unexpected in her own northern London decaying working-class neighborhood of Islington, a place whose path resembled that of Park Slope. A small bohemian-intellectual crowd—people much like her, in other words—were turning some of the area's "shabby modest mews and cottages" and subdivided Victorian townhouses into pleasing, bourgeois family homes. "[O]ne by one, many of the working-class quarters of London have been invaded by the middle classes," she wrote in a transformational 1964 article. "Once this process . . . starts in a district," she continued, "it goes on rapidly until all or most of the original working-class occupiers are displaced, and the whole social character of the district is changed." Not realizing that she was discovering the sociological equivalent of $e = mc^2$, Glass labeled the phenomenon "gentrification."[13]

Not coincidentally, this was the very moment when a young middle class was beginning to eye the forlorn brownstones of Park Slope. By that time, a modest-size group had already renovated the federal and Greek Revival homes of Brooklyn Heights; a few had even crossed the wild border of Atlantic Avenue, or the area that real estate agents had begun to call—hopefully—"Cobble Hill," with its own collection of potentially salvageable nineteenth-century townhouses. The "slum" of Park Slope was deeper yet into Brooklyn; but in 1963, a young couple by the name of Everett and Evelyn Ortner stumbled into the area, launching what turned out to be the multi-decade process of gentrification that Glass was just then discovering in London's Islington.

The Ortners were not just the first of Park Slope's gentrifiers; they were its prophets. (It's worth noting that no one at the time, or except a few academics for at least the next three decades, knew the word "gentrification," though "Quichification" made a brief, local appearance in the 1980s.)[14] They sent brochures to potential recruits in Greenwich Village and on the Upper West Side to advertise the beauty and affordability of this diamond in the rough that they had discovered deep in Brooklyn, a place where many of them had never been. They threw parties for friends and friends of friends at their home, and they organized house tours and lectures explaining the craft of restoration. They arranged for thousands of trees to be planted. With a growing number of coconspirators, some of them college-educated natives, they organized the Park Slope Betterment Committee, which would eventually become the still-active Park Slope Civic Council. Sensing a potential ally in the utility companies that had a strong interest in growing the population serviced by them, they enticed Brooklyn Union Gas Company to buy and refurbish a decayed brownstone—with the best modern gas appliances, of course. The gas company, in turn, worked with local banks on other "Cinderella projects" to bolster endangered blocks.[15]

The civic groups and comradely enthusiasm were crucial for those undertaking what in those days was the risky business of gentrification. No doubt the new Slope crowd was influenced by a housing shortage in Manhattan that was particularly affecting the middle class. Still, the "pioneers," as they sometimes called themselves, were choosing a harder route than their peers who were content with the 5:10 train to Larchmont, one that required a level of adventurousness not ordinarily associated with middle-class domesticity.

For starters, there was a financial risk. Most of the newcomers had little capital except for their educations and maybe a few good social connections. Banks had shown no interest in revisiting the 1938 decision to redline much of the neighborhood. Local bank managers frequently lived in the suburbs, and "Brooklyn [including Park Slope] was, in their mind, the land of crime, gangs and arson," Betterment Committee member Joe Ferris recalled decades later in the *New York Times*.[16] After receiving rejections from twelve banks, the tireless Everett Ortner wrote to David Rockefeller, asking why Chase Manhattan Bank wouldn't mortgage brownstones. Amazingly, Rockefeller responded, and the mortgage freeze started to thaw. Started to, at any rate; at least until the 1970s, when Brooklyn banks sensed that the pioneers were not just a temporary craze, Ortner frequently found himself making phone calls for buyers whose applications had been unaccountably rejected.[17]

After they cobbled together the funds, the gentrifiers' troubles started in earnest. The plumbing and electric wiring in their newly purchased homes was ancient and sometimes even dangerous. The furnaces were coal-burning behemoths the size of railroad cars, inefficiently jury-rigged to burn gas. Layers of lead paint and asbestos coated walls and pipes. Determined to preserve and restore, the new owners stripped the intricately decorated mahogany and oak on every door, window, and mantel. By 1982, writes Suleiman Osman in the best history of brownstone Brooklyn, "the area had three times as many [hardware stores] as the rest of the city."[18] Part of the adventure for early Slopers, much like their back-to-the-land hippie counterparts, was their "do-it-yourself" energy, though many also hired local workers. Wood-stripping products were as toxic as they were foul-smelling. After I moved into the area in the early 1980s, I called the go-to wood stripper to look at a job. I shuddered to realize that his twisted limbs and slow speech might well be a result of decades of contact with chemicals used to beautify the homes of affluent newcomers.

The brownstoners' aesthetic and preservationist impulse extended to the neighborhood at large. The Ortners spearheaded a campaign to gain landmark status for the area. When the poorly staffed Landmarks Preservation Commission showed some interest, neighborhood volunteers, following the model used by gentrifiers in Brooklyn Heights and Cobble Hill in the 1960s, researched and photographed 1,800 buildings to make their case. They were successful. In 1973, about a quarter of Park Slope was officially deemed a historic district, ensuring that no one could paint a façade or alter a cornice or put up another aluminum awning.[19] (In 2012, the district was expanded to include another 600 buildings in the South Slope.)[20]

The revivalists' effort to preserve Park Slope's brownstones set out to protect an invaluable historical legacy. Inadvertently, it also helped to make the prices less Brooklyn than Park Avenue. Throughout the 1970s and 1980s, a white middle class, now enough of a demographic force to earn the name "yuppie" (young urban professional), searched the real estate listings. Their numbers were small compared with the invasion that would be coming, but the demand was great enough to astound residents with regular reports of record-high prices. A large group of lesbians—Park Slope was said to have the "heaviest concentration of lesbians" in the United States[21]—attracted to the relatively low rents and safe streets also added to the demand. A few years after I moved to the area in 1982, outrage greeted anonymous flyers announcing that a five-story house on the park block of Carroll Street, one of the original Gold Coast blocks, had gone for $275,000—a number that could barely buy a studio today. During the decade as a whole, prices rose almost 300 percent.[22] Park Slope hadn't seen any developers since the turn of the century, but with demand like this, their return was inevitable. A number of them, realizing that the house prices had surpassed the bank accounts of many young families, began subdividing brownstones into cooperative apartments.

For all of its record house prices, Park Slope was usually described as "transitional" during those years. The main reason could be seen in the nightly sidewalk baptism of broken glass, the handprinted "You've already stolen my radio" signs on car windows, and the iron bars that protected ground- and first-floor windows. They were decorative bars, to be sure, often designed to fit window boxes for geraniums in the summer months. They were good for business for a diminishing population of Italian iron craftsmen in the area. But they also advertised the reality of daily break-ins, muggings, and worse. Outside schools at 3 P.M., in the aisles of the all-volunteer food co-op, at dinner parties in half-renovated houses, everyone talked about real estate prices, the best second-grade teachers—and the most recent mugging. In 1991, coming home from Christmas shopping, the mother of a preschool classmate of my younger daughter had a gun put to her head as she exited the subway. That's when you go home and consider calling the real estate agents in Westchester, and many did. Briefly, for a few years after the 1987 stock-market crash, prices plateaued, and Park Slope truly earned the label "transitional," though which way it was going was unclear.

And then, for a number of reasons, including police reforms during the administration of Mayor Rudolph Giuliani, crime dropped.[23] The trucks of decorative ironworkers became a less familiar sight. Car alarms went silent for nights and then weeks at a time. The safer streets and appealing new businesses unleashed a flood of middle-class housing demand, which had been kept in check by fear for their children and their investment accounts.[24] Before the 1990s, a lot of young families picked Park Slope by default; they needed space but couldn't afford a three-bedroom on the Upper West Side or, goodness knows, Soho. They especially couldn't afford it once they added private-school tuition into the household budget. No longer. "Brooklyn had been the destination of people who made an economic decision; it wasn't an ultimate destination. Park Slope's writers and journalists had moved there because they didn't have much money," says Stephen Raphael, a longtime Park Slope developer. "After the 90s they came because there was something about living in Brooklyn that they liked. . . . Writers were now moving to Brooklyn with their first large advance. They were willing to pay for the place." The *Daily News* reported a rise in median home prices in Park Slope of 20 percent to 30 percent in the one year between the fall of 1996 and 1997.[25] By 2000, $2 million listings were no longer raising eyebrows.

Real estate agents began nudging aspiring Slopers into tougher nearby brownstone neighborhoods of Prospect Heights and Fort Greene and, perhaps more surprisingly, into the working-class row houses and tenements below Fifth Avenue toward the toxic Gowanus Canal. Throughout the 1980s, northern Fifth Avenue had a 35 percent vacancy rate.[26] Even through much of the improving 1990s, Fifth Avenue was known for its 99-cent stores and its drugs and crime; cashiers in liquor stores, one of the few viable businesses in those parts, sat inside Plexiglas cages for protection from desperate crackheads. Yet by the mid-2000s, Fifth Avenue had morphed from an outpost of the South

Bronx into a capital of brunch. It has surpassed the more established Seventh Avenue as the edgier, more fashionable shopping and dining area, fueled by a crowd of young entrepreneurs and, as of 2009, its own Business Improvement District.

Even the worst economic crisis since the Great Depression couldn't stop Park Slope's upward mobility. After 2008, banks stopped lending and sales flattened, but only very briefly. By 2009–10, Slope real estate had recovered every drop in price. More remarkably, almost half the new buyers were offering mostly or all cash for the houses and condos; such transactions were rare before the recession. There was a lot of local grumbling about Wall Street money driving the craze, and indeed, researchers have noticed "third wave" or "super-gentrification," what English urbanist Loretta Lees describes as "the exorbitant rewards of the global finance and corporate service industries."[27]

But there was another kind of person with enough cash to buy a Park Slope brownstone or co-op: upper-middle-class parents willing to bankroll their grown children's housing. With interest rates at 1 percent, Stephen Raphael explains, those who had the money might look at investing in Park Slope real estate as a better idea than a stock portfolio. Ironically, the more cautious suburban peers of the early pioneers are now, via their children, subsidizing Park Slope's late-stage gentrification. Some of them are even using a floor of those houses for their own pied-à-terre.

With the housing demand remaining intense, developers and city planners saw the potential in the blocks nearest Fourth Avenue and even on that gritty, industrial avenue itself. The street was a dingy traffic corridor with fast food and auto-repair shops and a few tenements remote from any neighborhood. In 2003, the Bloomberg administration decided to rezone thirty-six blocks of Fourth Avenue, allowing developers to build apartment buildings as tall as twelve stories. The plan was promoted as the coming of the second Park Avenue: "It's the same width; it has the same medians that could use some beautifying," said Craig Hammerman, district manager of Community Board 6 and a supporter of the plan. "We think it's appropriate, that it could become a canyon of housing. . . . If it's good enough for Park Avenue in Manhattan, it's good enough for Park Slope."[28] The universal verdict was that the dismaying new buildings were closer to a "canyon of mediocrity," in the words of the *Wall Street Journal*,[29] though they did allow thousands more families to be close to the park, the shops, and small-town atmosphere that had drawn people like myself there in the first place.

The First World development horror on Fourth Avenue hasn't prevented the neighborhood from continuing to lure people looking for the urban village feeling and the architectural pleasures that the pioneers themselves wanted. French, German, and English yuppies, as well as television producers looking for cool backdrops for next season are drawn to the area. Park Slope must have more novelists, poets, and journalists per square mile than any place outside Yaddo. It has celebrities like Maggie Gyllenhaal and John Turturro and buildings by starchitects Richard Meier and Jean Nouvel. When Everett Ortner, the man who had founded the new Park Slope, died in 2012 (his wife, Evelyn, died six years earlier), their house, purchased for $32,500 in 1963, was listed for sale at $4.8 million, eventually selling for $3 million.[30]

PROFILING THE GENTRIFIER

One of the least understood aspects of gentrification—in Park Slope, Seattle, Boston, and every other urban district going from rags to riches—is the identity of the people who actually do the gentrifying. Who are these interlopers who, in the late twentieth century, suddenly began looking to move into areas that their kind had been avoiding for so long? Post–World War II America was an age of suburbanization, after all. The GI Bill, the interstate highway system, federal lending policies, rising crime, and racism were all conspiring to get the white middle class into the suburbs. Why was this particular Brooklyn crowd ignoring all the many reasons to get out of town in the 1960s and 1970s? For that matter, why are so many similar sorts of people still begging for entrance to gentrifying neighborhoods today? That the same thing began happening in London around the same time suggests that the answer has to have deep roots. So let's begin by setting it in the context of changes in the larger economy.

The first requirement before the gentrifying middle class moves into an area is, for better or worse, deindustrialization. The poor didn't have much choice in the matter, but as we've seen throughout Brooklyn's history, the middle class always preferred living at a distance from the toxic fumes, clanging machinery and trucks, foul smells, and rough manners associated with docks, slaughterhouses, gas plants, and machine shops. There was never going to be a mass middle-class homecoming to Brooklyn or any other city if it meant that their kids would be growing up next to a sugar refinery.

The decline of manufacturing was a necessary—though far from sufficient—precondition for Brooklyn to become more appealing to the middle class. There also had to be new jobs. At the same time that many factories were closing shop, white-collar offices were expanding. In 1958, 11 percent of America's population was working in jobs considered white-collar, Daniel Bell noted in his *The Coming of the Postindustrial Society*; by 1980, the percentage was still only 16.3.[31] But remember: the growth was concentrated in cities, especially in New York,[32] now turning into the Rome of white-collardom and the destination for strivers from the staid heartland and the slow-moving

South. New York had long been the nation's capital of finance, insurance, and real estate, as well as media, publishing, art, and philanthropy. Now with the trauma of the Depression and a world war fading into the past, the synergies between those industries was unleashing a huge demand for lawyers, accountants, bankers, managers, advertisers, public-relations workers, editors, and so on. At the same time, federal, state, and city governments were adding agencies and regulations, which led to more jobs in government, as well as in what Bell called the "third sector": schools, hospitals, research institutes, and voluntary and civic organizations.

These new sought-after workers could have just moved to the New Jersey, Westchester, and Long Island suburbs, and plenty (or maybe even most) of them did. But the arrival of the postindustrial economy was also about to change the domestic life of the educated class in ways that reduced the appeal of the suburbs. Jobs in sectors like media, design, law, education, and health services required little muscle power and could even be rather interesting; they soon proved to be especially appealing to educated women. At the same time, rising real estate prices in those cities where the best of the white-collar jobs were clustered were making two incomes a necessity. A 2015 paper, "Bright Minds, Big Rent," looked at the movement of two-earner families into twenty-seven of the largest American cities between 1980 and 2010. "[S]hrinking leisure time of high-income households" due to longer work hours *especially among women* explained much of the migration. "College-educated men and women saw a decline in free time, especially after 1990," the authors write, and "a notable increase" in the fraction of those working fifty or more hours per week.[33] Under those circumstances, the hour-long commute that might have suited their single-breadwinner parents became more untenable. For some of these college grads, the answer was places like Park Slope.

The education piece of the gentrification story can't be emphasized enough. While the United States has active fault lines that dominate the political news—between blacks and whites, whites and Hispanics—a college degree has become the most powerful indicator of socioeconomic status as well as a prerequisite for a middle-class future. In the respects that matter—income, achievement,[34] family formation and life script,[35] health,[36] not to mention cultural taste—the black and Hispanic educated middle class resembles the white educated middle class more than they do less educated people of their own race and ethnicity. The same goes for whites: the Cal Tech grad living in Seattle and the Tufts BA in Park Slope have more in common with a black University of Virginia grad than they do with a white truck driver or janitor in a nursing home. Gentrification is the spatial expression of this class divide: the educated move into accessible urban neighborhoods; the working class and poor move out. As of 1990, 49.5 percent of Park Slope's population was already college-educated, compared with 19 percent of Brooklyn as a whole;[37] by 2000, the Slope's number was over 60 percent.[38]

Already in the 1960s, the Park Slope pioneers foretold the interconnection between gentrification, education, and the postindustrial knowledge economy. A 1971 survey of brownstone owners showed that 99.9 percent had high school diplomas and 60 percent had attended graduate school; that's compared with 50 percent high school grads in the city as a whole.[40] "What kind of people are these, the invading army?," Park Slope brownstoner and *Warriors* screenwriter Sol Yurick asked in a July 1972 article in the *New York Times*. "Lawyers and professors and doctors and architects and psychologists and social workers and writers and newspapermen and city officials and Mayor Lindsay's daughter and poverty fund richies who've made the transition from idealism to hustler and investment analysts and artists and teachers." Suleiman Osman cites a 1976 survey of the occupations of the members of the Brownstone Revival Committee, confirming Yurick's general observation: the members were lawyers, editors, writers, architects, and psychologists. Osman sums up the trend: "The story of brownstoning is the story of the formation of a new postindustrial middle class."

The postindustrial crowd settling in Park Slope had a somewhat different profile from their educated suburban counterparts, a profile that continues to dominate gentrified neighborhoods everywhere. They were an artsy-literary bunch; today, we could call them the "creative class." Ortner himself was an editor; his wife, an interior designer. Another of the earliest settlers, the preservation expert Clem Labine, became a writer and publisher. His wife was a writer at the popular soap opera *One Life to Live*. The many writers and journalists among them—Yurick, Charles Monaghan, who wrote a number of articles in the *New York Times* about Brooklyn real estate, the novelist L. J. Davis—used their talents to spread the good news in major publications about the life that they had found in Park Slope.

The pioneers' artistic tendencies extended well beyond their professions. It was apparent in their aesthetics, their cultural attitudes, and their politics. Perhaps their college social-science courses made them write off the suburbs as "alienating." Perhaps the arrival of Kennedy-era European sophistication led them to scorn what they viewed as the mass consumer tastes of the mall-goer. Whatever the reasons, the original gentrifiers were in conscious retreat from suburban conformity. Though gentrifier tastes have veered back toward mid-century modern, the Tiffany lamps, stained glass, and Victorian antiques that the pioneers collected were a far cry from the harvest-gold kitchen appliances and plastic chairs and dishes favored by suburbanites. They were countercultural, an urban version of the era's hippies who were stripping away modernity's hyper-civilized deceptions by going "back to the land." As acolytes of Jane Jacobs, they despised the artificial, planned high-rise projects and superblocks associated with New Deal urban renewal. In *The Death and Life of Great American Cities*, Jacobs had memorably celebrated the organic "sidewalk ballet" of locals going about their business. That's what the gentrifiers were looking for on the sidewalks of brownstone Brooklyn.

The gentrifiers' politics also tended toward the countercultural. "They're of liberal temperament," Yurick explained in his *Times* article. "[T]hey've backed all the right causes from Kennedy to anti-pollution to integration." Looking for a way to transcend the impersonality and profiteering of corporate America, they organized cooperatives, including nursery schools; one young couple opened the area's first bookstore in 1971, which they called "Community Book Store." ("A bookstore in Brooklyn?," people said to the owners when they opened. "You'll go broke."[41] The shop, like other independent bookstores in gentrifying neighborhoods, continues to thrive today.) In 1977, the now-legendary Park Slope food co-op, the oldest cooperative supermarket in the country, opened its doors. The newcomers embraced diversity well before the word had become the touchstone of enlightenment that it is today.

Still, gentrification has a tendency to surprise even the most open-minded people with its revelations of *la différence*. Tolerant as it can be, educated middle-classness is its own culture, rich with unconscious habits and rules of behavior every bit as distinct as, say, Mexican or Chinese culture is. When the educated middle class sets up housekeeping amid people from a different culture—whether white working class, poor black, or immigrant Hispanic, Chinese, or whoever—tensions are inevitable.

The changing Park Slope, like most gentrifying areas, didn't resemble the Jets and the Sharks, or even Archie Bunker and his son-in-law, Michael. But as gentrification continues to teach us today, those tensions can irritate. In 1979, one Park Slope native described them thus: "The blue-collars hate the blacks and view the brownstoners as weird kids with money and no brains; the blacks and the blue-collars at the very least resent the brownstoners; and the brownstoners try to ignore the blue-collars and strain their liberalism all out of shape trying to adjust to the blacks and their culture of poverty." Speaking with Pete Hamill in 2008, one old-timer summed up the contrast between the two: "They're kids from dorms. My day, they came from barracks."[42] It's a distinction rich with political, generational, and class overtones and, in a general sense, one that continues to gnaw in gentrified areas everywhere.

The cultural distance between Park Slope's newcomers and the dwindling white working class can be captured in the latter's term for the former:

"beatniks." The word was, at best, imprecise, considering the lawyers or city managers among the beatniks, but it captured an aesthetic-cultural divide. The locals wanted to shop at big supermarkets like Pathmark and later at Costco; the newcomers preferred smaller, more personalized shops. The blue-collars enjoyed McDonald's; the newcomers vilified the golden arches. The middle-class people who were lovingly stripping the mahogany trim in their Victorian homes were put off by the aluminum siding and the linoleum floors that the working class used to modernize their elderly homes, while the latter were amused at the gentrifiers' habit of hanging macramé holders with spider plants instead of curtains in their windows.[43] In 1961, well before the Landmark Commission could stop them, a tailor and his wife had painted their brown-stone pastel pink. Years later, when it was time for a fresh coat, the paint they purchased turned out to be even worse, a shade that could be most accurately marketed as Pepto-Bismol. The pink house sat on the well-tended block—a genuine, if unwelcome, reminder of one kind of neighborhood diversity, until 2012, when the tailor moved and the house was finally sold and repainted by someone whose taste conformed to local norms.

Still, the differences between the "beatniks" and the remaining Park Slope Irish and Italian proletariat went far deeper than window treatments and paint color and will probably ring a bell for many gentrifiers today. Cooperative nurseries and supermarkets aside, the middle class tends to have a pronounced sense of personal boundaries and privacy. In Park Slope, gentrifiers oriented themselves toward their prettily landscaped back gardens; many built cedar decks to extend their private space in the outdoors.

Not so the old-timers. Growing up in small apartments, sharing a bedroom or the pullout couch in the dining room with siblings, grandmothers, and aunts, the working class was used to a more collective way of life. The backyard was where they dried laundry, stowed junk, and maybe grew some grapevines and fig trees, still on view in many Park Slope gardens today. It was the block—not the yard—that was their social arena. That's where their kids played and where adults sat in lawn chairs at the top of the stoop or on fire escapes or even on the sidewalk gossiping through to sundown. Today, a major complaint among longtime locals about newcomers, some of them perhaps accustomed to Manhattan skyscraper anonymity, is that they seem too busy or guarded—or is it snobby?—to say "good morning" and chat with their neighbors.

That same acute sense of personal boundaries leads to gentrifiers' discomfort with industrial-era smells, litter, and noise. Some of the older men in this part of Brooklyn liked to play checkers or chess in local parks; now neighbors complained about their cigarette smoke. In Carroll Gardens, a brownstone area close to Park Slope that had long been home to Italian immigrants, newcomers objected to the smell of roasting coffee at an Italian-American café called D'Amico's. D'Amico's had been roasting coffee in the same spot since 1948, probably before most of the complainers had been born. The Department of Environmental Protection threatened to close D'Amico's unless it upgraded its venting system, which it ultimately did—at considerable cost.[44]

There have been other unexpected sources of class tension. Brooklyn civic groups had been fighting poorer residents who kept goats and chickens since the middle class first spread south into the city in the mid-nineteenth century. Likewise, Puerto Ricans in Park Slope, like Italians before them, occasionally kept training pigeons on their roofs, something that didn't go over well with a lot of gentrifiers. As late as 2014, the *Guardian* profiled the Park Slope son of Puerto Rican immigrants from the 1950s. He owns the house that his parents purchased long ago, but he can no longer keep training pigeons on his roof. "These new folks love their animals and spend crazy amounts on them," he observed, "as long as it's cats and dogs."[45]

The class divide was at odds with the early gentrifiers' hope of becoming part of an "authentic" urban village. Authenticity: it's a term without an easy definition, but it comes up frequently in the debates over gentrification. It appears to refer to a people and a specific way of life rooted in a place over a long time, the opposite of the standardization of modern mass society. That's a big part of what attracted early middle-class gentrifiers to neighborhoods like Park Slope, Logan Circle in D.C., Northeast Portland, and Islington, London, and continues to do so today.

One lesson from Park Slope's recent history is that the project is bound to fail, at least in those terms. The working-class locals who created the Park Slope that the early gentrifiers found in the 1960s and 1970s had defined themselves by the block, the parish, the family, and the ethnic group, *not* the neighborhood. The educated middle class—mobile, secular, and individualistic—relied on voluntary, self-chosen bonds, the very opposite of the people they wanted to attach themselves to. Insofar as the gentrifiers were able to create an urban village, it wasn't the geography of the neighborhood that gave it to them. It was the chosen cultural identity that the newcomers shared with one another—a very specific form of quasi-bohemian, educated, progressive middle-classness—that has brought cohesion to the new Park Slope and so many neighborhoods like it. It may not be "authentic," but it is true to the educated middle-class experience and sense of self.

DISPLACEMENT AND TURNOVER

When most people hear about the tension between gentrifiers and local residents, they think "displacement." In fact, some of them seem to assume that the two—gentrification and displacement—are the same thing. They are not. Gentrifiers might move into formerly abandoned buildings or homes that they purchase from owners who are retiring to Florida or moving to be near family in Texas. In those cases, they are not "displacing" a resident in the way the word is generally understood. However, gentrification can drive out tenants by increasing evictions, demolitions, and landlord harassment, and raising rents to heights that existing tenants cannot afford.

This kind of displacement has a decades-long history in gentrifying Park Slope. In the early days (and despite their countercultural sympathies), brownstoners made no bones about wanting to evict tenants whom they often inherited with their newly purchased brownstones. Civic groups published advice on the relevant laws and regulations,[46] and neighbors shared telephone numbers of savvy lawyers. For the most part, these were people who wanted to add on, or reconfigure, space for their own families. Park Slope brownstones often have separate entrances in the basement or "garden" level that made it easy to create rental apartments. Among the early gentrifiers were plenty of teachers, social workers, and public-interest lawyers who relied on that extra income to pay for mortgages or child care that they otherwise couldn't afford.

But it wasn't long before Park Slope's gentrification attracted people who were interested in local real estate for reasons other than homesteading. Opportunities to make money, which providing housing for the relatively well-to-do presents in abundance, attract not just individual buyers but small real estate investors, big-time developers, individual risk-takers, and alas, more than a few sharks. One of the first landlords in the neighborhood to try to turn his Garfield Place apartments into condominiums reportedly cut off the heat and hot water of existing tenants in 1981.[47] The *Village Voice* described the eviction of an elderly tenant when the owner sold development rights to the building that she lived in after Fourth Avenue was rezoned in 2003. A seventy-six-year-old pensioner who had lived in her $550-a-month apartment for twenty years: there was no way she was going to find a similar deal in the area. "The result of this rezoning is they're kicking all the minorities out of here," one African American local told the paper. "And my God, they're giving the seniors hell."[48] A recent oral history of gentrification in New York, *The Edge Becomes the Center*, by D. W. Gibson, profiles unscrupulous and even outright illegal dealings by landlords and their attorneys. One of the worst examples took place in Crown Heights, a rapidly gentrifying neighborhood near Park Slope, where a landlord demolished a rent-regulated tenant's bathroom for "renovation." Months passed when she was forced to use a neighbor's facilities, and it becomes clear that the landlord had no intention of completing the job—at least not as long as she is living there.

It's hard to know just how many bad actors like these are prowling gentrifying neighborhoods. From the anecdotes in Gibson's book and from activists like those at the Fifth Avenue Committee—Park Slope's community development corporation, whose mission includes helping low-income tenants being harassed by their landlords—you'd have to conclude: "a lot." But the picture that you get from the research doesn't support that proposition. Nor does it confirm the widespread assumption that gentrification causes widespread displacement.

Consider the mounting evidence: in a study of gentrifying neighborhoods in New York City between 1986 and 1999, Columbia professor Lance Freeman and coauthor Frank Braconi found a displacement rate that was only 0.5 percent higher than in low-income areas that stayed that way.[49] A paper from NYU's Furman Center actually found *less* turnover and more renter satisfaction among poor households in "gaining" or gentrifying neighborhoods in New York during the 1990s than in stagnant, nongentrifying areas.[50] The bleakest image comes from a University of Toronto study, and even that one fails to qualify as dystopian. The authors calculate an average annual 10,000 displacements a year among all renters in New York City—not just those in gentrifying neighborhoods—between 1991 and 2002. Most of the displaced blamed costs. A small number of them did become homeless. The findings are troubling, but keep in mind that those 10,000 represent 6 percent to 10 percent of intra-city moves among renters (depending on the year).[51]

These studies all have problems: some have questionable definitions of "neighborhood" or "gentrification"; others don't capture the more intensive gentrification of the 2000s before the Great Recession; others fail to follow individual residents over time. A more recent Federal Reserve paper, tracking Philadelphia neighborhoods between 2002 and 2014, tries to correct for these issues, recording annual mobility, financial well-being, and new place of residence for movers. Once again, the results don't begin to support the bad news reports about gentrification. The authors found that low-income residents of gentrifying areas are no more likely to move than similar residents in nongentrifying neighborhoods. Moreover, those in gentrifying neighborhoods report more satisfaction with their living conditions and experience higher credit scores. Most of those who *do* move find new homes in "comparable or better economic conditions," though the few people who do land in worse neighborhoods—those with lower home values and higher rates of unemployment—are more likely to be lower income.[52] We'll delve into those neighborhoods in more detail in later chapters.

Why these surprisingly low numbers? The public discussion about displacement rarely takes into account this crucial fact: the urban poor have always moved far more than the affluent, and—with the exception of tenants of public housing—they continue to do so today. Anti-gentrification fervor is frequently accompanied by a belief in a time when neighborhoods sprouted organically out of the industrial-ethnic-urban soil, when neighbors helped raise one another's children, when the city was diverse and hummed with energy, and when families stayed put over generations. Gentrification, goes the thinking, upset this urban idyll.

But that belief is largely fantasy. "For all the rhetoric of neighborhood attachment," Josh Freeman writes in *Working-Class New York*, "most working-class New Yorkers had only recent roots in their immediate communities, two generations or less." The poor living in bad neighborhoods have always moved a great deal—in search of better jobs, or to escape abusive spouses, in-laws, or landlords. Economist Joe Cortright, who studies mobility and urban development, observes that even today, "far more of the long-suffering poor move out of high-poverty neighborhoods that stay poor than move away from high-poverty neighborhoods that see a significant reduction in poverty."[53]

If there is one lesson to be found in the history of Park Slope, it's the ephemeral nature of urban communities, especially in an immigrant-rich society like the United States. There's no question that gentrification means that people of modest incomes are priced out of neighborhoods like Park Slope, which they once might have been able to afford. Nor is there any doubt that, as Ruth Glass put it, "the social character" of these neighborhoods changes or that established social networks are sometimes disrupted. There are things cities can do to ease some of the disruption. They can, for instance, protect vulnerable tenants from unscrupulous, lawbreaking landlords. They can preserve buildings, street grids, and districts.

But there's a huge cost to trying to make time stand still and a limit to what urban governments can do to protect communities and ways of living grounded in particular moments of social and economic history. Anyone who doubts it should take a good, hard look at Detroit.

· 4 ·

Haute Hippie Williamsburg

$\mathcal{I}$n 2013, *Travel + Leisure* named Williamsburg's recently opened Wythe Hotel one of the year's "It Hotels," but don't go expecting the Ritz. The already-iconic spot is set on a grim warehouse-lined intersection. The lobby has no plush sofas or polished marble floors; instead, wooden stools shaped like tree stumps surround an austere wooden bench sits on a bare concrete floor. Look up for the customary crystal chandelier, and you'll find instead an oddly angled iron track in a rough timbered ceiling. The unshaven doorman is not in livery; no, he is wearing jeans and scuffed work boots. If, like me, you're confused about contemporary sumptuary rules, you might assume that he will be shaking a grimy paper cup into which compassionate passersby have deposited a few coins.

The steerage motif continues as you pass from the lobby to Reynard's, the celebrated hotel restaurant. The room has no drapes or wallpaper covering the distressed walls, nor does it have any uniformed waiters or waitresses. The servers are kids in pajama bottoms or jeans who seem to have wandered in off the street that morning—with the doorman, I guess. There is butcher paper in lieu of linen tablecloths—leftovers, perhaps, from the kitchen where the staff butcher specially raised grass-fed animals for the restaurant's steaks and burgers. If you stop off at Marlow's, the hotel gift shop, you'll find not the usual tourist tchotchkes but satchels and handbags crafted from the hides of the cow whose progeny you might have just eaten on a brioche bun at lunch.[1] When you go to your bedroom and check out the minibar, you'll look in vain for a Snickers bar. The Wythe version is stocked with granola, small-batch liquors, and ice cream—all produced locally. It's all high quality, but one caution: the hotel beds sit so close to the floor that anyone over fifty is going to have to plan her ascent to avoid throwing out her back. God forbid there is a fire.

Like the hipsters walking the streets nearby, the Wythe's style, simultaneously downmarket and precious, is an easy sarcasm target. But the designers were perfectly reading the zeitgeist. The Wythe bypasses conventional elegance in favor of the "authenticity" and industrial drama of "old" Brooklyn. The designers kept the bones of the original 1901 cooperage, that is, a factory for making barrels and casks, from an era when North Brooklyn hummed with active breweries and bars for the guys getting off work at the Domino's refinery. The floor-to-ceiling steel-framed windows, soaring ceilings, and the three-story glass Tetris block on the top of the building with stunning views of midtown Manhattan create a contemporary language of grandeur humbled by the staff's informality and the faint recollection of proletarian toil.

In short, the building perfectly captures New Brooklyn's origins in—and transfiguration of—Old Brooklyn. The result is a shabby-chic, neo-industrial style now associated with Brooklyn and, in particular, Williamsburg. It's a style that has gone global and taken the Brooklyn label with it. Everyone, including people who might have once aspired to the Ritz, whether in Tokyo, Stockholm, Berlin, Philadelphia, or Chicago, wants to be cool in a Brooklyn sort of way.

The story of how Williamsburg turned from an industrial orphan of a neighborhood into the galaxy's hippest corner is usually oversimplified as run-of-the-mill "gentrification." But the recent history of Williamsburg reveals much more about what's happening in contemporary economies and cities than can be captured in that single word.

IMMIGRANTS AND ARTISTS

This is not to say that Williamsburg's newcomers aren't, like those in Park Slope, members of the genus *gentrifier*. Middle class (by education, if not by income), they have chosen to live in formerly down-and-out urban neighborhoods in search of a kind of community and authenticity they find lacking in strip-mall America and commuter suburbia. Their unconventional living preferences are bound up in an artistic sensibility. They are fiercely preservationist when it comes to their neighborhoods, though avidly progressive in their politics and social values.

Yet Williamsburg's gentrification—now taking root in the even more unlikely Bushwick to the south and Greenpoint to its north—seems as though it belongs in a different category from the Park Slope version. For one thing, bad as their condition was in the mid-twentieth century, townhouse neighborhoods like Park Slope and London's Islington, with their bourgeois Victorian aesthetic, at least had a compatible history: after all, they were originally designed for an affluent middle class. Williamsburg, on the other hand, had always been a hard-knocks industrial district. It's striking to see this historical legacy live on in the differences between the two groups of gentrifiers. The newcomers of working-class Williamsburg may be middle class, but they are generally outfitted in vintage (i.e., used) clothing and frequently tattooed, pierced, and counterculturally coiffed. Park Slope's gentrifiers, by contrast, are likely to be more conventionally dressed as they push double strollers and drive their Subarus.

Williamsburg's working-class history remains a powerful presence on the area's streets. The hulks of the Pfizer chemical factory, the Domino refinery, the massive Cass Gilbert–designed Austin and Nichols warehouse, and remnants of the smaller foundries, ironworks, and breweries loom even today. Germans and Irish worked in these buildings and occupied some of the tenements and small townhouses nearby. The steely functional towers of the Williamsburg Bridge, so sharply contrasted with the romantic Gothic turrets of the Brooklyn Bridge, are also integral to the local scenery. The span carried so many poor Jews escaping the tenements of the Lower East Side after its opening in 1903 that it was referred to as "Jews' Bridge." Churches attest to the large Italian community that introduced the beloved festival Giglio over 140 years ago; even today, local Italian men carry on the tradition of marching a multistory pillar decorated with flowers through the streets. The writer Henry Miller, the grandson of German immigrants, is widely remembered as a son of Williamsburg. He spent part of his childhood in a cold-water flat on the unpaved Driggs Avenue in what was then called Northside but today is known as North Williamsburg. Though he doesn't appear to have met her, he was a near-contemporary and neighbor of Betty Smith, the author of the classic 1943 novel *A Tree Grows in Brooklyn*, set in the misery-filled Williamsburg of the early twentieth century.

The decades following World War II brought new groups of immigrants, who continue to dominate parts of Southside, or South Williamsburg. The largest were Hasidic Jews of the Satmar sect who had escaped Romania and Hungary; and Hispanics (first Puerto Ricans, and later Dominicans)—who referred to the area as *Los Sures*. Williamsburg still had a few notable bank buildings and churches from its distant days as a small city commercial center, but with factories beginning to close, the always-poor area was now in big trouble. Northside streets were barren while Southside's were brutal; the *Times* described some of the locals as "Marauders armed with machetes, baseball bats, guns and chains."[2] During the blackout of 1977, Williamsburg stores were looted for days; nearby Bushwick was practically torched to the ground.

This is where things stood until the mid-1980s, when Williamsburg began to see a new group of migrants. They were rock musicians, painters, sculptors, conceptual artists, writers, and unclassifiable creatives. Their arrival was not quite as odd as it might seem. Artists had long gravitated to down-and-out parts of big cities like Paris and London; in New York, it was the Lower East Side and Brooklyn. They were attracted to people living on the margins, the lively streets, and, of course, the cheap rents. After World War II, with a housing shortage in the artist-friendly Greenwich Village, Truman Capote, Norman Mailer, Arthur Miller, and Carson McCullers called Brooklyn Heights home, at least for a while. By the 1960s, a scattered group of artists, which included the fluorescent-light sculptor Dan Flavin, had worked in some of the large loft spaces of Williamsburg.

But the Williamsburg artists arriving in the 1980s and early 1990s were different from *les Greenwich Village bohèmes* of yore. For one thing, this crowd was very young—and very single. In the previous chapter, we saw how, as educated mothers took associate and managerial positions in downtown offices, young families began to see more appeal in urban living. By the 1980s, another change in social life was propelling gentrification to include not just brownstone Brooklyn but more unlikely spots like Williamsburg. Young people—particularly, educated young people—were putting off marriage and children well into their twenties and early thirties, a consequential phenomenon I describe in my book *Manning Up.*[3] Instead of spending the young adult years paying off new mortgages and warming baby bottles, college grads were going to grad or professional school, trying on different careers, or drifting in and out of lifestyles.

The latter group, in particular, may have wanted to join their older comrades in the East Village; but by the late 1980s, that area was becoming too expensive for new graduates. Word got out that right across the East River was a place with large, empty loft spaces—large enough for their art installations and six-piece bands—that were affordable. Though grimy and unreliable, the L train could take them back and forth between "Billyburg" to the simpatico bars and clubs of the Village. True, a lot of Williamsburg was, to put it bluntly, toxic. Childhood leukemia rates were among the highest in New York City.[4] Radiac, the only facility in the city licensed to handle radioactive waste, sat adjacent to the Domino refinery; it was also within breathing distance of a local elementary school. Newtown Creek, a tributary long renowned for its pollution, was nearby. But that was the thing about young singles, particularly those with an artistic bent: with no children or spouses to worry about, they were willing to risk dangers and industrial effluents that would have made their middle-class parents shudder.

Also distinguishing the Williamsburg crowd from their bohemian forerunners were their preferred crafts. Though there were plenty of aspiring novelists, memoirists, and poets, the Williamsburg tribe had more extroverted types than earlier artists' enclaves: sculptors working with unconventional materials, especially found objects; multimedia and conceptual artists; and, most of all, rock musicians. More than cerebral, low-key folk music, rock thrives on young, uninhibited audiences—in other words, the very people moving into Williamsburg.

The scene in the nascent gentrification era of the late 1980s and early 1990s was a magnetic mixture of art school, Woodstock, and proletarian dystopia. The young artists were drawn to the adventure of the razor-wire and oil-tank landscape and the waterfront, with its broken piers, abandoned burned cars, and occasional random body parts in the high grasses; walking ten blocks to the Laundromat while dodging the more than occasional rat made for good war stories and polished their starving-artist cred. The more adventurous among them might even snort cocaine at Kokie's, whose name was a sly allusion to its favored inebriant, with Puerto Rican toughs.[5] After perestroika, a new wave of Polish immigrants arrived in nearby Greenpoint, spilling over into Williamsburg; they added another layer of exotic color to the surroundings.

The artists had a different relationship to their grim surroundings than did the Latinos, Hasidim, and Poles who lived there, too. Using their ingenuity and manual skills, they made a playground out of the detritus of the industrial era. They turned rubbled factories into living space—or tried to, at any rate; without money or experience, they sometimes blew out their buildings' power while tinkering with electrical panels. They squatted near vagrants or the still-operating sweatshop, or rented from eager landlords. (With little demand for the desolate buildings, they were happy to rent to the twentysomethings. Who else could be trusted not to complain to authorities about rampant code violations and a lack of hot water and heat?) For entertainment, they held impromptu film screenings on vacant building walls. Robert Moses had built the enormous McCarren Park pool in 1936 for the enjoyment of local German, Irish, and Jewish immigrants. By the 1980s, it had closed, victim of government neglect, deindustrialization, and racial tension. The Williamsburg artists resurrected the graffitied cavern as an astonishing performance space for local dance troupes and bands.

The inside of those abandoned, trash-filled warehouses that no one else had any use for became the site of some of 1990s Williamsburg's most memorable events: all-night multimedia "immersion" bacchanalias. The genre-bending parties brought together video artists, punk bands, stilt walkers, painters, sculptors, sword swallowers, contortionists, conceptual artists, whatever other imaginative soul who could possibly be included in the category "artist." The cavernous spaces were decorated with "found" objects: scrap-metal streamers, forests of plastic strips to create the impression of "plastic fog."[6]

The impresario of "Organism," one of the most famous of these extravaganzas, was Ebon Fisher, an MIT media-lab graduate and gnomic conceptual artist. Fisher and his coproducers held their event in the Old Dutch Mustard Factory, a brick pile built in 1908. It started life as a warehouse for rags and paper, until 1930, when two Czech immigrants turned it into a factory for making vinegars, mustard, and juices. They stayed for over fifty years— though, like so many other Brooklyn factory owners, they eventually moved to a more welcoming location (in their case, Long Island).

The departure turned out to be a boon for the arriving artists. The cavernous space was ideal for letting young creative people go wild. "Hang your stuff. Read your stuff. Play your stuff. Project your stuff. GET INVOLVED," read one poster for the 1993 Organism. One hundred artists and 2,400 guests wandered the space all night, watching exploding watermelons and performers rappelling down silos.[7] "The fine arts are dead," one organizer told *Newsweek*, "and we're taking advantage of decentralized media to create a new cultural forum."[8] The idea was not just to entertain local artists but to use art to shape a bedraggled community; Fisher called it a "web jam." The artists were small in numbers—in 1990, there were probably only 2,000 or so in Williamsburg— but some people were convinced that Williamsburg at that moment was still the largest enclave of artistic talent ever to congregate in one community in American history.[9] They may have been right.

THE RISE OF THE ARTIST-ENTREPRENEUR

But the artists' adventure among the ruins couldn't last. "We're under siege from all sides," Eve Susman, a well-known local artist, told *The Brooklyn Rail* as early as 2001. "The neighborhood is at war."[10] Most people put the blame for the "war" against Williamsburg's avant-garde on real estate developers, trust-fund hipsters, and Wall Street wannabe bohemians, who were bringing their minimalist furniture into the mediocre condominium mid-rises and towers springing up in the area by the first few years of the new millennium. That interpretation is not wrong—more on this soon—so much as incomplete. Already in the early 1990s, articles in *New York* magazine and *New York Press* were bringing establishment attention to the intriguing happenings across the East River.

The larger threat to the scene turned out to be the entrepreneurial energy of the artists themselves. Changes in the culture and the economy that they themselves barely understood were giving them the power to spin their passions into a decent income. Creativity, the arts, and innovation were becoming integral to a shifting economy and expanding opportunities.[11] In a 2002 paper, the urban theorist Richard Florida explains: "Capitalism, or more accurately new forms of capitalist enterprise . . . are in effect extending their reach in ways that integrate formerly marginalized individuals and social groups."[12] In effect, the revolutionary Williamsburg arts scene was destined to be devoured by its own.

One of the first of the new breed of artist-entrepreneurs was Andrew Tarlow, a struggling painter/bartender who had moved from Manhattan to South Williamsburg for loft space. He had a crowd of friends, other artist refugees from Soho and the East Village, but the area was as empty of places to hang out together as a junkyard. He and a friend did something similar to the warehouse scene setters; they found a derelict space—an ancient train dining car—did some do-it-yourself preparations, and started a small restaurant. In a foreshadowing of hipster irony and retro styling, they called the place Diner.

It was a crazy kid idea: they had no business experience or plan. They hadn't even hired a chef. But their timing and location were ideal. Shortly before opening in the winter of 1998, they happened to meet a young cook who had trained at the Savoy, one of the first locavore restaurants in Soho. Almost immediately, Diner became a key part of the local scene; actually, it *invented* the scene—at least, in that part of Williamsburg. The place was packed; people hung out there at lunch, having drinks or coffee in the afternoon, staying through dinner. When a *New York Times* food critic gave Diner a glowing review, it wasn't just a great advertisement for the restaurant; it was great publicity for this forgotten neighborhood and its enclave of offbeat artists. So many people wanted to see what was happening that five years later, Tarlow and his partner were able to open an equally successful second spot, which they called Marlow & Sons, just a few blocks away. (Tarlow would eventually go on to open the aforementioned Reynaud's at the Wythe Hotel.)[13]

Diner was not the first restaurant to focus on perfectly fresh ingredients and unfussy surroundings and preparation; Alice Waters had done just that when she opened her legendary Chez Panisse in Berkeley, way back in 1971. But Tarlow did play an important role in creating a Brooklyn restaurant style: casual-seeming but meticulously cooked food in downmarket surroundings. The Brooklyn vision and its aesthetic vocabulary—exposed brick, naked Edison bulbs, distressed wood—have spread all over the developed world, including the gastronomic capital of Paris. You can eat wonderful food in a junked train car on plebeian plates served by waitresses more likely to start dancing with the bartender to the beat of the indie music playing on the sound system than to inquire, "More Dom Pérignon, sir?" Truffles and oysters can still appear on the Brooklyn menu, but more common is old-fashioned "comfort food" turned into something haute: burgers made from grass-fed cattle from a New York farm, butchered in-house, and served on a perfectly grilled brioche bun; mac 'n' cheese made from heritage grains and artisanal cow and sheep's milk.

Tarlow was not the only Williamsburg artist unknowingly helping to define a Brooklyn brand at the turn of the millennium. Around the same time he opened up Diner, twenty-six-year-old Lexy Funk and thirty-one-year-old Vahap Avsar were stumbling into creating a successful business in an entirely different discipline. Their beginning was just as inauspicious as Diner's: a couple in need of some cash found the canvas of a discarded billboard in a Dumpster and thought that it could be turned into cool-looking messenger bags. The fabric on the bags looked worn and damaged, a textile version of Tarlow's rusted railroad car, but that was part of its charm. Funk and Avsar rented an old factory, created a logo with Williamsburg's industrial skyline, emblazoned it on T-shirts, and pronounced their enterprise Brooklyn Industries. ("We wanted it to sound like a steel plant," Funk told CNBC.)[14] At first, they sold mostly to friends and friends of friends; but today, with sixteen stores in three states and a successful online business, the website announces that the brand "fills a void in the clothing market with artistic clothing for urban dwellers."[15] Just as in the case of Diner, Williamsburg—the place and its artists—was crucial to the company's identity and its eventual success.

Through a combination of high animal spirits, lucky timing, and a clustering of innovative peers, these entrepreneurs were able to tap into—and to promote—several related cultural trends. First was a change in public taste. Industry's decline was expanding the popular aesthetic vocabulary;[16] what was once associated with deafening, dangerous, and stultifying work could now be admired as historic creations and greeted with reverential, if only quasi-informed, nostalgia. The taste for outré street culture like grunge and hip-hop had already spread into youth culture. Now industrial style was becoming another major signifier of urban hipness. With so many artists moving to formerly industrial neighborhoods not just in Brooklyn but in Wicker Park in Chicago, Chelsea in Manhattan, and Belltown in Seattle, the industrial style was becoming closely associated with young artists and their way of life.

Another trend working in the artist-entrepreneurs' favor was the growing cultural power of artists. After World War II, artists had gained some visibility in popular culture—though they were still largely a marginal, elite concern.[17] But by the late twentieth century, with more Americans going to college, making more money, and, thanks to more affordable airfares, traveling to Europe and Asia, the market for art was expanding, as were the number of artists.[18] A growing educated middle class had the money to support the ballooning number of galleries. David Brooks had noticed the blending of bohemian and bourgeois—or "bobo"—sensibilities in 2000.[19] Gentrified neighborhoods are the urban habitus of the bobo, and art galleries are about as good a signifier of gentrification as wine and coffee bars. In fact, many wine and coffee bars in gentrified areas *are* art galleries where a revolving cast of local artists display their work.

By the mid-2000s, "a new kind of ambition was taking hold," writes Ann Fensterstock of Williamsburg in *Art on the Block*, a history of the turn-of-the-millennium New York art scene. There was "a thirst for critical attention in the wider, increasingly international art world. The notion of producing art for profit was no longer anathema."[20] Anyone with a modicum of irony couldn't help but notice the symbiosis between the artists and the affluent gentrifiers. Even as the latter changed Williamsburg in ways the artists either hated or could not afford, they also enlarged the pool of money sloshing around for galleries and art. When it comes to the prosperous newcomers, the Williamsburg artists can't live with 'em and can't live without 'em.

Along with an interest in gallery-hopping, middle-class Americans were growing intrigued by the artists themselves: in post-1960s America, their autonomy, ingenuity, and fealty to free self-expression had become aspirational values. But whereas the early 1990s Williamsburg's warehouse scene was too drugged-out and anarchic to have mass appeal, twenty-first-century Williamsburg was producing a more accessible artist-model. Artist-entrepreneurs like Funk and successful indie bands like LCC Sound System were pragmatists demonstrating that work—even work that made a lot of money—could also be a passion project. "Live, Work, Create" was Brooklyn Industries' motto, printed on the front window of its stores. The ethos gave birth to the multitude of artisanal businesses percolating in Brooklyn, especially in areas near Williamsburg.

As the success of Diner and Marlow & Sons foretold, food has become one of the most popular media for this new generation of creative entrepreneurs. They have started businesses for locally made pickles, beer, mayonnaise, and chocolate, often with a nod to their home borough. "We make small-batch charcuterie using sustainable meat and fine-dining technique, with a bit of Brooklyn swagger thrown in for good measure," reads the website for Brooklyn Cured, maker of cured meats. Some of the entrepreneurs are drop-outs from the Manhattan establishment who were able to take "Live, Work, Create" to heart. Daniel Sklaar left his position as a financial analyst to open Fine & Raw, a company that produces raw chocolate with what the website calls "conscious ingredients." A disaffected Chase Bank employee named Tom Potter partnered with an ex–Associated Press reporter to found one of Williamsburg's most famous companies and a top Williamsburg tourist destination: the Brooklyn Brewery.

By this time, what seemed like a significant percentage of the nation's art-school students and graduates were pouring into Williamsburg, Bushwick, and Greenpoint. Many of them were joining, or launching, fashion and graphic design firms; between 2003 and 2012, Brooklyn as a whole saw a 101 percent increase in design businesses, according to the Center for an Urban

Future.[21] The art grads fit right in to the artisanal scene. The chocolates, pick-les, and music groups coming out of North Brooklyn almost always have mag-nificent logos and packaging, thanks to all that design talent within a few miles, or perhaps even next door. Other do-it-yourselfers made furniture, clothing, lighting, and decorative *objets*. They sold their products at crafts fairs in Wil-liamsburg and other Brooklyn street markets. Ironically, a decaying industrial neighborhood was reviving preindustrial modes of production. The number of businesses in Williamsburg grew by nearly 32 percent between 2003 and 2011, compared with a 21 percent gain borough-wide.[22]

It wasn't just individual artist-entrepreneurs making things happen. It was the density of talent and energy. Ideas were shared, visions imitated and trans-formed. Justin Moyer, a musician, described the process in an article in the *Washington City Paper*: "[There] are galleries, and loft parties, and record stores. A dude who presses vinyl lives there. So does a dude who makes stickers and a woman who books a venue. Because there's an infrastructure that supports getting shit done, people do shit, and a lot of the shit they do is cool. Someone is a recording engineer. Someone is a graffiti artist. Someone has a blog. There's a lot of energy, and a lot of people to know. Information—'Know a cheap place to print posters?' or 'Who can play the tambourine in my Jefferson Airplane cover band?'—is the coin of the realm."[23]

The turn of the millennium saw one other significant force that would shape the new capitalist-friendly Williamsburg: the arrival of the "brogram-mers." Like other gentrifying cities at the turn of the millennium—Seattle, San Francisco, Boston—North Brooklyn was attracting a large number of tech-savvy college grads. Williamsburg's veteran artists grumbled about these new-comers for some understandable reasons. After all, your typical computer-science grad is likely to outearn your average sculptor or performance artist by considerable amounts. That earnings gap has helped turn San Francisco into a virtual war zone between Silicon Valley commuters and more long-term resi-dents; it likely did drive up costs for housing and local retail in North Brooklyn as well. It stung even more that higher-income techies were often barely out of their teens, while many of the artists were going gray.

Despite the antagonism, there turned out to be a creative synergy between the techno-types and the artists that was a boon to both groups and helped complete the transformation of Williamsburg and its neighboring dis-tricts into the New Brooklyn. Computer technology hugely expanded the possibilities for making money through creative endeavors, especially with the rise of Web 2.0 around 2004. Web-design businesses opened all over Brooklyn as the Internet gave local businesses a global reach. An obvious confluence of interests between video artists, musicians, and techies allowed artists to experi-ment with new projection and audio techniques. More generally, the web was turning out to be a visual and audio playground. "The Internet entailed not only the explosion of information but also the *aestheticization of information*," writes Vanderbilt sociologist Richard Lloyd in *Neo-Bohemia: Art and Commerce in the Postindustrial City*.[24]

For all of their right- and left-brain differences, the digital newcomers and the analogue old-timers shared a certain sensibility. Richard Florida has found a close connection between "bohemian clusters" and high-technology industry in American cities.[25] Like artists, techies prefer autonomy and flexibility; they needed space to pursue their project-based passions, and warehouses fit the bill. Some of the warehouses of North Brooklyn began to be "repurposed" yet again, this time not for Organism events but for coworking spaces. Programmers shared rent, coffee-making equipment, Internet access, TGIF rooftop barbecues, and ideas with aspiring info-graphic designers, illustrators, graphic artists, and aspiring start-up founders.

Two successful start-ups perfectly reflect North Brooklyn's symbiosis of technology and the arts. First is the website Etsy. In 2005, three NYU grads—two of them coders and one an eccentric dreamer-craftsman living in Fort Greene, a bit to the south of Williamsburg—launched an online marketplace where craftspeople who made everything from pillows to knives to posters could set up online shops. Etsy is, in effect, a flea market, but online; and just like analogue flea markets, it has the potential to bring a lot more customers than would individual stores' websites. Craftspeople from all over the country—and even some from abroad—were soon paying the small fee to sign on. Within three years after its launch, 400,000 vendors sold $100 million worth of goods on Etsy.[26] "Rob is an accidental businessperson," said Fred Wilson, an early investor in Etsy, about Rob Kalin, the craftsman and one-time public face of the company. Kalin left the company he founded in 2011, but Etsy is now housed in Brooklyn's Dumbo, another tech and design warehouse neighborhood a short bike ride from Williamsburg. (The firm is one of Brooklyn's top two tech employers.) It's an apt description for so many of North Brooklyn's entrepreneurs—Tarlow, Brooklyn Industries' Lexy Funk, and many others. In 2008, Kalin was invited to lecture the Masters of the Universe at Davos. In April 2015, Etsy debuted an IPO; it was only the second Brooklyn company to go public.

The other tech company greatly expanding opportunities for artistic types is Kickstarter. Kickstarter "crowdfunds" creative projects like films, music groups, or the Pebble watch. The idea originated with Perry Chen, a sometime Brooklyn musician who was making a living as a waiter at Diner (early 2000s Williamsburg was a small world). One frequent customer was the editor of an online music site, and, together with a web designer, the three kickstarted Kickstarter. The start-up moved into its first offices on the Lower East Side of

Manhattan in 2009 but by 2013 had set up shop in its spiritual home of North Brooklyn. The company renovated the renowned nineteenth-century Eberhard Faber Pencil Factory with meticulously sustainable materials. Etsy and Kickstarter have not just hired hundreds of locals to staff their offices, a benefit for Brooklyn in and of itself. They have launched the careers of Brooklyn artists and, in fact, of innumerable people with an idea and a penchant for making things, all over the country and the world.

As North Brooklyn and Dumbo developed into centers of innovation, other young Internet companies have been clamoring to join the scene. A number of these companies employ more than 500 people. Amplify invents data-driven instruction and digital curricula, while Huge creates brands and digital presence for businesses. Perhaps the most well-known is Pitchfork, which was invented by Minneapolis teenager Ryan Schreiber in 1995. Schreiber had located his company in Chicago before finally moving his offices to the inevitable Greenpoint. (The company was purchased by Condé Nast in 2015.) Vice Media, which began as a street paper in Montreal, has also grown up and come to Williamsburg. Rupert Murdoch has a 5 percent stake in the company, now estimated to be worth over $4 billion.

With parts of Williamsburg now as pricey as Manhattan, Bushwick has become the hot destination for companies looking to give their brand a more youthful, with-it identity. Real estate agents find "a growing preference for edgier and more industrial environments in office design," according to the real estate paper *The Real Deal*. "Every firm from Manhattan checking out Brooklyn expects an outdoor space or something unique like twenty- or thirty-foot-high ceilings."[27] *Crain's* interviewed a real estate investment firm owner who counted out-of-state license plates as he drove around Bushwick one day in the fall of 2015. He stopped when he got to thirty states.[28] Across the street from the former Rheingold brewery (purchased for conversion to residential lofts), the sixty-five-year-old Schlitz beer-bottling factory is being revived as a "cool, sexy and strong" work space. Meanwhile, Dumbo developers are also responding to the new demand for spaces for start-ups ready to grow by reconfiguring condos into offices. Plans for a new complex called Dumbo Heights have attracted a lot of press attention because one of the developers is Jared Kushner, Donald Trump's son-in-law, and also because it's an enormous project dedicated to the technology, advertising, media, and information, or TAMI, fields. A partner in the venture has described it as "our little hipster kibbutz."[29]

North Brooklyn's explosion of youthful entrepreneurial energy and successful innovation, its global recognition, the appeal of its industrial aesthetic, and its flood of new money have turned a crumbling, decaying district into a dynamic—and increasingly expensive—cultural, business, and tourist center.

To give just two small examples: North Fourth Street between Kent and Bedford once had next to no retail in the old Brooklyn; it has now become one of the most expensive shopping corridors in the borough.[30] In 1991, when Brooklyn Brewery first came to North 11th Street, across the street from the Wythe Hotel, they could expect around eight people to show up to drink beer on a good night, and many of those were relatives or close friends of employees. Now there are 3,000 to 4,000 on a good weekend, and a good number of them are from abroad.[31]

THE GREAT REZONING

It's an immutable law of human civilizations that when a neighborhood becomes cool, everyone wants to move there. Inevitably, Williamsburg's remarkable metamorphosis and the exploding numbers of educated young singles drawn to its delight-filled streets led to a huge demand for housing that the existing local supply couldn't possibly satisfy. The result was housing shortages, eye-popping rents, apartment waiting lists, pressure on existing tenants, a packed calendar of community protests, and intense spillover demand into neighboring districts, especially Bushwick and Greenpoint.

As we saw in the previous chapter, the problem of housing the growing hordes of middle-class urbanites is widespread in the United States. The problem of high demand is not even limited to the United States. Google almost any city name in Europe or Australia, along with the phrase "housing shortage" or "soaring rents," and you'll find enough examples to fill an ambitious bucket list. The *New York Times* reports that 40,000 new workers arrive to join one of Stockholm's tech and financial firms annually; the city's housing shortage threatens to send them elsewhere.[32] Berlin, which has become "a magnet for European youth," was seeing more than 40,000 people moving in each year, well before the 2016 migrant crisis. Meanwhile, the city is building only about 8,000 units of housing annually.[33] The housing pressure has brought out some bad behavior. According to *Der Spiegel*, Berlin landlords in the former immigrant district of Neukölln sometimes double the rent once they get a glimpse of the well-heeled "students, families, and young professionals" scouting the area.[34]

City officials had one major tool in adapting the old Williamsburg to the growing demand: a zoning code written in 1961, over a generation before the area's redevelopment became the issue. Over the years, the code had been amended, refined, clarified with various setbacks, height limits, and approval processes; yet it still manages to be a blunt instrument. Basically, an area could be districted for one of three uses: commercial, residential, or manufacturing. It could also be upzoned (increasing the size and density) or downzoned (reducing allowable density). The Williamsburg waterfront and several blocks along it were zoned for manufacturing. However, the vast majority of Williamsburg was zoned residential for row house–size buildings.[35]

Officials also confronted the wide range of interested and, in some cases, passionate parties they might find in any other gentrifying city. There were renters, who assumed that more development would mean higher rents. There were also residents who wanted to keep Williamsburg "authentic," which appeared to mean, more or less the way it seemed when they moved in. People were right to worry: unlike Park Slope, Williamsburg was not landmarked. Change could easily come in dramatic form. The other formidable group was developers who would celebrate rising rents and were not especially sentimental about the area. Then there were community organizations representing various overlapping subgroups: in Williamsburg's case, Hasidim, Latinos, Poles, the poor and working class, local manufacturers, artists, preservationists, and environmentalists.

Intensifying the emotions surrounding the debate was Williamsburg's industrial decline. North Brooklyn's derelict factories, rotting piers, and poverty had epitomized the misery of the borough's mid-century deindustrialization. As industry decamped, vast stretches of land were left vacant or underutilized; but there was still no easy access to the waterfront, with its incomparable views of the Manhattan skyline.

Yet to rezone the area was tantamount to admitting defeat to the powerful forces arrayed against the blue-collar economy, forces represented by the very middle-class young people clamoring for Williamsburg digs. In the later 1990s and early 2000s, developers had "infilled" vacant parcels on residential or mixed-use streets and converted industrial buildings; one of them was the Smith Gray building, a former menswear manufacturer, one of the few Soho-style cast-iron buildings in the neighborhood. These efforts were nowhere near meeting demand. To the great pleasure of New York City's powerful real estate interests, city planners concluded that more housing was needed. A lot more.

Ultimately finalized in 2005, the city's plan for Williamsburg was a time bomb that would bring despair to anyone hoping to hang onto the Williamsburg of the past. The Department of City Planning (DCP) rezoned a 200-block area of Williamsburg and Greenpoint to allow not just modest-size residential buildings but skyscraper residential buildings of up to thirty stories. Some said, reasonably enough, that the plan was larger in scope and more radical in its implications than anything since the Robert Moses era, with the possible exception of Manhattan's Battery Park City. Almost everyone hated it.[36] Even an aging Jane Jacobs came out of semiretirement to weigh in against it, with a letter to the city from her home in Toronto. The plan seemed to confirm the worst suspicions about government's ties to Big Real Estate and its disregard for neighborhood little guys. It didn't help the city's case that the mayor, Michael Bloomberg, was one of the richest men in America or that Amanda Burden, head of DCP, was a socialite with an impeccable Upper East Side/ East Hampton pedigree.

As so often with gentrification, the big guy versus little guy narrative couldn't explain everything. Some community groups like Churches United welcomed the large buildings because they would include "affordable"—or, to be more precise, below-market-rate—housing.[37] Following some of the recommendations made by local community boards, critics were able to chisel away a bit at the original city proposal. The city agreed to keep thirteen of the affected blocks zoned for manufacturing. It added incentives for developers to create more below-market-rate housing. It also threw in five more acres of parkland, $20 million seed money for new factories, and $4 million to help existing companies on the site relocate.

Nevertheless, by 2006, the fifteen- and twenty-five-story towers of Schaefer Landing (approved before the 2005 rezoning) had begun the transmutation of the North Brooklyn waterfront. Ten years later, the process is ongoing, but there has been enough construction to confirm at least some of the critics' concerns. Most egregious is a two-block multi-tower project called, in a nod to Williamsburg's artsy allure, the Edge. A forty-story glass tower, next to a thirty-foot tower, next to yet another forty-story in the works are, as Jane Jacobs predicted, "visually tiresome, unimaginative and imitative of luxury project towers" (though that didn't stop the throngs from buying; for several years running, the Edge was one of the top-selling developments in New York City).[38] The towers create a massive wall between the community and the waterfront park. The park may be public space, but it feels like a private front lawn for Edge residents. "Affordable" housing has yet to materialize in anything like the quantities predicted. A 2012 statement by the local community board resorted to biblical depictions about the "tide of grief" caused by the "forced exodus" of commercial and residential tenants.[39] Meanwhile, the area's infrastructure remains inadequate to the new population. Even after an upgrade of the signal system, L train commuters sometimes have to let three or more trains go by before they can find enough space inside a car into which they can shove themselves.

Yet blaming Bloomberg and developers ignores the constraints inherent in the existing zoning and approval process. While the uproar over the upzoned waterfront raged on, few seemed to notice that most of residential Williamsburg had been "downzoned," or "contextually zoned," which amounts to the same thing. Any new building would be limited to the same three or four stories that already existed in the immediate context. By making even incremental increases in housing impossible in large swaths of the district, downzoning limited the supply of housing and gave rise to towers (where permitted), higher rents, and advancing gentrification. "The city's ubiquitous six-story tenement would be illegal to build in most of Williamsburg today, as would many of the neighborhood's coveted loft buildings," Stephen Smith, an acerbic critic of the city's housing policies, has written. "Because the amount of housing in the neighborhood is effectively capped through zoning, demand has spilled out of the neighborhood much faster than it would have if Williamsburg had been allowed to grow."[40]

The widespread use of downzoning is a perfect example of good intentions gone awry. Traumatized by Robert Moses's slash-and-burn approach to urban renewal, the city created fifty-nine community boards with their own—albeit nonbinding—say in local planning and budgetary matters. Designed to decentralize an impersonal and unresponsive decision-making process, the boards were, in many respects, a needed innovation. The boards give locals power to limit development for good reasons; they also give them power to act out of self-interest, with little regard for the city's broader needs. They might understandably worry about overcrowded schools and subways. Or they might just dislike interlopers. One thing's for sure: they empower people's natural aversion to change. Despite Mayor Bloomberg's reputation for wanton development, between upzoning and downzoning, the city increased residential capacity by only 1.7 percent between 2003 and 2007, according to a report from the Furman Center.[41] More worrisome, most of the downzoning took place in white, relatively affluent, areas. If upzoning the waterfront was a big win for developers, then downzoning residential areas was the same for well-off homeowners.

NEW BROOKLYN'S ELITE

The original artist settlers in Williamsburg came for the area's low rents but also happily seized on the outsider status provided by their gritty, outer-borough home. As a group, they were proudly antiestablishment, defining themselves in opposition to what they viewed as Soho's commercialism, with its snooty curators, slick galleries, and capitalist greed. Their close, self-contained community gave them the freedom to be indifferent to the absence of the mainstream press and sparsely attended gallery openings.

That was then. Williamsburg's outsiders have now not only been drawn into the mainstream: they are redefining its terms. Their tastes and lifestyle have become normcore and have migrated from small start-up efforts by locals to the development and marketing offices of large corporations. Urban Outfitters has opened a "concept" store in Northside; it has all the familiar Williamsburg/Brooklyn fixtures, including a rooftop bar, brick and exposed beams, goods by local designers, and so on. Levi's has opened a 3,000-foot store selling "authorized refurbished vintage" jeans as well as its usual collection. For months, the store was advertised on Brooklyn streets with thumbnail portraits of young men and women of various hues and the enticing words "We are Brooklyn." Millions of white suburban girls have watched *Girls*, an HBO series created by Lena Dunham, a Brooklyn artist-filmmaker, about a group of aspiring young artists hanging out in cafés and warehouse parties in a proto-Williamsburg setting. Young opportunity-seekers find imaginative ways to latch on to the Williamsburg allure. One of the most unself-conscious is surely an anti-gentrification-messaged "Affordable Brooklyn" T-shirt made by a company called Standard Brooklyn and Wardrobe for sale on the Etsy site. Made from the same cotton as old Brooklyn's "wife beaters" that you could find for a few bucks, it's printed in Soviet realist–style with a muscular hand gripping a protest flag. It costs "only" $30.

You could say that these are all merely examples of the market co-opting of the counterculture that drove so much marketing in the 1960s and 1970s.[42] There's a big difference between the "Pepsi Generation" ad campaign and the success of Lena Dunham, however. In the latter case, a high-tech, creative economy is nourishing the actual artist (or designer or digital innovator), not just appropriating a countercultural style. That economy has consummated a marriage of art and commerce going well beyond anything that the world has seen before. Artists become CEOs lunching with lawyers and bankers, throwing around terms like "leverage" and maybe even "IPO." Indie musicians front for Beyoncé and fill venues in Paris and Tokyo. Those who don't strike it rich may still find market space to pursue their craft. "[T]he space between starving artists and rich and famous is beginning to collapse," Jack Cont, member of the band Pomplamoose and cofounder of the crowdfunding platform Patreon, observed in a controversial 2014 article.[43] Williamsburg's creative class has learned the ways of Wall Street capitalism. Some old-timers complained because their grungy old haunts were shutting down. It wasn't just due to high rents; the rising generation had raised the bar for good food, thoughtful service, and appealing surroundings. Profits, distribution, business plans, customer satisfaction, vertical markets along with sustainability, organic materials, and community responsibility: meet the economic engine of New Brooklyn.

Williamsburg's prosperous bohemia brings us back full circle to the Wythe Hotel. The Wythe takes the aesthetic objects of Williamsburg's recent development—the derelict factories and warehouses, the artisanal foods and soaps, the roughhewn and retro furniture, the industrial décor, and the art (the hotel has its own curator)—and polishes them into establishment glamour, ready for their close-up in *Travel + Leisure*. Ironically, the hotel—and Williamsburg, more generally—represents the triumph of a new, alternative, Brooklyn elite. Instead of Anna Wintour lunching at Michael's, we have *Vice* editors lingering over cappuccino at Reynard's. Town cars cruise these streets. True, the Wythe makes gestures toward keeping the alt faith: the hotel keeps several modestly priced rooms with bunk beds for band members playing at the famous warehouse entertainment venue across the street, Brooklyn Bowl.

That can't change the fact that Williamsburg shows History once again playing with us: the very people who shunned modern commerce and establishment rules have created a new global style and notable power center. They are the prime movers behind the "Brooklynization of the World."[44]

· 5 ·

The Brooklyn Navy Yard

New Brooklyn's New Manufacturing

$\mathcal{I}$ doubt that many Thomas Piketty or Bernie Sanders acolytes know what a 5-Axis CNC router is, but they probably should. Strictly speaking, the router is a robot, though if you're expecting R2D2, you'll be disappointed. This robot is more like an extra-wide, open-sided MMR machine. The patient— usually a slab of plastic, metal, or wood—lies on the bed, where it is "operated" on by a giant drill-like machine suspended from a track above. Following computerized instructions (CNC stands for Computer Numerical Control), the drill grabs the needed "bit" as it moves along the track to cut, trim, and shape the slab/patient into a seat, a domed architectural detail, or whatever it is that its human master is trying to make. The more ordinary and less expensive 3-axis has a drill that can move left to right, right to left, and up and down. Ah, but the 5-axis can go around and create swirly, curving, complex forms. Done by mere humans, these forms would be so time-consuming as to consign them to the category of one-of-a-kind sculpture rather than manufactured object.

I saw the 5-axis router in action at Situ, a fabrication company housed in a massive garage still enclosing the train tracks attesting to its former identity as a locomotive repair shop. The space is located in the 300-acre Brooklyn Navy Yard on an East River inlet between the Williamsburg and Manhattan Bridges. A mere twenty-five years ago, the Yard was the perfect symbol of the ruins of the American working class, its forty or so structures strewn like industrial carcasses from a Mad Max movie. The buildings, used as warehouses and by a smattering of small manufacturing firms, endured regular blackouts, stuck elevators, and roads so cratered that truckers referred to the area as Dodge City. Occasional wild dogs and dead bodies (mob related, one assumes) completed a scene that was more film noir than site of legitimate business.

Enter through one of the five gates of the Yard today, though, and you'll find scores of young companies like Situ humming with deliveries, projects, plans, and digital machinery. The Yard is now home to 330 small to medium-size manufacturing firms employing 7,000 workers, double what it was fifteen years ago. Many of those companies are traditional, or "analogue," in their approach, but firms emerging out of the local North Brooklyn design, crafts, and tech scene—or the "maker movement," as it is sometimes called—knock on the door of the Yard every day for vacancies that don't exist. City and local officials have their fingers crossed that the Yard's rise from Old Brooklyn's smokestack ashes will reverse decades of manufacturing decline and have a real impact on the joblessness and poverty that continue to trouble nearby areas. But for reasons related to that 5-axis router's creative destruction, they're likely to be disappointed.

THE NAVY YARD: THEN AND NOW

A recovery of the manufacturing sector, insofar as that's what's happening, couldn't find a more fitting spot than the historically resonant Brooklyn Navy Yard. Purchased by President John Adams in 1801, it was one of the young country's first military bases at a time when international stature was defined largely by naval power. During the Civil War, the laboring men of the Yard launched the USS *Monitor*, famous as the first ironclad warship, and later the *Maine*, whose 1898 sinking led to the Spanish-American War. At its peak during World War II, the Yard was Brooklyn's largest employer, sustaining 70,000 men and women who were electricians, mechanics, welders, and sheet-metal workers and, by extension, their nearby neighborhoods.

But in September 1945, the Japanese surrendered in a ceremony on the USS *Missouri*, launched from the Brooklyn Yard just a year earlier. The event turned out to be symbolic, for as the war ended, so did the jobs of thousands of Brooklyn workers. Given the Yard's history and its centrality to the Brooklyn economy, it took some time for the federal government to bow to the inevitable; but finally in 1966, Secretary of Defense Robert McNamara announced its closure. Deindustrialization was already eating away at Brooklyn's blue-collar economy by this time, as companies looked for homes with less punishing wages, taxes, energy, and real estate costs, as well as truck-friendly streets and bridges. By the early 1960s, most of New York's port areas were in decline as well, as costs and outdated infrastructure chased the industry to New Jersey and more distant parts. Still, with its historical significance and its size—not to mention the loss of the borough's beloved Dodgers a decade earlier—the closing of the Yard came as a serious blow to the borough's pragmatic, but optimistic, identity.

The closing aggravated the well-known effects of deindustrialization on cities—white working-class flight to the suburbs, rising minority unemployment and welfare dependency, budget crises—which would soon reach a crisis point in Brooklyn. The Ingersoll, Walt Whitman, and Farragut Houses, built by New York City in the 1940s and 1950s to house Yard workers, had coincided with the arrival of poor blacks and Puerto Ricans. Yard workers now had limited job prospects and they became dependent on an overstretched city. Retailers, restaurants, and small contractors in adjacent neighborhoods like Fort Greene, Williamsburg, and Greenpoint shriveled up and died. Things didn't improve when the Yard reopened in 1971 under city management. While a few tenants had stuck through the bad times (such as, until recently, Sweet'n Low), the Yard's condition mirrored that of its fraying home borough. Throughout the 1970s and 1980s and even into the early 1990s, the area was primarily known to car owners as the site of the city tow pound.

So what led to the resurrection of this old dinosaur of a shipyard? The first real sign of life came in the mid-1990s, when the Yard caught the attention of a Giuliani administration pondering ways to increase the quality of the city's lower-skilled jobs. They began with a $15 million infusion for updating the crumbling infrastructure, some of it dating back, if you can believe it, to the Civil War. The administration also revamped the Brooklyn Navy Yard Development Corporation (BNYDC), which was managing the Yard. The non-profit, acting as the Yard's leasing agent and landlord for more than a decade, had been stuck in an old-industry mind-set. Now with a bit of nudging from the administration, they got creative. Instead of large manufacturers and warehouse distributors, they focused on finding small, light industrial firms and niche manufacturers that would need workers, hopefully including some from nearby depressed communities. By 1998, BNY had just about fully leased the 4 million square feet of its available space to 200 businesses—though, compared with past numbers, the 3,000 jobs that it generated were worth only a few tepid high-fives.[1]

There was a sign, however, of more, though less traditional, Navy Yard blue-collar jobs to come. Shortly after taking the reins at the BNYDC in 1996, Marc Rosenbaum, a former white-shoe-firm lawyer, was on a trip to Los Angeles when he had a eureka moment. There was plenty of space, and the Yard needed some sex appeal: Why not build a movie studio there? In the minds of doubters, there were many reasons, including that no one, least of all Hollywood *machers*, was interested in commuting to work in North Brooklyn before the era of hipsters and Jay-Z. "There was a lot of skepticism," Rosenbaum admits. "People said that sound stages in L.A. were sitting vacant, that digital advances threatened to make the sound stage obsolete. And because sound stages don't bring in that much, they wondered why anyone would want to lend money for such a project." Rosenbaum proved them all wrong when Robert De Niro and Miramax studios began negotiating for the acreage;[2] and although that particular deal fell through, it wasn't long before the city was signing a sixty-nine-year lease with a local family real estate firm called Steiner NYC.[3]

If there are people who don't believe that the results have been, in Rosenbaum's words, a "monumental success," they're not saying so. Employees, including camera grips, sound engineers, set decorators, seamstresses, directors, producers, and actors, drive daily through Steiner Studios' dramatic entranceway, flanked by World War II radio towers, now lit and painted bright blue like the poles of a giant circus tent. With its ten sound stages, Steiner is the largest television and movie studio on the East Coast. It has been the birthplace of numerous films, such as *The Producers*, *Spider Man 3*, and *Sex and the City 2*, and television series including *Boardwalk Empire*, as well as commercials and music videos. "People with talent want to be in New York," Rosenbaum observes. "In fact, they'd rather shoot here than in California. Plus we have a tremendous stock of actors. The city had been losing business because of the lack of facilities."

Equally, if not more important to BNY's upward mobility was the new population of design-inspired, tech-savvy college grads we just read about in nearby Williamsburg, Bushwick, and Fort Greene. Tom Maiorano, the BNY's veteran leasing agent, says that he noticed a change in the kinds of tenants looking for space in the late 1990s. "It was a generation looking for security," he said of the older firms owned by immigrants or the sons of immigrants who were now moving toward retirement age. "They did what they had to do—provide for their wives and kids, who eventually became doctors, lawyers, teachers. In the late 1990s, the new tenants were woodworkers, designers, metalworkers. And they were young, just starting their businesses."

Maiorano was noticing something much bigger than he might have realized at the time. Manufacturing—owners, workers, products, and the process itself—was undergoing a dramatic change. Technology like routers, computer-assisted design (CAD) programs, and 3-D printers were making it possible to create not just apps and websites but physical objects quickly, on a small scale, to engage in what is sometimes called "mass customization." Unlike mass production, mass customization blurs the lines between design and production. Young "creatives"—designers, artists, and engineers—could dream up an idea, cobble together a relatively small amount of capital, buy a router, and open a small fabrication shop. Computers also cut down in the making of prototypes: what used to take months or years can now be done in hours or minutes.

This new manufacturing has considerable advantages for Brooklyn and other "creative" cities. "Because manufacturing today takes much less space, it can become part of the city again," explains Nina Rappaport, an architectural historian and author of the 2016 *Vertical Urban Factory.* "You don't need to keep a large inventory or warehouses, and that can keep you close to clients."[4] (It also keeps manufacturers within biking distance of employees' lofts and apartments, an important plus for Brooklyn's breed of millennial worker.) A study by Pratt Institute found that 88 percent of Navy Yard tenants sell goods inside New York City; those transactions make up an average 71 percent of these tenants' total sales. These days, a lot of Brooklyn manufacturing is local.[5]

MAKERS AND THE NEW BROOKLYN

And that brings us back to Situ, a perfect example of the new manufacturing. Founded by four millennial Cooper Union architecture graduates, Situ is more like a combination crafts shop, conceptual art studio, and tech company than conventional factory or architecture firm. "Cooper Union gave us a lot of time in the shop; we got used to drawing and making things," says Brad Samuels, one of the company's founders. "It helped us to erase the distinction between designing and making. We bought our first router in 2004." At first, the company did commissions for older artists and architects who didn't have their "maker" know-how. They went on to produce their own designs: a granite memorial for Flight 587, which crashed in 2001 near JFK airport, exhibit-display systems for stores and events, mannequins for Marc Jacobs, and a "design lab" in the 11,000-square-foot Grand Hall at the New York Hall of Science in Queens. In 2015, the company got its highest-profile job yet: a redesign and reconceptualization of the entrance pavilion of the Brooklyn Museum.

The Yard's newer tenants also include Ice Stone, a company that makes countertops of recycled glass; Rockpaperrobot, a "kinetic" furniture and lighting company run by an MIT robotics grad; and Ferrara Design (founded by a Pratt graduate priced out of Williamsburg), which makes metal railings and signage, such as the whimsical schooner-shaped bike racks used throughout the Yard. Other Pratt graduates have opened such businesses as OgoSport, a manufacturer of "play products"; and December Box, a producer of custom furniture, lighting, and display. In addition to numerous individual fine artists, furniture-restoration studios, jewelers, and muralists, the Yard now houses Kings County Distillery ("New York City's oldest operating distillery . . . founded in 2010," the company's website puckishly declares)[6] and Brooklyn Grange, which is the largest rooftop farm company in the United States. Andrew Kimball, the highly lauded CEO of the BNYDC between 2005 and 2013, summed up the atmosphere at BNY: "Making things is cool again."[7]

If manufacturing 2.0 was only about providing a customized entrance table for the new Park Hyatt Hotel in Manhattan (Situ) or baby kale for Brooklyn locavores and their fave restaurants (Brooklyn Grange), it would be good for high-end consumers and perhaps inspiration for an episode of *Portlandia.* That's an exaggeration, though, especially at the Navy Yard. There are plenty of companies at the Yard using technology for innovations with more crucial uses, including several that recall the Yard's military origins. Honeybee Robotics, for instance, has developed robots for NASA, hospitals, and mining companies; Atair Aerospace makes advanced self-guiding parachutes; and Pliant Energy Systems has received a grant from the Navy to develop an underwater device that generates power from moving water for eventual use with drone submarines.

Another military contract business, Crye Precision, may be one of the biggest success stories at BNY. Crye designs and manufactures advanced protective military clothing, including helmets with cameras for Special Forces, removable chemical weapon protection, communication devices, and "Multi-Cam," a newly designed all-terrain camouflage used by the Australian military and the United States in Afghanistan. Rag and Bone, a high-end designer eager for a novel fashion statement, also uses Multicam for some of its products. Caleb Crye, who has been called the "Steve Jobs of tactical gear,"[8] and his partner moved to a 1,000-square-foot space in the Yard in 2002. As their company grew, it was forced to scatter its operations to different buildings, a situation that was rectified when they were able to consolidate into a new 85,000-square-foot space in the Yard in 2016.[9]

Brooklyn's new manufacturing isn't close to recouping the city's blue-collar losses over the past sixty years. In fact, according to Jonathan Bowles of the Center for an Urban Future, between 1997 and 2010 New York was continuing to shed at least 5,000 manufacturing jobs a year. But by 2010, the decline had halted in New York City as a whole and actually reversed itself in Brooklyn.[10] Now if the Navy Yard has one problem, it's too little usable space. Several large renovations in the works, including the 2016 opening of the Green Manufacturing Center, will help. In November 2014, Mayor Bill de Blasio pledged $140 million to another addition, "Building 77," a million-square-foot concrete hulk that will house Shiel Medical Laboratory, employer to 600 people at BNY, along with other larger companies.

And there's more coming. Because BNY is a good twenty-minute walk from the nearest subway stop, the management is bringing in Citi Bike, New York's bike-sharing company, and introducing free shuttle service to local subway stops—with free Wi-Fi, of course. Steiner Studios is also enlarging into a fifty-acre annex where nineteenth-century buildings, including a magnificent antebellum Greek revival hospital, will be modernized to house media offices.

The annex is also slated to have the first underwater soundstage in the country, along with a graduate school of cinema under the auspices of Brooklyn College. All told, the new additions are expected to add 12,000 jobs to the Navy Yard.[11]

So does all this signal Brooklyn's coming working-class revival? On the surface, it might look that way. "We are probably at an all-time low in vacancy rates in habitable industrial space," says Bowles of the Center for an Urban Future. "It's the tightest industrial market in years or decades." No wonder public and private developers have been betting on other fallow industrial areas of Brooklyn.

The 660,000-foot former Pfizer pharmaceutical factory, located in the middle of hipsterville (on the border of Bed-Stuy and Williamsburg and close to Bushwick), is another icon of the transformation of the old to the new industrial Brooklyn. Pfizer chemical works opened in 1849, to become one of the largest pharmaceutical companies in the world, inventor of Zoloft, Lipitor, and Viagra. Reluctant to leave Brooklyn in the mid-twentieth century even as dozens of other local manufacturers were moving their facilities elsewhere, Pfizer hung on until 2008, costing Brooklyn 600 relatively high-paying jobs when it closed.[12]

Today, the Pfizer building has been transformed into a production facility for one of New Brooklyn's primary growth industries: food. Dozens of trendy and hoping-to-be-trendy companies and a food innovation lab occupy an up-to-code space in the Flushing Avenue building. Kombucha Brooklyn makes its popular fermented health drinks there, near where Brooklyn Soda Works concocts its hibiscus, cinnamon, and clove beverages, among other "high-quality, healthy sodas." People's Pops—makers of cantaloupe and tarragon frozen treats—Steve's Ice Cream, McClure's Pickles, and Madécasse Chocolate all have their kitchens at Pfizer. Brooklyn Food Works, a food incubator for the borough's seemingly limitless number of aspiring culinary entrepreneurs, is now located in the building. Michelin-endorsed (and Bill and Hillary Clinton–blessed) Roberta's Pizza, based in Bushwick, has a kitchen at Pfizer, where it produces a frozen version of its famous pies. Their outpost is right near Sfoglini Pasta, whose products also happen to be on Roberta's menu.

It's all a little incestuous, but that's the idea. Economists tell us that the clustering of creative companies allows them to cross-pollinate ideas and innovations and also, if the competition stays friendly enough, to help one another.[13] That appears to have happened at Pfizer. "Steve's Ice Cream lets People's Pops piggyback on its trucks when deliveries are headed to the same place," writes a reporter for *Edible Brooklyn*. "[One tenant] even hosted a hard-to-score visit from Whole Foods buyers, who ended up meeting everyone on the floor—plum opportunity for all. The tenants take inspiration from each other's products (exhibit A: Steve's Kombucha sorbet, or a test run of Bloody Mary ice cream with a mix from McClure's Pickles, a company with office space down the hall), swap supplier tips, and hope to combine orders for common ingredients, such as organic fair-trade sugar."[14]

That's the kind of synergy that other Brooklyn manufacturing centers hope for as well. Greenpoint Manufacturing and Design Center, a nonprofit industrial real estate development corporation, has purchased six buildings—including a former auto-parts warehouse in Crown Heights, a nineteenth-century jute and rope factory in Greenpoint, and another in East Williamsburg. The spaces are home to producers of items that sit on the boundary between manufacturing—or "making"—and art: traditional crafts workers like woodworkers, glassmakers, ceramicists, and metalworkers, as well as special-effects designers and filmmakers, GMDC rents space to more than 100 businesses that, in turn, employ well over 500 workers.[15] Italian developer Est4te Four is planning the 1.2 million-square-foot "Innovation Studios" in Red Hook. In the old industrial section of Gowanus, similar Brooklyn-style new businesses increased by 44 percent between 2000 and 2012, including the lines-out-the door ice-cream factory and retail shop Ample Hills Creamery, an electronics manufacturer, an artisanal cutlery maker, and Soakwalla, a skin-care company housed in one of Gowanus's former can factories.[16]

ALL THAT IS SOLID MELTS INTO AMPLE HILLS'S OOEY GOOEY BUTTERMILK ICE CREAM

The borough's largest and most innovative cluster of new manufacturing firms has been taking shape in a more surprising form in Sunset Park, five miles south of the Brooklyn Navy Yard. So far, there are three enormous waterfront complexes: the city-owned ninety-seven-acre complex of warehouses built in 1919 known as the Brooklyn Army Terminal; the privately developed Industry City (IC); and Liberty Plaza, constructed during World War I as a navy warehouse. Industry City, in particular, suggests that what is happening in Brooklyn is actually something closer to the "gentrification of manufacturing" than the reemergence of a blue-collar economy.

Established in 1895 by Irving T. Bush, a descendant of one of Brooklyn's earliest Dutch settlers (and no relation to the political family), Bush Terminal manufactured, warehoused, and distributed goods for Manhattan wholesalers. Ridiculed by contemporary business folks as Bush's Folly, the complex, which could ship and receive from the water and from train tracks directly outside, eventually grew to sixteen hard-used buildings. Its success couldn't last. Like that of just about every other company on the New York waterfront, Bush

Terminal's customer base began to fade after World War II. Only Topps Base-ball Card Company kept its operations there, and after it departed in the mid-1960s, the terminal complex—indeed, the entire Sunset Park waterfront—degenerated into a wasteland of abandoned cars, broken piers, and denizens of the neighboring red-light district looking for unpatrolled areas to do their business. Other than that, no one went there; it's a good guess that most Brooklyn-ites were completely oblivious to the peerless views of the Statue of Liberty and Governor's Island hidden by the terminal's decaying hulks.

It wasn't until 2013 that a development company, Jamestown Properties, saw the potential in this prime acreage at this special moment of Brooklyn's evolution. Now the largest privately owned industrial complex in the city,[17] it is, like the Brooklyn Navy Yard, easily accessible to the Brooklyn-Queens Expressway but close to subway lines as well. In need of hundreds of millions of dollars in infrastructure improvements, Industry City has been coming online under the guidance of CEO Andrew Kimball, the former impresario at the Navy Yard. At the Yard, Kimball had already seen the energy ignited by bringing together New Brooklyn's artists, designers, techies, and entrepreneurs. When he arrived at IC, he found a small population of artists, stalwarts from the bad old days when no one else wanted to risk Sunset Park no matter how cheap the rents. Soon enough, Kimball was able to attract young maker firms into the carved-up spaces: lighting designers, furniture makers, and the like. Today, 3-D printer Makerbot has a 135,000-square-foot facility on the premises. This being twenty-first-century Brooklyn, there is also an assortment of artisanal food manufacturers—Li-Lac Chocolates, Colson Patisserie (a favorite of Mayor de Blasio's), and Blue Marble Ice Cream, to name but a few.

Kimball placed the food makers on the ground floor of one of the main buildings so that the companies might also attract retail customers and diners. It was the first step in redefining a manufacturing district as a pleasure-filled shopping, dining, and entertainment experience on the waterfront. At IC, companies can make and sell their products, to be sure. But in contrast to factories past, customers can also buy, eat, and watch the products being made, and even learn how to make them. They can shop at an ultracool design store with a focus on Brooklyn-made products; other retail outlets are on their way at a passageway to be named—rather dubiously, for a shopping area— "Innovation Alley."[18] The effect of the space is an unusual and surprising maze of shopping and eating venues. To entice more customers and visitors, the complex has hosted wine festivals, fashion shows, tenant mixers, a Saturday Cinema Club for children, and, in the summer, family- (and dog-) friendly "Mister Sunday" outdoor parties, accompanied by techno and disco music selected by hometown star DJs Justin Carter and Eamon Herman. Brooklyn Flea and Brooklyn Smorgasburg, the borough's trademark outdoor flea market and food market, have their winter quarters here. IC has added celebrities to the mix: the Brooklyn Nets basketball team now has a glamorous new 70,000-square-foot official training facility in the complex. The actual practice space is on the eighth floor, with floor-to-ceiling windows so that players can enjoy the view, but who's to say a Colson Patisserie patron, lounging by the waterfront on a sunny day, won't catch a glimpse of them as well?

How did a manufacturing zone come to resemble a gentrified bit of current-day Williamsburg? In the smokestack days, factories were generally kept far from commercial, office, and middle-class residential districts. The reasons were many: those factories were dirty, toxic, noisy, and dangerous. By contrast, Brooklyn's new manufacturing is cleaner, less toxic, safer, and quieter. It also frequently produces aesthetically pleasing products such as sweet-smelling cupcakes and fine-grained wood shelves. These appealing qualities have allowed the maker movement to develop a proletarian-meets-artist chic. And it all means that the new manufacturing can be a good neighbor to other sorts of commercial, entertainment, retail—and possibly even residential—activity.

In fact, IC's newest and biggest-name tenant is Time, Inc. The magazine's new offices' high ceilings, large windows, and fantastic views are a big draw, but so is its Brooklyn cool, especially useful for a company not generally associated with trendsetting youth. Though its main editorial offices will still be in Manhattan, Time has made sure to trade on the Brooklyn brand. There are desks from a Red Hook–based furniture maker, custom-designed neon lights from Gowanus-based light designers (one custom-made neon light reads "I Create, Therefore I Am" in Latin), ironwork from a Brooklyn-based metal fabricator, and a pièce-de-résistance chandelier from a Brooklyn Navy Yards–based artist. There are also showers for bike commuters.[19]

A similar gentrification of manufacturing is now taking place up the East River at the Brooklyn Navy Yard. The soon-to-be completed Building 77 will turn a concrete, windowless hulk of a warehouse/ammunition depot into offices and shared work spaces. The Navy Yard is hoping to attract a "marquee tenant" to the building's penthouse with an accompanying terrace. On the ground floor will be a food hall anchored by Russ and Daughters, New York City's renowned smoked-fish and caviar emporiums. An event space will be for rent. Nearby, another group of developers are planning a spectacular modernist glass-and-concrete seventeen-floor building called Dock 72. Workers in the offices and shared work spaces will be able to take advantage of a basketball court, a specialty food market and cafeteria, a bike valet, a rooftop conference center, and health and wellness facilities. "Our target market is the creative market, the millennial knowledge workers . . . who are in demand by many of the expanding businesses," said John Powers, New York regional manager for Boston Properties, one of the developers.[20] Not far away in the Yard is another event space called Duggal Greenhouse. The company's promotional materials promise customers that they can arrive by car or "yacht . . . steps from the Duggal Greenhouse and its private waterfront patio." The site has been used for a Lady Gaga release party, designer Alexander Wang's fall 2014 runway show, and a 2016 presidential debate between Hillary Clinton and Bernie Sanders, among other glamorous occasions.

It scarcely needs to be said that this is not your grandfather's Navy Yard. During its manufacturing heyday, Brooklyn was able to employ generation after generation of poor immigrants and bring them to the threshold of the middle class. At least on a large scale, that scenario seems unlikely today, though not because gentrified manufacturing is displacing old-timers.

No, the problem is that new manufacturing doesn't rely on a low-skilled workforce in the same way that old manufacturing did. For one thing, it needs far fewer workers; that 5-axis CNC router and other productive technologies consign many low-skilled jobs to history. In 1999, Scott Jordan, whose eponymous company has been making Shaker-style wood furniture in a former cannon factory at the Yard since 1988, brought a 3-axis router that cuts one of his trademark chairs in twenty minutes. That and a slow economy reduced his staff from twelve to six in 2015. Since the beginning of this century alone, the number of people hired by businesses has been sinking; Brooklyn averaged 11.2 workers per business in 2011, compared with an average of 16.8 workers in 2000. In 2012, manufacturing made up only 4.1 percent of Brooklyn's labor market.[21]

Until recently, Cumberland Industries, manufacturer of Sweet'n Low, was one of the few remaining "analogue" businesses at the Yard. A family business, Cumberland has been around since the time when workers in their overalls sweated through the day building battleships and stopped for a beer at a nearby dive bar before trudging home for dinner in their tenements and row houses. The company was said to have a loyal group of unionized employees, some of whom had been working there for decades. The Eisenstadt family, who founded and manages the company, has been so worker-friendly that they resisted installing machinery that could reduce the number of jobs. Yet in early 2016, Cumberland announced that it will be closing the facility at the Navy Yard and outsourcing those jobs to other "co-packing" facilities that manufacture goods for several companies at once. That means another 300 more low-skilled but unionized jobs gone from Brooklyn. Cumberland does intend to keep offices nearby for product development, marketing, distribution, and sales. They are all white-collar positions.[22]

Another reason for doubting the revival of a familiar blue-collar economy is that manufacturing jobs require more advanced skills than the smokestack-company grunt work of the past. In a 2012 profile of Jergens, a Cleveland manufacturer of clamps and fasteners, the *National Journal* stated: "There are no more siloes between physical labor and white-collar work—everyone, from the factory floor to the sales office, is expected to talk the same language."[23] Brooklyn's new manufacturers often have trouble finding workers with the skills they need—not a college education, mind you, but just the skills specific to their company.[24] The Navy Yard's Situ partner Brad Samuels notes that each project they take on uses different materials and different processes; he needs people who can adapt. Recently graduated artists and architects looking for experience in advanced manufacturing often take those lower-level jobs. The day that I visited Situ, I saw about fifteen workers; they were almost all young and white, straight out of Williamsburg central casting. The Yard's employment center places only about 200 people a year; 25 percent of those are from nearby housing projects. It's not much.

This doesn't mean that there are no opportunities for low-skilled Brooklynites in gentrified manufacturing centers. Crye Precision's Multicam vests, for instance, are hand-sewn by seamstresses, most of whom commute from Sunset Park's Chinatown; the same goes for the Alexandra Ferguson pillows made in Industry City. IC is launching a "community-based skills training center" designed to prepare and place locals for jobs both in the complex and elsewhere in Sunset Park. Administrators expect to double the workforce to 14,000 in the next five years. Though it's unclear what percentage of those jobs will be unskilled, David Ehrenberg, the newest CEO of the Brooklyn Navy Yard Development Corporation, was upbeat when I interviewed him in 2015: "Modern manufacturing . . . requires more and more skills, but it still has a wider skill band than in other sectors. And these are skills that lend themselves to on-the-job training. People progress from lower down watching and learning, graduating to laser cutter." The organization partners with local schools like City Tech and offers internships for high school and college students. But with so much office versus maker space arriving in the Yard, it's hard to see who is going to provide those solid manufacturing jobs.

Even should the jobs appear, the Brooklyn Navy Yard's promise for the hardest-to-employ Brooklynites is ambiguous for two reasons. One is that the lowest-skilled jobs, even in manufacturing, just don't pay that much. Food manufacturing is the biggest area of manufacturing growth in Brooklyn, with a total NYC workforce of a little over 16,000. But food manufacturing is the lowest-paying niche in the sector—often paying about $12 an hour and only rarely with benefits.[25]

The other reason for pessimism about manufacturing's ability to help the least advantaged of Brooklyn is a deficit of social skills and work habits. Furniture maker Scott Jordan has seen all sides. His deliveryman who grew up in the projects has been with him for over 29 years; his knowledge and expertise have become indispensable. Other local employees have left him wary. "Look, I don't want to generalize. I've seen Pratt grads smoking crack in the bathroom. But you need skills to hold a job that are not learned in a week or a month or a year, like the skill of getting to work on time every day."

"Hiring from the projects requires a lot more sifting," he continues. "Right now, I've got a guy working for me who comes in late all the time. He knows how to work. I like him. When I warn him, he just shrugs his shoulders, and says 'I'll try better tomorrow.'" Jordan pauses. "I'm not doing social work. I'm running a business."

·6·

Bedford-Stuyvesant

A Ghetto in Transition—or Is Gentrification Racist?

$\mathcal{O}$ f all the changes I've witnessed in Brooklyn since I settled in the borough over thirty years ago, none has been more surprising than the blossoming reputation of Bedford-Stuyvesant. For decades after 1950, in the minds of outsiders, and many residents as well, Bed-Stuy's nickname "Do or Die" captured the spirit of the place. It was a neighborhood of hopeless black poverty, mean streets, meaner housing projects, and a homicide rate that had reporters reaching for war metaphors. Now, if you are to believe newspapers' style, real estate, and food sections, Bed-Stuy is the next Park Slope and Williamsburg. It is becoming the latest destination for young professional and creative-class whites on their ceaseless prowl for appealing housing, lively walkable streets, and express subway lines to Manhattan. Inevitably good coffee, Danny Meyer–inspired restaurants (one, with the winking name Do or Dine, was known for its foie-gras doughnuts before it closed in 2015 and reopened as a bar called Do or Dive), and prenatal yoga classes have followed close behind.

In some circles, changes wrought in neighborhoods like Bed-Stuy and other black communities like Columbia Heights in Washington, D.C., or Oakland, California, are routinely described as "ethnic" or "racial cleansing," or, more bluntly, "white people stealing shit." In a famous 2014 rant, the filmmaker Spike Lee railed against the white newcomers in the once-black Brooklyn neighborhood of Fort Greene, accusing them of being part of a "motherfuckin' Christopher Columbus syndrome."[1]

But a closer look at Bedford-Stuyvesant reveals the usual drama of white oppressor meets black victim/professional meets working stiff/yuppie meets homeboy to be a cartoon picture of a much more interesting story of economic, social, and racial transformation. No one would deny that the blighted black area has seen both an influx of white professionals and creative types as well as the sort of designer coffee cum croissant cafés and restaurants that keep them well lubricated and content. Talk to locals and look closely at the census and crime data, though, and you'll find that gentrification's familiar tensions around class and inequality are also intra-racial, reflecting the rise of an energetic, new black class, on the one hand, and the persistence of a ghetto underclass, on the other.

BLACKS COME TO CENTRAL BROOKLYN

To understand the disputed territory that is Bed-Stuy, as of 2016 one the fastest-growing neighborhoods in the fastest-growing borough of New York City, the first thing to appreciate is its location. Bedford-Stuyvesant sits in the middle of Brooklyn, abutting Williamsburg to the north, Clinton Hill and Fort Greene to the west, Crown Heights to the south, and Bushwick to the east. As we've seen, those once-poor and working-class neighborhoods are now in flux as professionals, artists, managers, and nonprofit employees (most of them white) are not only priced out of Manhattan but of the proto-yuppie neighborhoods of Park Slope and Cobble Hill and hipster meccas like Williamsburg as well. Bed-Stuy was bound to succumb to the educated-class invasion, if for no other reason than it is near these other rising areas and, not to be forgotten, it has excellent subway connections to Manhattan.

The area's biggest draw, however, is its legendary brownstones. Nineteenth-century architecture is to Bed-Stuy what oil is to Saudi Arabia. In the mid-nineteenth century, a growing German and Dutch upper middle class, wanting to escape the grimy tenement districts of Manhattan, began to build homes in the once-rural village of Bedford. A few decades later, with the opening of the Brooklyn Bridge, the Italian, Jewish, and Irish middle class moved in as the original Brooklyn burghers took off for the suburbs. Bed-Stuy's "starchitect" of the time, Montrose Morris, built the first apartment building in Brooklyn, the Alhambra, at the southern end of the area in 1889. It was a risky venture, since the aspiring middle class tended to equate apartments with poverty-filled tenements. But Morris's extravagant Romanesque and Queen Anne pile—think nine-room apartments with maids' quarters and a croquet court in the building's garden—was far from that. Morris was part of a building spree that resulted in block upon block of single-family homes with a riot of intricate masonry that, while in varying degrees of disrepair these days, still delights: Romanesque arches, bays, Byzantine columns, Queen Anne–style pediments and gables, terra-cotta tiles, carved mahogany doors, castle turrets, stone swirls, cupids, flowers, and grotesqueries of animals and human faces. Metalworkers added wrought-iron fences and gates and decorated cornices. Churches and community groups were plentiful. Add newly planted shade trees, and you had the infrastructure and civic energy for urban living at its best.

Bedford and nearby Stuyvesant Heights were not to remain so fine for very long. Between the two world wars, the original German upper-middle-class homeowners—manufacturers, merchants, and brokers—moved out, to be replaced by working-class Jews, Italians, Irish, and others. The area's brownstones were already showing their age, and so was the area's reputation.

Still, as the area turned white ethnic working-class in the 1920s, there was no sign that Bedford and nearby Stuyvesant Heights would become "Brooklyn's Harlem," as it was named in a 1961 *Times* article. By comparison with other northern cities, the shift in Brooklyn's racial geography was late in coming. The great migration northward after the Civil War had already given Chicago, Philadelphia, Detroit, and Manhattan's Harlem a substantial black population by 1920. Brooklyn's black population grew more slowly.[2]

When they did arrive, Southern blacks found that they were settling in a city with a curious racial history. As we saw, in its agricultural days, Kings County's economy depended on slavery every bit as much as the South's. It took two centuries before slavery was finally outlawed in New York State, in 1825. Yet within a few decades, antebellum Brooklyn became a hotbed of abolitionism, especially in Brooklyn Heights, where the immensely popular Henry Ward Beecher preached an antislavery message at Plymouth Church. Not far away, Weeksville, one of the first free black villages in the country, provided refuge for blacks fleeing the Civil War draft riots that rocked Manhattan in 1863 as well as safety for a few early refugees from the Southern states. Weeksville was a thriving community, supporting several newspapers, churches, an orphan asylum, and a home for the aged, but it was tiny, an urban hamlet of only 500 people. Now a protected historical site just beyond the boundaries of Bed-Stuy, it remains a point of pride for black Brooklynites.

The earliest signs of Bed-Stuy's black future came in the first two decades of the twentieth century, when migrants from the South joined a group of Caribbean blacks settling on the edges of the area, along Fulton Street and Atlantic Avenue. Their numbers remained small: until the 1930s, blacks made up less than 1.4 percent of the borough's population. There was no official Jim Crow in Brooklyn, but discrimination shadowed the newcomers through their daily lives. Segregation was commonplace in hospitals and schools; movie theaters refused to sell orchestra seats to black customers.[3] Though many congregations strenuously objected, a few white churches refused black members. In one notorious incident in the mid-1920s, a hooded Klansman spoke at the Washington Avenue Baptist Church, very near the boundaries of Bedford.

Bed-Stuy's racial identity shifted more notably during the Depression. In 1936, the A subway line was finally completed, giving Harlemites easy access to their brethren in Kings County. They liked what they saw in that small settlement in Bedford. In the eyes of blacks taking the A train, the houses around Bedford and Stuyvesant Heights were superior and the neighborhood far less packed than their home district in northern Manhattan. It's unclear how alarmed Bedford-Stuyvesant's German, Italian, and Jewish residents were at the growing black presence at that time, especially since that presence remained too small to trigger a "tipping point." But we do know that they, much like Park Slope's bourgeoisie at the time, were already being drawn to greener pastures in eastern parts of Brooklyn. The Harlem and Jim Crow refugees may have seen in the area's brownstones a luxury that they could never afford in Manhattan. The established white residents, on the other hand, saw obsolete, fraying structures no longer suitable for their modernizing lifestyle. The more restless of them headed off to newer housing developments in Flatbush.

The Depression brought about another change—a federal program that would eventually help drag Bedford-Stuyvesant and other minority communities around the country into desperate straits. In the early 1930s, the Roosevelt administration, attempting to head off mass foreclosures and bank failures, created the Home Owners' Loan Corporation (HOLC), whose main purpose was to subsidize imperiled mortgage holders. To gain more information about the problem, they surveyed 239 cities across the country and created "residential survey maps." The surveys rated neighborhoods based on a number of characteristics: the age and type of housing and residents' occupations and incomes, as well as the number of foreign-born residents and blacks. Most momentously, it created maps ranking neighborhoods from A, for desirable areas, to D, for risky ones. It's not clear how widely disseminated the maps were—they came to public attention only in the 1970s, when they were uncovered by historian Kenneth Jackson.[4] But their color coding—A areas were colored green, B and C in blue and yellow, and D in red—gave birth to the term "redlining."

That the long-term consequences of redlining and the exploitative lending practices following in its wake for aspiring black homeowners like those of Bedford-Stuyvesant—and their descendants—would turn out to be calamitous is beyond dispute.[5] However, if race was the guiding principle behind the HOLC's rankings, it's hard to see it in the 1937 Brooklyn map. Much of Brooklyn was redlined: white, manufacturing areas like Williamsburg and Dumbo; and as we saw in chapter 3, parts of Park Slope, though, at the time, it was over 90 percent white. Redlined Bed-Stuy itself was about 12 percent black in 1930, about the time when the maps were first being researched.[6] It's possible that the HOLC was alarmed by that 12 percent, but it's also the case that lenders and officials at the time didn't care for the white ethnic groups in the neighborhood, either. The agency shared widespread contemporary assumptions about the limited material value of older, urban, and ethnic neighborhoods as well as racial suspicion—especially, as was certainly the case during the Depression, when people didn't have the funds to renovate outdated plumbing and crumbling stonework. Investors aren't looking for ways to lose money, after all.

Indeed, over the next decades, many brownstones already scarred by the Depression went into deep decline. As in Park Slope, struggling residents, white and black, stripped gracious parlors and decoratively plastered bedrooms to create rooms for boarders, as windows rotted and stone washed away. By the 1940s, frequently panicked into selling at a discount by "blockbusting" real estate agents, the remaining Jews and Italians packed up and left for Long Island and other points in Brooklyn and Queens. By 1950, Bed-Stuy was already 50 percent black. Ten years later, it was 74 percent, growing to a stunning 85 percent in the 1980s.[7]

THE GHETTO AND THE BLACK MIDDLE CLASS

By the mid-1960s, with Bedford now merged with next door's Stuyvesant Heights, the community was bulging at its seams. Some 450,000 mostly African Americans, the size of the population of a medium-size American city, were crammed into less than three square miles. It was the most populous neighborhood in Brooklyn and had one of the largest concentrations of African Americans, the vast majority of them poor, in the United States—second only to South Chicago. As in Chicago, the city government turned its back: garbage pickup was listless, at best; and the schools were dilapidated and disorderly.

The large majority of Bed-Stuy residents at the time—80 percent—were high school dropouts. The lucky ones had jobs at the Sheffield milk-bottling plant on Fulton Street, but their numbers were small; as of 1962, only seven of the 367 employees were black.[8] During World War II, things were better at the Brooklyn Navy Yard; Local 968 of the longshoremen's union had a membership of a thousand African American men, though union solidarity did not prevent blacks from being last hired, first fired.[9] In any event, those jobs were disappearing for whites and blacks; after the Brooklyn Navy Yard was decommissioned in 1966, Sheffield also shut its doors in the mid-1960s, a victim of changing distribution methods in the dairy industry.[10] Already 36 percent of children were born to unmarried mothers, a number that would continue its relentless rise into the twenty-first century. Rates of venereal disease and infant mortality were among the highest in the nation.[11] Juvenile delinquency, gangs, and heroin added to the misery; merchants on the once-vibrant Fulton Street closed their doors; holdups and muggings were chasing away customers and making employees fear for their lives.

By the 1960s, the blight of Bed-Stuy brought the neighborhood a national reputation as a poverty-and-crime-stricken black ghetto. In July 1964, Harlem was torn by riots after a white police officer shot and killed a fifteen-year-old black youth, James Powell. Two days later, the flames spread to Bed-Stuy, where an estimated 4,000 rioters ransacked hundreds of local stores and pelted police and firemen with bottles and bricks.[12] The memory of those days of chaos, which would flare up sporadically in "long, hot summers" through much of the 1960s, led New York's newly elected senator Robert F. Kennedy to take a walking tour of the area. In 1966, journalist Jack Newfield, who accompanied the senator, described their excursion as "filled with the surreal imagery of a bad LSD trip."[13] Kennedy gathered a group of high-powered businessmen and Bed-Stuy community leaders to create the Bedford-Stuyvesant Restoration Corporation, the first community-development corporation in the country, whose meager results were evident on the neighborhood's dangerous streets for decades following.

Black poverty, crime, drugs, underclass misery: that's the picture that most outsiders have had of Bed-Stuy since the 1960s—until very recently. But there was always another Bedford-Stuyvesant whose considerable strengths had the potential to serve as the foundation for an eventual revival. Even as whites and banks began to flee in the middle decades of the twentieth century, the neighborhood had a tight-knit, neighborly working-class spirit that lingers in the local ancestral memory and remains a source of local pride. Throughout the 1940s and 1950s, black teachers, mailmen, firemen, and nurses lived on those fraying blocks. Many of them, through a mixture of luck, hard work, and penny-pinching—and despite redlining—were able to buy and live in those precious brownstones; some would hand down their houses to their children and grandchildren, who continue to live there today. Compared with other poor communities like Harlem, where renting was the norm, Bed-Stuy had relatively high levels of homeownership. Even in the 1960s, after decades of neighborhood downward mobility and damage caused by an abundance of negligent absentee landlords, 22.5 percent of area buildings were owner-occupied, according to a study by the nearby Pratt Institute; another 9.7 percent had owners living nearby.[14]

The combination of those enticing brownstones, human-scale streets, and neighborly residents nourished a civic orientation that carried at least some of Bed-Stuy through miserable times. The neighborhood's Southern blacks had brought with them not just hopes of a better life but the habits of friendly, slow-moving, small-town living. Bed-Stuy residents still boast about blocks where folks always say "good morning" to passersby and warm evenings where residents sit on the stoops of their homes, passing the time and watching children playing on the sidewalks. During those more mannerly times, adults felt free to scold misbehaving children without fear because kids, you could be sure, always listened to their elders. In an interview in *New York* magazine, city comptroller and mayoral hopeful William C. Thompson, Jr., who grew up in a brownstone on a shady block of Jefferson Avenue with his politician father and schoolteacher mother, remembered being scolded by a woman whose daughter had been in his mother's third-grade class for "cussing" during a pickup football game. "I don't remember what I said, but it contained some rather spicy language," Thompson says. "I remember Audrey giving me what for. There was a sense of what was acceptable and what wasn't."[15]

A 2015 *New York* profile of a single Bed-Stuy block over the years captures the essence of civic-minded, looking-out-for-your-neighbor bonds. The brownstone-lined 400 block of McDonough lost more than half of its white population between 1930 and 1940, going from 90 percent white in 1930 to 40 percent in 1940. By 1950, it was only 6 percent white. But the churchgoing black homeowners remained a resilient, family-oriented group. Block-association parties for special occasions combined with an instinctive sense of responsibility toward the children crowding the stoops and sidewalks as they tussled and played. "Every parent from that corner to that corner knew each other," explains a fifty-two-year-old who grew up on the block. "So if I did something on the corner, I'd get dragged all the way up to here. . . . And then you got home and they'd tell your mama, and your mama'd put you on punishment until your daddy got home. . . . Look, that's how we were raised. Because if something bad happens to your kid and I'm out there, you're going to wonder why I didn't help your child." Another former resident, eighty-four-year-old Ulrich Hayes, is old enough to remember the block when it was half white. His observations of Bed-Stuy evoke an alternate universe compared with the 'hood of popular imagination: "All the black kids on the block went to college. And I do mean all, though I can't say that for the white kids. . . . On the part of the black families on that block, there was a conscious effort to improve one's self. I would attribute our feeling to a kind of immigrant zeal. We all knew, even those who came from the American South, that we had to work hard—not just to make a living but to make a place for ourselves in American society. And the white kids in the neighborhood didn't have that feeling, that zealousness."[16]

"We were very much a group of strivers," he concludes. Hayes is understating, at least in his own case: he himself served as U.S. ambassador to Algeria.

Throughout the decades that Hayes and his peers were growing up, Bed-Stuy was alive with civic activity: there were homeowners' associations,

African American–run banks, block associations, food co-ops, and house tours. After years of lobbying, local strivers were able to gain landmark status for the Stuyvesant Heights historic district in 1971. The Bedford-Stuyvesant Neighborhood Council lobbied for better sanitation, bus, and subway service. The Paragon Progressive credit union was established in 1941 and provided residential and commercial loans for forty years.[17] Churches, too, organized credit unions and mediated with government agencies for better schools and health care. The civic ethos was distinctly middle-class: organizations pleaded—unsuccessfully—with police to close down brothels and supported Boy Scout troops to give children "a wholesome atmosphere."[18] Perhaps it helped a little that amid widespread discrimination, Brooklyn in the 1940s and 1950s was the home of Jackie Robinson's Dodgers, a hopeful sign of integration. Kids "went to movies together, fished together in Prospect Park, and sat together in Ebbets Field," writes Brian Purnell in *Fighting Jim Crow in the County of Kings*.[19]

Bed-Stuy's African American population built the neighborhood into the cultural center of black Brooklyn, which, by the 1950s, had expanded into Fort Greene, Clinton Hill, Brownsville, parts of Bushwick, and Williamsburg. That culture may not have had the national reputation of the Harlem Renaissance, but it was nonetheless a source of solidarity, pleasure, and commerce that still shapes the local population's sense of itself. By the 1940s, Bed-Stuy had dozens of restaurants and movie theaters, including the 2,500-seat Brevoort, one of the largest in New York City, which entertained children at Saturday matinees and made a specialty of black-directed films starring black actors. According to historian Clarence Taylor, though whites owned many of the local establishments, black-owned businesses were commonplace. They hired black waiters, bartenders, managers, hosts and hostesses, ticket takers, projectionists, and ushers, helping to create a lively, if woefully inadequate, self-contained economy.[20] Lena Horne and the master drummer Max Roach learned their art in the mid-century. In the 1950s, jazz greats Freddie Hubbard and John Coltrane played at local clubs; Dinah Washington and Carmen McRae performed there as well. Even today, area venues attract up-and-coming jazz artists pumped up to perform for older aficionados who once heard Duke Ellington—whose "Take the A Train" celebrated the Harlem–Bed-Stuy subway line—play live.

Even during the dark, crack-filled days of the 1980s, black performers sparked feelings of local pride. By setting some of their most memorable work on the blocks of Bed-Stuy, Spike Lee and Chris Rock helped the area to usurp Harlem as the center of black energy and style in the American consciousness. By the 1990s, Bed-Stuy had become hip-hop's Nashville, the birthplace and inspiration of Lil' Kim, Notorious B.I.G., and the rapper-impresario Jay-Z, who was born Shawn Carter, the bard of the gun-tormented Marcy housing projects, equally well known for his roles as Beyoncé's husband and entrepreneur.

THE NEW BED-STUY

Given this history, it's not hard to see why some locals would glower at the white or biracial couples pushing wooden toy-bedecked strollers, or bike riding, or parent-dependent musicians and Pratt students moving into their territory. There's no question about it: the newcomers, priced out of Park Slope, Fort Greene, and Clinton Hill, have helped make $2,000-a-month one-bedroom apartments and $2 million houses the new normal in the once-cutrate neighborhood. Unwittingly, they have been party to the departure of low-income locals from apartments that they've called home during a time when the rest of the world wanted nothing to do with either them or their neighborhood. A lot of poor renters have been reduced to scouting the ads in the far less richly endowed Brooklyn neighborhoods East New York and Brownsville. Bed-Stuy saw a 633 percent increase in the white population between 2000 and 2010; according to the *New York Times*, that's the biggest increase of any racial or ethnic group in any New York City neighborhood. As of 2010, the share of black Bed-Stuy residents had shrunk from 81.9 percent in 2000 to 64.6 percent.[21]

Still, Bed-Stuy's fortunes do not fit a simple story of gentrification's white colonialism. For one thing, Bed-Stuy was becoming less black in part because of a rising number of Hispanics; their portion of the population increased by 17 percent in the decades between 1990 and 2010. For another, there were so few whites in 2000, that while the white influx was huge, percentage-wise, they still added up to only 15 percent of the Bed-Stuy population in 2010.[22] Moreover, the large majority of those whites are clustered in two census tracts in the northwest corner of the neighborhood, abutting Williamsburg.[23] Walk along those streets, and you'll jostle neither white hipsters nor Iphone-toting lawyers but bewigged women in long skirts pushing double strollers to kosher food establishments past new apartment buildings with staggered balconies where Jews can build their Sukkoth huts. More than yuppies, the Hasidim are the white newcomers—though "newcomers" seems inaccurate, given the Jewish presence in the 1920s and 1930s. As if commenting on the unpredictability of history, some of the Christian churches nearby still feature mezuzahs and Jewish stars from when they were first built as synagogues in the early decades of the twentieth century.

Also muddying the stereotypical gentrification story are the numerous signs of black success. Older, longtime black homeowners who held on through the worst times are now cashing in. Many of them are moving to greener pastures. In 2006, Claire Hussain, a half-Bangladeshi, half-Irish woman and her Irish husband purchased a three-story brownstone on Madison between Tompkins and Throop from a couple in their mid-sixties who had lived in the house for thirty-five years. After vetting Claire and her husband to be sure that they were going to be suitably respectful of their beloved house, the owners purchased a new large home with a pool in Georgia, where their daughter and her family lived. Clare is now vice president—and the only non-black member—of her block association. She and her husband have made friends with many upwardly mobile couples with young children on nearby blocks. "They are almost all black or mixed-race," she says. Most have moved from other parts of the country, but more than a few are prodigal sons and daughters who grew up in the 'hood.

In fact, black college-educated professional men and women, or "buppies," as they are sometimes called, are the underappreciated engine behind Bed-Stuy's gentrification. In researching his book *There Goes the 'Hood*, Lance Freeman found a similar trend in both Harlem and Clinton Hill. "By the 1990s," Freeman writes, "Fort Greene/Clinton Hill was a mecca for black creative types and entrepreneurs" who dismissed the suburban aspirations of previous upwardly mobile groups.[24] These were the black counterparts of the yuppies who, by the 1990s, were upscaling Park Slope and Cobble Hill. And they are now drawn to what Freeman calls the "neo-soul" aesthetic and culture of Bed-Stuy. In Bed-Stuy, something similar was happening. Between 1990 and 2000, the percentage of households earning over $50,000 a year went from 12.3 percent to 28.3 percent, while the number of households earning over $100,000 went from 947 to 3,293 (a 350 percent increase). The number of owner-occupied buildings soared by 633 percent in the same ten years.[25] Yet, unlike the large white increase in the following decade, the racial composition of the neighborhood hardly changed.

This new black gentry—and their white counterparts, for that matter—often take their business to one of several pockets of gentrified commerce in the area, much of it black-owned and black-run. Bed-Stuy suffered badly from the subprime mortgage crisis; the area had among the highest rates of foreclosure in the city. Still, even during the recession, new cafés, bakeries, and lounges were opening, especially along a commercial corridor taking shape along Classon Avenue, adjacent to Clinton Hill and the four-block stretch of Lewis Avenue between Halsey and Decatur. Walking from the north along Lewis Avenue, you get a feel for the separate worlds of old and new Bed-Stuy. North of Gates Avenue, where the neighborhood's infamous housing projects loom, is a rough area, largely avoided by the new class. Keep walking south past the projects, and almost every block, some with storefront churches or empty, graffitied hulls, is anchored by a mini-mart with torn awnings, ATMs, and signs saying, "We Accept Food Stamps."

Once you get to Halsey, however, you come across Saraghina, a brunch and pizza café and a perfect example of gentrification, Bed-Stuy-style. Though owned by two Italians, Saraghina couldn't be further in spirit from Sal's, the classic Brooklyn family-run pizza joint in Spike Lee's *Do the Right Thing*, with its pictures of Joe DiMaggio and Frank Sinatra on the walls and its scowling, racist cook in his "wifebeater" T-shirt. Instead, Saraghina seems to have been imported straight from *Portlandia*. One weekday morning around 11, I got to the meandering white painted space, with retro icebox doors, vintage glass bottles, long picnic-style tables, benches, and Wi-Fi, to find three black women in their twenties and thirties and another older, mixed-race couple sipping coffee as they worked on their laptops and checked their iPhones. One of the three freelancing women was a yoga teacher who grew up in Ohio; another, a media producer recently moved from Michigan; and the third, a food consultant in the area who runs a wholesale distribution of food and groceries with fifty or sixty members.

The food consultant, Melissa Danielle, is a sharply observant, blunt-speaking third-generation Bed-Stuy resident whose maternal great-grandparents arrived in Weeksville in the 1920s. She herself grew up in her mother's nearby brownstone. She remembers first noticing signs of gentrification in the late 1990s in Fort Greene, where she went to high school, and a bit later in Bed-Stuy, when a new population of twenty- and thirtysomething black men and women moved back to the area from college or from time spent abroad. "You want to re-create the experience you had in college," she explained. "You socialized in bars and cafés; you want something like that where you live." Contra the conventional wisdom, "It was black folks who opened up the first three-dollar coffee shops—and black people who complained about it."

Though she didn't mention any names, she might well have been thinking of a local minor celebrity named Tremaine Wright, a Bed-Stuy native and University of Chicago–educated lawyer and onetime city council candidate, who opened up the "fair trade," "environmentally sound" Common Grounds café on Tompkins Avenue in 2007. In a 2009 interview with her alma mater's alumni magazine, Wright remembered that, like most students, she survived law school on coffee. When she got back to Brooklyn, she found that she couldn't find a decent cup of the stuff outside her friends' living rooms. Borrowing money against her grandfather's brownstone, whose mortgage she had taken over when he moved away, she brought university-educated coffee to Bedford-Stuyvesant.[26] Wright closed the shop in 2015 but not because of the usual problems facing small-business owners in gentrifying areas. She stopped pouring coffee in order to run for the state assembly.

Anthony Williams, co-owner of the Therapy Wine Bar, one block down from Saraghina, tells a very similar story. A handsome, friendly Bed-Stuy native, Williams opened up the bar four years earlier, after he and his partner noticed that in order to sit for a while and sip a good pinot noir, they had to go to Harlem or New Jersey. They found a space in the neighborhood—one that hadn't been rented since 1985—and started renovating it in the upscale style that they had seen during their meanderings. Therapy has stylish, small glass globes hanging over its long polished bar and, on the exposed brick wall opposite, framed album covers of jazz and hip-hop artists; black music—jazz, soul, and rap—was a big part of the plan for the bar. (Sometimes they play the albums of Santigold, a local hip-hop star, brownstone owner—and 1997 Wesleyan graduate.) Williams says that his clientele comprises upwardly mobile blacks, mostly college-educated, many from the Midwest and some Bed-Stuy returnees, who like the "rich" look of his bar. He has been surprised by the number of tourists stopping in for a drink. They may be staying at the nearby Akwaaba Mansion (a bed-and-breakfast opened in 1997 by a fortyish editor at *Essence* who is now owner of four other B&Bs between D.C. and the Jersey shore) or the boutique Brooklyn Hotel (offering L'Occitane shampoo and conditioner in its bathrooms), which opened in 2015 on Atlantic Avenue.

On the next block of Lewis, Peaches, fast growing into a neighborhood franchise, is a perfect distillation of black and white strains of gentrification. Peaches is jointly owned by Craig Samuels, a black man, born and bred in Bed-Stuy, who trained at the haute Philadelphia restaurant Le Bec Fin; and Ben Grossman, white and from the Flatbush section of Brooklyn. The food reflects the hybrid nature of their establishment no less than the owners: on the one hand, Brooklyn foodie-style lists of sustainable sources on the menu; on the other, Southern favorites like grits and jambalaya. The clientele is similarly integrated: I sat next to a tattooed, black-booted couple speaking Italian and a white couple with a toddler asleep in her stroller; at the bar, several women with Afros chatted animatedly. Other black-owned Lewis Avenue establishments include Brooklyn Beso, serving a combination of Southern and Latin American fare; and Emeline's, a diner named after the Bed-Stuy native owner's grandmother, who grew up in Weeksville. There are many others: Rustik Tavern, Bed Vine Brew, Bedford Hall, Brooklyn Swirl, Bushbaby, Essence Bar, Island Salad, Khemistry Bar, Vodou Bar, and the Black Swan, in a former auto-repair shop, all owned by young black entrepreneurs, many of them children of Bed-Stuy. One 2014 survey found thirty-three new retail establishments, twenty-eight of them restaurants, cafés, or bars.[27]

For all the lively commerce of Lewis Avenue and the encouraging signs of black upward mobility, tensions do mar the changing Bed-Stuy. White gentrifiers sometimes raise hackles when they tell longtime residents that the neighborhood is "coming back" or when they frown at the locals' "stoop culture." As in Park Slope, stoops—and noise levels—remain a cultural flashpoint between newly arrived whites and locals. Given that gentrifiers are almost always in their twenties and thirties, there are generational tensions as well. Danielle says that a lot of old-timers are wary of giving liquor licenses to restaurants or upscale bars. "Why does a restaurant need a bar?," they ask with annoyance. "They still think of bars as hangouts for drug dealers and down-and-out winos," she says.

THE PERSISTING GHETTO

But the biggest problem facing the area is not class and racial tension; it's the fact that many parts of Bed-Stuy still merit the term "ghetto," with all the problems that term implies. The numbers make alarm about gentrification seem beside the point. Over 30 percent of the population is below the poverty line; that represents a decline from 35.2 percent in 2000, but it's still very high by regional standards.[28] An April 2012 report from the Citizens' Committee for Children put the percentage of poor children in the area at a catastrophic 47 percent. Bed-Stuy families with children under eighteen had a median income of about $28,000 in 2010, compared with a citywide average of about $61,000, not exactly what you would expect from an up-and-coming neighborhood. There is an obesity rate of 63 percent, 7 percentage points higher than the city as a whole; reported levels of child abuse are twice as high as other parts of NYC.[29] In 2012, unemployment was 16.6 percent, also well above the rest of Brooklyn and the city as a whole.[30] Fair-trade coffee shops and designer pizza joints are not going to do much to change that.

Nor are gentrifiers likely to be able to help the educational prospects of the area's children, a prospect that doesn't look markedly better than it did fifty years ago, the striving Ulrich Hayes and his neighbors aside. Fewer than 18 percent of third-graders passed the Common Core reading test; that's about 12 percentage points worse than for the whole of Brooklyn.[31] An earlier report described the area's middle schools as "in a crisis state," with fifteen- and sixteen-year-olds wandering the hallways. Two of the area's largest and best-known high schools are on life support. The community landmark Boys and Girls High is among the bottom 5 percent of schools in the state in terms of achievement. It had a 3 percent Advanced Regents Diploma graduation rate in 2015; 60 percent of students were "chronically absent."[32] At Paul Robeson High (officially in Crown Heights, though serving many Bed-Stuy kids), one in every eight students was homeless or in temporary housing in 2010; as many again were identified as having special educational or emotional needs, and one in seven was held back at least one grade.[33] The Department of Education deemed the school so hopeless that by 2011, it was no longer accepting new students. It shut its doors for good in 2014.

The most important threat to the neighborhood's well-being is crime. Articles on Bed-Stuy nearly always tout the large percentage drop in crime. They're right to do so. The numbers are astounding. Murders in the 79th Precinct went down by 67 percent between 2010 and 2016. "Crime," Claire Hassain tells me, "mostly involves gangs. It stays among certain groups. In seven years of living here, we've had no problem." Anthony Williams of the Therapy Wine Bar agrees. "Knock wood. Nothing in four years."

But the truth is, improved or not, Bed-Stuy crime rates remain among the worst in the city. Headlines about shootings remain commonplace. On chat boards, commenters draw elaborate maps for people thinking of moving to the area, detailing the best routes to shopping areas and subways, as well as lists of no-go zones. Don't settle too far from the subway stop, they advise. You're safe about two blocks north, but don't go west. Not after ten at night. And so on. Bijoun Jordan, an African American high school teacher who grew up in Georgia, and his wife, a publicist, were enjoying the Bed-Stuy vibe: "I would go to random concerts on Fulton. We lived above Peaches Hot House [owned by the people at Peaches on Lewis Avenue], and I would go there to grade papers or have a drink." But when the couple was awakened by shots one night in 2014, shortly after their daughter was born, they wasted no time. After studying crime statistics in nearby neighborhoods, they decided to move to Kensington, a quiet neighborhood south of Prospect Park. "We were paying the rent of an upper-echelon neighborhood," he says resignedly, "but had none of the security." In 2013, the area was in shock over the shooting of an eleven-year-old girl by a seventeen-year-old out on bail from a separate gun-related charge. Doctors say that she will be paralyzed for the rest of her life. The shooting took place about three blocks away from Claire Hassain's house; only a block away is the playground where the police caught the alleged shooter. Until now, Claire tells me, she and her friends used the park regularly.

In a landmark study, William Julius Wilson argued that the civil rights movement of the 1960s had one tragic unintended consequence for urban blacks: it gave the middle class the ability to exit black ghettos, leaving behind, as the book's title puts it, the truly disadvantaged. In Wilson's telling, the middle-class departure concentrated the ills of poverty into a single hopeless geographical space. The black middle class had created pockets of relative stability and normalcy within the sorrowful ghetto. Not only did teachers and accountants patronize local businesses, Wilson wrote in a 2012 afterword of his book; they "reinforced societal values and norms" and gave the poor a chance to "envision the possibility of some upward mobility."[34] Now a black middle class is returning to some of the very neighborhoods that their parents either escaped or aspired to escape.

But the ability of the black educated class to inspire the down-and-out of today's Bedford-Stuyvesant partly rests on a notion of racial solidarity that may not hold up in the twenty-first century. In *Black on the Block*, her book on black gentrification in the North Kenwood–Oakland area of Chicago, sociologist Mary Pattillo McCoy describes the "divergent class interests" that confound widespread assumptions of a unitary "black community."[35] For the prodigal black gentrifiers as well as the young educated who grew up there, living in the whitening 'hood inevitably leads to spells of existential vertigo. "Walking by the Marcy projects with a bag full of Trader Joe's groceries," as one Bed-Stuy blogger describes her life, has a way of exploding popular ideals of a single "black identity." Young black lawyers and journalists explore their divided worlds in articles with names like "Reflections of a Black Gentrifier." The dilemma is not entirely new; other upwardly mobile groups—immigrant Jews, Italians, and Irish—have struggled with a similarly split self. In their case, class identity has ultimately submerged race identity.

That dynamic may well play out differently among blacks. But though complaints about perceived racism in the workplace and suspicion about white motivations remain fairly common, black gentrifiers tend to be a cosmopolitan group.[36] They are generally at ease when a white English professor or nonprofit administrator moves into the apartment upstairs.

The same cannot be said about either Bed-Stuy's old-timers who came of age during the days of black power or the younger activists. "You can't just come in when people have a culture that's been laid down for generations and you come in and now shit gotta change because you're here?" the filmmaker and Bed-Stuy neighbor Spike Lee ranted in a now-famous 2014 diatribe. "Get the fuck outta here. . . . How you walking around Brooklyn with a Larry Bird jersey on? You can't do that. Not in Bed-Stuy."[37] If you think about it, Lee's comments are troublingly reminiscent of the way Irish and Jewish Bed-Stuy residents might have sounded in the 1930s.

Lee's bunker mentality isn't likely to triumph over the forces of economic and social change bringing about gentrification. For at least four decades, white was the dominant color of Bed-Stuy; black has been the primary color only a bit longer than that. Now, once again, things are changing. "You've got the most unexpected, diverse people moving into the neighborhood now," Morgan Munsey, a Bed-Stuy native and real estate agent, told the *New York Times*.

"I'm getting a lot of Europeans, and actually lots of Germans." Those were the very people, Munsey muses, who built Bed-Stuy in the nineteenth century.[38]

Still, the gentrification battle continues in cities everywhere. "If you want to stop a place—anywhere—from becoming gentrified, don't move there, don't even go there—leave it the hell alone," a self-identified London "hipster" wrote in the British newspaper *Metro*. We'll see in the next chapter what happens when people follow that advice.

·7·

Brownsville

The Permanent Ghetto

$\mathcal{E}$ ven if you have never heard of the Van Dyke Houses in Brownsville, Brooklyn, chances are that you know a lot about them. The thirteen scowling brick towers are interspersed with a smattering of squat six-story accomplices with their pissed-in elevators, littered stairwells, and gangs of minority boys and girls, some as young as twelve. The murders, shootings, knifings, the fear, the black isolation: these have been familiar tropes of media stories about U.S. housing projects for many decades. You could find a version of Van Dyke—or, at least, you could have before some cities gave up and simply tore them down—in Chicago, St. Louis, Philadelphia, Manhattan, the Bronx, Newark, or Los Angeles. Actually, you could just go across the street from Van Dyke to the Brownsville Houses or down the next block to the Howard Houses, or a few blocks away to Langston Hughes, Tilden, Woodson, Seth Low. There are plenty to choose from in Brownsville: eighteen groupings of public housing. Brownsville has a greater concentration of public housing projects than anywhere in the United States.

Brownsville isn't all public housing; there are blocks of semidetached multiunit row houses. But the projects are the spatial symbol of the area's deep minority poverty and all its associated ills. Brownsville has one of the lowest-performing school districts with the lowest high school graduation rates in the city—and one of the highest poverty and welfare rates. It ranks the highest of any area for elementary school absenteeism, and second in terms of incarceration rates. It has among the highest number of teen births and assault rates in the city.[1] For many decades now, and with seemingly no end in sight, the grim march of extreme numbers has proceeded.

Forget about gentrification, shady landlords, soaring rents, and displaced renters. That the Van Dyke projects and their Brownsville comrades hunker but a mile from the clinking cocktail glasses and luxury sheets at the Wythe Hotel, that it is equally near the busy entrepreneurs and eager developers of Williamsburg, Bushwick, and the Navy Yard, that it languishes adjacent to the streets enjoyed by the growing black gentry of Bed-Stuy is the major challenge facing Brooklyn and American cities like it.[2] While so much of the rest of Brooklyn is in motion, Brownsville and its residents are static. People generally use terms like "inequality" or New York mayor de Blasio's campaign motto, "a tale of two cities," to capture the socioeconomic distance between places like Brownsville and the borough's affluent neighborhoods. But concentrated, multigenerational black poverty of the sort you find in this section of east central Brooklyn belongs in its own category. In Brownsville, America's slave-holding and Jim Crow past bumped into larger cultural, economic, and governmental forces in the early and mid-twentieth century. It's a collision that continues to isolate the neighborhood and too many others like it.

A JEWISH SLUM

Many of the better-known African American ghettos of the mid-twentieth century—Bed-Stuy, Harlem, Chicago, and North Philadelphia—were originally white and comfortably working- and middle-class but came on hard times as poor blacks moved in to center cities and the white middle class left. Brownsville's poverty, though it has changed color, lies deep in its neighborhood DNA. There was no rise and fall of this small 1.9-square-mile district, "nearer the ocean than the city," as native son and man of letters Alfred Kazin wrote in his famed memoir, *A Walker in the City*.[3]

Toward the end of the nineteenth century, a farmer who owned one of the few lonely farms scattered around New York City's largest waste dumps in the marshes of east central Brooklyn decided to put up a few miserable shacks of two to four rooms. When he went bankrupt, another developer, Charles Brown, took over the land and grandly bestowed his name upon it. Soon, Russian Jewish immigrants moved in, followed by a few garment factories—or sweatshops, as they were more cynically known. The factory owners built more housing, and then came the opening of the Williamsburg and Manhattan Bridges. The number of Russian Jews grew so much that this Brooklyn outpost earned the name "Little Jerusalem." Few Americans and not all that many New Yorkers knew much about the place, but for the forty years between 1910 and 1950, the former waste dump held probably the largest concentration of Jews in the United States.[4]

From early on, Brownsville was described as a slum, and for good reason. The original wooden tenements were cramped, dark, and stuffy; the area had no high school; residents were typically provincial, uneducated, and Yiddish speaking; steady work was far from certain; and infant mortality and TB rates were among the highest in New York. Still, it was a step up from Manhattan's Lower East Side, the more common destination for poor Jews in New York. Residents could at least find some space and air. More important, unlike the polyglot East New York just to the south, where Jews lived among Germans, Poles, Russians, and Italians, Brownsville provided a partial haven from widespread anti-Semitism. At its peak, Brownsville was bustling with seventy synagogues, numerous Yiddish theaters, kosher butchers and delis, a Woolworth's, banks, and pushcarts, many of whose owners would soon graduate to shopkeepers.

Philanthropists also boosted the community's viability. Some of their gifts still benefit Brownsville today. The Betsy Head "playground," gift of a nineteenth-century philanthropist, was within its borders. Though later, its facilities included a pavilion, wading pool, field house, track, tennis courts, and swimming pool (upgraded to a Deco-design, Olympic-size pool in 1936 by Robert Moses), it was far too small for the growing population. In 1914, Andrew Carnegie bestowed the first children's library anywhere in the world, on Stone Avenue (now Mother Gaston Boulevard); it was so popular that local merchants complained about the lines of children blocking their businesses.[5] Prominent Manhattan Jews opened a branch of the Hebrew Educational Society (HES) in Brownsville in 1899. Along with a gym and a music room, it provided English and citizenship classes; the organization donated enough books to lead to the founding of yet another in a crowd of local libraries. In 1916, Margaret Sanger introduced the nation's first birth-control clinic in this section of Brooklyn; though the storefront attracted crowds of women from as as far away as Massachusetts, it was raided so often by police that the landlord shut it down after only a few months.[6]

Brownsville Jews themselves started a wealth of civic groups. Residents from the same village or town organized aid societies known as *landsmanshaftn* to help their "landsmen" learn English and find places to live. Each member paid dues to create a communal pool for unemployment insurance and funds for burial plots. A chronic worry among the poor was of their loved ones spending eternity in a mass grave in potter's field. Steeped in socialist teaching and organization, Brownsville public schoolteachers, who were almost all Jewish, organized the first teachers' union in New York City in 1916;[7] it was an invention that would later add a note of bitter irony to Brownsville's most divisive historical moment.

Brownsville's civic and commercial vitality did not spare it from a criminal element that has always plagued impoverished neighborhoods. We already looked at some of exploits of Murder, Inc., the local "Kosher Nostra."

Fortunately, Jewish Brownsville also brought the world many reputable sons and daughters. Entertainers like Danny Kaye, Zero Mostel, Larry King, and the original Three Stooges—Moe, Curly, and Shemp Howard—nurtured their talents there. A number of prominent intellectuals, in addition to Alfred Kazin, found inspiration on the local streets: the left-wing historian Howard Zinn, son of two factory workers, first learned his politics in Brownsville. Art historian Meyer Schapiro and Norman Podhoretz, a leading conservative thinker, grew up near the Bed-Stuy border. Upward mobility was a communal Brownsville dream. Kazin describes local Jews as desperate for their children to succeed. "My father and mother worked in a rage to put us above their level; they had married to make *us* possible. We were the only conceivable end to all their striving; we were their America."[8]

BROWNSVILLE INTEGRATES

Jewish aspiration may have sometimes taken a more bookish form than that of other immigrant groups, but the general desire to make it in America was a powerfully shared ideal. First-generation Brooklynites, many of them peasants escaping near quasi-feudal conditions, had been struggling to move out of poverty for many generations: in this sense, the Irish of Vinegar Hill, the Italians of Gowanus, the Poles of Greenpoint, and the Norwegians and Finns of Sunset Park were all fellow travelers of Brownsville's Jews. Civic institutions like churches, societies, hospitals, philanthropic groups, and schools saw their mission as assimilating newcomers to the language, habits, and values of mainstream American society. In addition to providing a living, the industrial workplace and the waterfront taught immigrants language and the modern discipline of the clock. The attitudes of the native-born toward the greenhorns ranged from paternalistic to condescending to cruel, but the formula for assimilation worked well enough. The course could be slow—the Irish and Italians took several generations to escape the borough's shanties and tenements[9]—but by and large, by the mid-twentieth century, most of Brooklyn's first or second generation had joined America's mass middle class.

For a variety of reasons, the formula would largely fail several generations of African Americans, the first of whom moved into the area in the 1930s. Like Brownsville's Jews, the Southern arrivals were desperately poor rural folk, ill-suited to an industrial urban existence. But like their counterparts who moved to Harlem, Chicago, or Newark, Brownsville's blacks carried with them a number of burdens unknown to previous generations of Brooklyn poor. Most obvious was the legacy of slavery. The middle passage and generations of servitude had ripped away sustaining cultural memory and traditions of civic cohesion. The black family, though still far stronger than it would become in the latter part of the twentieth century, was seriously weakened, and while the large majority of black children were born to married parents after the Civil War, black communities included many abandoned mothers.

The Irish, Jews, and Italians had faced punishing discrimination in the borough; by the time blacks started arriving, restrictive immigration laws had already begun to slow the growth of Russian Jews. But antiblack animus proved more stubborn and more severe. Adding to the trials of Northern urban existence was an accident of timing: the earliest black arrivals moved into Brownsville's shacks during the Depression; the larger wave of arrivals in the 1950s transported their belongings into the projects and tenements as the borough's factories were closing en masse. In fact, black Brooklynites never achieved an appreciable niche in New York City's industrial workforce.[10]

Nevertheless, if anyplace offered a hopeful urban destination for poor blacks, it should have been Brownsville. Inspired by the revolutionary movements of their native Russia, Brownsville's Jews were proudly socialist, dedicated to the ideal of class solidarity and universal brotherhood. (In the 1940s, a Brooklyn boy named Bernie Sanders would imbibe the same politics in another Jewish neighborhood a few miles west of Brownsville.) Their universalistic principles extended to people of color. Brownsville Jews were pioneers as well as avid organizers of the civil rights movement, writing petitions against the poll tax and holding rallies to protest Jim Crow and school segregation. One of the premier social agencies, the Brownsville Boys Club, actively recruited black members; when the travel teams were greeted with racist taunts, as they predictably were, the white members remained stalwart.[11]

This is not to say that racial discrimination was unknown or even rare in Brownsville. Jews as well as blacks were banned from many occupations and companies, but Jews had no trouble getting admitted to the neighborhood's landmark Loew's Pitkin Theater or being served in local restaurants; blacks often did. Jewish youth were not immune to rough treatment by local police, but it was undoubtedly worse for blacks.

Brownsville looked well positioned to pass the first big test of residents' integrationist principles in the mid-1940s. The return of GIs from World War II battlefields, the first wave of slum clearance, which had displaced a considerable population of poor New Yorkers and a growing number of black refugees from the South, had worsened a chronic housing shortage all over New York City but especially in cheaper districts like Brownsville. Not that the neighborhood's extant housing was worth pining for. Brownsville had always been known for its miserable living conditions; now those dwellings had declined even further. Some housing still had windowless rooms and outdoor toilets that predated a 1901 tenement-reform law. By the mid-1930s, an influx of federal funds from the New Deal brought the city relief in the form of public housing on the Lower East Side and Harlem and, a bit later, in Williamsburg and Red Hook. The Brownsville Neighborhood Council, whose socialist Jewish members were particularly enthusiastic about public housing, lobbied heavily to get their district included on the list. Robert Moses and his entourage visited the area and agreed with them: Brownsville needed public housing and lots of it.[12]

With the hindsight wisdom of Jane Jacobs, author of the transformational 1961 *The Death and Life of Great American Cities*, it's easy enough to shake our heads at the wrongheadedness of bulldozing "slums" that happened to include the homes and businesses of a great many New Yorkers. The "tower in the park" design of the buildings—tall apartment buildings surrounded by playgrounds and grassy areas—intended to house some of those whose homes had been "cleared"—may also seem to have been destined for trouble.

Within the constraints of the time, however, the decisions seemed humane. It wasn't only aristocrats like Robert Moses who found the tenement slums appalling. Progressive-era reformers believed that the condition of housing both reflected and promoted the "loose morals" of the residents; Jacob Riis believed that the tenements were themselves poison for the spirit. The Lower East Side had such high rates of TB, diphtheria, and cholera that they were called "Lung Blocks." Eleanor Roosevelt was there to celebrate the opening of the city's first project. Building tall was the only way to meet more of the demand with the limited funds available. Mayor Fiorello LaGuardia, who blamed the TB death of his first wife on the evils of tenement living, celebrated slum clearance and the new public housing in 1944 in a famous speech: "Down with rotten antiquated rat holes. Down with hovels, down with disease, down with firetraps, let in the sun, let in the sky, a new day is dawning, a new life, a new America!"

Brownsville got its new day in 1946, when the city began razing several blocks of the neighborhood, including, in a bit of poetic foreshadowing, one of Brownsville's oldest synagogues: Chevra Thilim Kesher Israel. Despite that, residents greeted the twenty-seven (relatively benign-seeming) six-story brick buildings like the world's fair. Some 16,000 people applied for the 1,300 units; of those lucky enough to be chosen, 52 percent were white and 48 percent black, a rate of integration unknown in other projects. (In cities like Chicago and Detroit, public housing was almost immediately known as a black program; New York had many predominantly white projects, though they were de facto segregated, as were the neighborhoods around them.) Skeptics noted that other Brooklyn projects had not found many spaces for blacks in Williamsburg and Red Hook, while Brownsville Houses, where the "community residential pattern" at the time was only 20 percent black, was disproportionately black. They suspected, not unreasonably, that Moses had calculated that Brownsville's Jews wouldn't protest their "colored" next-door neighbors, though the Irish of Red Hook and the Italians of Bushwick probably would.[13]

Brownsville civic groups celebrated the opening with an Easter/Purim festival to welcome newcomers and honor the "brotherhood of man." They launched recreational programs for the project's youth and organized marches demanding new schools to replace the decrepit existing ones and the appointment of an African American to the New York City Board of Education. Though some grumbled that black and white adult residents didn't socialize with each other very much, that was not true for their children, who played skelly, a hopscotch-like street game, and stickball together.[14]

The Brownsville Houses were enough of a success that plans were put into place for an extension. But compared with the relatively low-rise Brownsville Houses, the extension, which became the aforementioned Van Dyke Houses, was a twenty-two-acre behemoth, "tower in the park" design. At first, residents reported the buildings to be well managed and comfortable enough. But Van Dyke turned out to be a sign of the end of Brownsville's era of integration and of relative neighborhood success. More blacks moved in from other neighborhoods; more Brownsville whites left.

A BLACK GHETTO

Why were Brownsville's integrationist hopes dashed? Racial discrimination, the obvious and patently true answer, turns out to be only a partial one. Blacks were unwelcome in most white neighborhoods; by contrast, many of Brownsville's whites were dedicated to an ideal of cross-racial unity. The specter of declining property values didn't play a role: as Wendell Pritchett notes in his history of the area, few of Brownsville's whites actually owned their living quarters.[15] But by the early 1960s, the New York City Housing Authority (NYCHA), the agency overseeing the city's public housing, made a number of poorly considered decisions that also helped pave the way toward what has come to seem like permanent ghettoization.

First were NYCHA residency rules. NYCHA residents were required to move out once their income surpassed a certain ceiling. That made sense; public housing was supposed to be for those who couldn't afford to live in private developments. The problem was that most of those who reached the income ceiling were white. Antipoverty advocates argued that it was only right to give preference to the most disadvantaged on housing waiting lists. Perhaps; but as a result, upwardly mobile whites were replaced by poor black refugees from both the South and the cleared slums of other parts of New York.

For a time, the compassion that inspired advocates to help the most needy was balanced by official NYCHA rules reflecting the still-powerful consensus around middle-class customs, which, judging from their behavior until 1960 or so, were widely aspired to by both the poor and the working class. Public housing families with children were supposed to include two parents; in fact, unwed pregnant women could be—and sometimes were—evicted. The head of the household had to be working. There were spot-checks to ensure that apartments were being well kept and that they included no unofficial tenants.

To the contemporary ear, the rules sound, at best, paternalistic; and, at worst, cruel to the very people most in need of help. By 1968, NYCHA reached the same conclusion and announced that tenant selection would no longer "deal with the morals of the applicants."[16] The unintended consequences of these humane policies were anything but kind: single-parent black and Puerto Rican welfare recipients replaced any remaining better-off white tenants, thus isolating the minority poor from the largely white lower middle class and creating the conditions for the spread of "underclass" culture.

New York's academic and governing elites were also getting behind policies that would distance the emerging ghetto from long-established middle-class norms. First was welfare. As first conceived, Aid for Families with Dependent Children (AFDC), the official welfare program, was meant to counter the severe hardship of the Depression by giving aid to abandoned and widowed mothers and their children. Necessary as the program was at the time, people recognized the "moral hazard," as economists would put it, of welfare: it could undermine America's pioneer creed of familial and community self-sufficiency. Though AFDC was a product of his own administration, Franklin Roosevelt himself warned that welfare was a dangerous "narcotic, a subtle destroyer of the human spirit."

In 1960s, that once-prevalent ambivalence seemed to vanish in a New York minute. The Kennedy-esque reform-minded Republican mayor John Lindsay joined forces with the National Welfare Rights Organization and activist-academics dedicated to expanding the city's welfare rolls. They scoured the city for potential recipients, held sit-ins, and issued ultimatums for more money and fewer restrictions. Activist lawyers and liberal judges diluted or, in some cases, overturned some of the rules and sanctions that had kept the rolls in manageable budgetary territory. The administration simplified the welfare application to a meaningless one-page form of self-declared need, no questions asked. By 1968, says historian Fred Siegel, welfare benefits plus Medicaid surpassed the salary of a minimum-wage job. Even as the rolls swelled, employers complained that they couldn't find enough workers.[17]

Indeed, New York's welfare spree, which coincided with a rapidly improving labor market, appeared to be as much a matter of ideology as economic need. In the 1960s, just about everyone, including most racial minorities, was finding work. By the late 1960s, black male unemployment in the United States had plunged to between 5 and 6 percent, half of what it had been in the 1950s.[18] The city had created 183,000 jobs during Lindsay's first term.[19] By 1970, Brooklyn blacks were significantly more likely to resemble whites in terms of their occupations than they had been in the past. In 1950, only 18 percent of Brooklyn blacks were in white-collar positions, compared with half of Brooklyn whites. By 1970, that black number had jumped to 43 percent. The percentage of working black women who were domestics plummeted from two-thirds in 1940 to less than a tenth in 1970—in large measure because so many of them were moving into government clerical jobs.[20] Throughout the country, the black middle class was growing apace.[21]

Yet by the end of that decade, when the city had 7.9 million citizens, more than *1 million* of them—disproportionately black—were receiving public assistance. In a mere three years following 1965, the portion of the city budget spent on welfare soared past the historical highs of 12.5 percent, already considerably higher than other large cities, to 23 percent. The administration's generosity, if that's what it was, would contribute to the near-bankruptcy of New York City in the 1970s,[22] leading to even greater hardship in ghettos like Brownsville.

New York City's welfare exuberance was intertwined with a spreading shift in attitudes toward unmarried parenthood. From our current perspective, when over 40 percent of American children are born to unmarried mothers, it's easy to forget the magnitude of the change. "Legitimacy," the community's recognition of a father's bonds and responsibilities to his children through marriage to their mother, was a norm in virtually every human society. The reasons were not merely a matter of stodgy convention; they were grounded in human social evolution. Mothers and their dependent children had a better chance of survival with the aid of an adult with a genetic connection to the children. Furthermore, large numbers of unattached young men with no personal ties to the next generation were not good for a society; neither was the situation good for the individual men themselves.

Both bourgeois "propriety" and working-class "respectability" were vehicles for reinforcing these truths in social life. As explained by Richard Hoggart, an eminent historian of the British working class, the proletarian culture "was embodied in the idea of, first, the family, and second, the neighbourhood. . . . [T]he most highly prized social virtues were 'respectability'—an amalgam of thrift, sobriety, and dignity, born of a determination not to succumb to what was always a harsh and tenuous economic environment."[23] In other words, the social "skills" that helped sustain families and communities were especially crucial for those struggling in arduous circumstances.

Yet the universal rule of legitimacy—and of the "propriety" and "respectability" that upheld it—began to unravel in poor, minority neighborhoods. In 1965, Daniel Patrick Moynihan warned in his famously infamous report, "The Negro Family: A Case for National Action," that single-mother families were spreading among blacks. The national figure cited by Moynihan at the time was 24 percent. In Brownsville and East New York, the number was already 45 percent.[24] That the response to the report was so bruisingly hostile—the phrase "blaming the victim" first emerged at the time—foreshadowed the end of the consensus about how to bond men, women, and their children—at least for the poor.[25]

Though neither was designed for that purpose, AFDC and public housing were to provide the economic infrastructure for the future generations of single-parent families. Under the guiding assumption of the time that mothers should stay at home with their children, the government moved into the business of supporting large numbers of never-married mothers just as most husbands did their wives; with the new relaxed NYCHA rules, those mothers would also have a place to live. Intellectual support for the new demographic came from a variety of academics and public officials who, if we didn't know better, appeared intent on widening the gap between the ghetto and traditional working and aspiring middle class. They argued that the nuclear family was a white middle-class invention—and a toxic one, at that. "One must question the validity of the white middle-class lifestyle from its very foundation because it has already proven itself to be decadent and unworthy of emulation," wrote Joyce Ladner (who would later become the first female president of Howard University), in her 1972 book *Tomorrow's Tomorrow.* Justice William Brennan carried the theme into a 1977 concurring assent in *Moore v. the City of East Cleveland.* In that decision, Brennan connected the nuclear family with delinquency, addiction, crime, and "neurotic disabilities," all of them more prevalent in societies where "autonomous nuclear families prevail."[26]

Clearly, Ladner and Brennan never tested their theories in Brownsville. Family breakdown hit Brownsville early and hard, and nowhere more than at the Van Dyke Houses. In 1956, shortly after its opening Easter/Purim celebration, 43 percent were white and 57 percent were black. Only twenty-four of more than 1,600 residents were on welfare, and 13 percent were from "broken families." By 1963, Van Dyke's population was 72 percent black and 15 percent Puerto Rican. The houses had the highest arrest rate in the city. White tenants reported being called "poor white trash" and "dirty Jew" and becoming the targets of rocks and punches. Pritchett found that "only twenty-five white families . . . remained at Van Dyke houses, and all of them were trying to get out."[27] It wasn't just "white flight": minority families also asked to be transferred. The novelist Richard Price, who grew up in the integrated Parkside Houses in the Bronx, recalls a similar pattern; welfare families moved in, and white and stable working-class black families moved out. "In our building alone, twenty-one out of the twenty-eight families . . . both white and black, put down their deposit and left—including my own," he wrote, in a mournful reminiscence in *Guernica*.[28]

The Van Dyke Houses continued to epitomize Brownsville's downward spiral. By 1966, it was one of four projects in all of NYC pronounced "unsatisfactory because of vandalism and crime." The buildings "suffered abnormally high tenant abuse, no tenant cooperation"; a full-time carpenter can't "keep pace with damaged doors and hardware." NYCHA hired social workers to help the many "multi-problem families" and added substantial numbers of caretakers, as well as a full-time elevator mechanic.[29] Conditions improved slightly for a time, but at that point, the damage to local morale and reputation was done.

These ominous outcomes were not enough to halt the numerous Brownsville projects already either in construction or in the planning stages. For city officials, Brownsville offered a path of least resistance for housing that, while increasingly scorned by the working class, remained in great demand. Many New York neighborhoods had learned to fight the Robert Moses power, but a struggling community like Brownsville could do little to stop the massing of large and increasingly dysfunctional projects in their midst. By 1970, Brownsville's identity as the dumping ground for the most welfare-dependent, least capable of Brooklyn's black poor seemed literally set in stone and brick.

THE WAR ON POVERTY'S BATTLE OF BROWNSVILLE

Brownsville needed help; that was for sure. As the War on Poverty geared up in the early 1960s, the neighborhood became an obvious battleground. The state, the city, and large foundations joined the federal government in pouring millions of dollars into the area, mobilizing community members and civic groups, training activists, building more housing and day-care centers, launching youth programs, reforming school governance, and hiring culturally sensitive principals and teachers. The efforts, predicated on a misunderstanding of the ghetto's new genus of social breakdown, were bound to disappoint. And they did.

The most notorious of the area's War on Poverty–inspired initiatives flared up in the Ocean Hill–Brownsville school district. Brownsville activists, black and Jewish, had long protested the growing segregation of New York City schools and especially the poor teachers and facilities of minority schools like those in Brownsville. They had reason to be unhappy. "You'd walk in, and the kids were out of control," Sandra Feldman, an organizer with the United Federation of Teachers and later the UFT's president, said. "The hallways were wild. They were dirty."[30] Local leaders and parents came to believe that the schools were failing the area's children because they were run by white principals and teachers who neither cared about, nor understood, black children. Tired of what they viewed as racist indifference and bureaucratic stonewalling, they demanded that local stakeholders, including elders, ministers, and parents—not the distant bureaucracy and self-interested teachers' union—should be able to hire and fire principals and teachers, determine budgets, and even design curriculum.

The unheard-of demands reflected the collision of two ideas coming into their own at the time. First was community control, a mainstay of War-on-Poverty thinking. It made its first official government appearance in the 1964 Economic Opportunity Act, ruling that programs would be "developed, conducted, and administered with the maximum feasible participation of the residents of the areas and members of the groups served." The second idea emerged from the black power movement: blacks needed to reclaim their own identity from the hands of a white majority implacably hostile to their well-being.

The white powers-that-be were surprisingly quick to agree with Brownsville's community-control contingent. Mayor Lindsay signed on to three experimental districts, one of them in Ocean Hill–Brownsville. The blue-chip Ford Foundation, then under the leadership of McGeorge Bundy—by many accounts, the brightest of President Kennedy's legendary "best and brightest"—funded the program. The *New York Times* was enthusiastic. A black educator, Rhody McCoy, was put in charge of the Brownsville initiative, and after installing a community board, he began cleaning house.[31]

One of McCoy's first acts was to fire nineteen principals and teachers, most of them Jewish, and then to hire several replacements. McCoy did hire Jewish teachers who agreed with community control and Afrocentric curriculum, but there were ominous signs that the activists' goals were radically separatist. One of McCoy's new principals, Herman Ferguson, was a founder of the Revolutionary Action Movement. Ferguson was under indictment—and later convicted—for conspiracy to murder Roy Wilkins and Whitney Young, the respective heads of the NAACP and the Urban League. Both organizations had voiced support for the Ocean Hill effort, though that was presumably before they got wind of the alleged conspiracy against their leadership. Local scuttlebutt had it that the FBI had framed Ferguson; but even without a rap sheet, he was a questionable choice, being a prominent follower of Malcolm X and a racial provocateur who believed that community control should be "a training ground for actual nationhood."[32]

In dismissing nineteen teachers, the board was violating a union contract, which led 350 of the district's personnel to go on strike. A mediator—Francis Rivers, a widely respected African American judge—concluded that four of the teachers originally dismissed by McCoy were let go not because of pedagogical incompetence but because of their lack of enthusiasm about community control. While some of the other dismissed teachers, Rivers continued, were less than stellar, they were not so different in that regard from a significant number of teachers who were never given pink slips. When the dismissed teachers returned to their classrooms in the fall of 1968, following Rivers's decision, McCoy loyalists encouraged students to disrupt the classrooms. Union members were enraged, and 60,000 NYC teachers, about 93 percent of the total number, took to the picket lines in an action staggered over a period of two months.

Whatever the theoretical virtues of community control—and in a huge, bureaucratic system like the New York City schools, there are bound to be some—Brownsville's version was a disaster not just for unionized teachers but for the area's kids. Community control can only be as effective as the community itself; Brownsville, however, was a community in poor health. In what was becoming a familiar theme in race politics, community controllers condemned the very bourgeois characteristics that had helped generations of poor, including many blacks, to escape places like Brownsville. "White middle-class values are harmful to black schoolchildren" were the words of a resolution made at a black school-official conference chaired by Rhody McCoy.[33] Charles Hamilton, a political scientist and influential writer on Brownsville's new pedagogy, questioned whether reading scores weren't a way of "induc[ing children] to emulate the culture of another racial or ethnic group." He proposed replacing verbal skills with black "normative values."[34] The approach all but guaranteed student failure in adapting to the most basic tenets of civic life in a diverse city and ensured that they would not be learning the foundational skills of reading and math—never mind the complex thinking needed for an emerging white-collar economy. After the media finally uncovered student scores— McCoy had refused to release them—the results of this particular experiment in community control were in: between 1967 and 1969, student scores cratered. To cite just one example, third-graders started out four months behind in reading and math; they ended up twelve months behind.

The wretched incident also brought to light a strain of black anti-Semitism that would have jolted Brownsville's socialists. Leaflets protesting the recent Six-Day War between Israel and the Arabs announced that black children should be taught by black teachers, "not the Middle Eastern murderers of colored people."[35] In the aftermath of the strike, Les Campbell, a history teacher hired by McCoy, read a student poem called "Hey, Jew-Boy" on WBAI radio.[36] By the end of the strike, Ocean Hill–Brownsville had accomplished what outer-borough Jews, with their memories of pogroms, ovens, and everyday bigotry, probably assumed could only arrive with the Messiah: it made them part of the white mainstream majority.

The War on Poverty brought an additional experiment to Brownsville with only marginally better results, this one yet another attempt to improve neighborhood housing. The chronic problems at projects like Van Dyke had not been lost on officials administering Model Cities, one of the many initiatives of the poverty war. One increasingly popular strain of thinking blamed those problems on the architecture of the projects.[37] City planners of the 1950s and early 1960s had based their design on "towers in the park," skyscrapers set in an extended green space, inspired by the French planner Le Corbusier. The new, new theory, most closely associated with Jane Jacobs, was that communities thrive with a walkable, lively street grid, lined with human-scale but high-density buildings that allowed for plenty of ordinary activity and "eyes on the street." With additional funding and oversight from New York State, a group of hand-selected, Ivy League architects and planners, after traveling to study a dozen European social housing models, put their heads together in the late 1960s. Progress was sluggish, as government projects tend to be. Patronage and turf battles plagued most of the Model Cities programs; legislation requiring neighborhood-based groups to do the construction, a difficult proposition in such a decimated community, added to the boondoggle.[38] It took four years before contractors broke ground, in late 1972.

Completed in 1975, the Marcus Garvey Village might have seemed worth the wait. The 625 one- to five-bedroom apartments, arranged in four-story rows along six square blocks, appeared to be everything that the Van Dyke–type houses were not. The houses had semiprivate entrances to avoid the criminal appeal of empty stairwells, elevators, and hallways. Adults would be able to keep close watch on their children and passersby, something they couldn't do from the tenth floor of one of the towers in the park. Pedestrian-only streets that the architects called "mews" were designed to encourage sociability among residents. Instead of just providing a roof over heads, Marcus Garvey was to be a holistic community with a community center, day-care facility, and parking. Hopes ran so high that around the same time the first tenants were hauling their beds and kitchenware into Marcus Garvey, the Museum of Modern Art held an exhibit in its honor, called "Another Chance for Housing: Low-Rise Alternatives." From the halls of Washington, D.C., the Department of Housing and Urban Development declared the project "of national importance," given its neighborhood identity as a "coast to coast symbol of physical deterioration of a neighborhood."[39]

Alas, it was neither community control nor enlightened architecture that Brownsville needed. Crime, disorder, civic apathy, and exhaustion plagued Marcus Garvey Village just as they did Van Dyke. By the 1980s, few residents socialized in the mews—unless they happened to be drug dealers or gang members. A 2005 study published in *Progressive Planning Magazine* found that the day-care facility and the community center, which was, by necessity, locked most of the time, were both rarely used by residents; the hoped-for tenant groups remained a planner's dream. Surveillance cameras became MGV's version of eyes on the street. "[T]he role of management has shifted from supporting community development and maintaining the physical structures of MGV to . . . securing and sustaining the development against external criminal influence and simply patching, but not fixing, the physical deterioration of the development," the authors wrote. "Social history trumped the architecture."[40]

Bad as crime and family life were becoming in Brownsville in the 1960s, the following decades were worse. It seemed as if civic life was completely unraveling. The celebrity preacher-activist Al Sharpton moved into a Brownsville project from middle-class Hollis, Queens, after his modestly successful father left his mother for his older half-sister. His mother's humiliation haunted him, especially in his new surroundings. "It was rough for me growing up in Brownsville in the mid-sixties," Sharpton told the journalist Jack Newfield. "I wasn't street. I was church."[41]

By the 1970s, if the childhood of heavyweight champion Mike Tyson recalled in his memoir, *The Undisputed Truth*, is at all typical, Brownsville had descended into a lower level of purgatory. Tyson moved with his mother and sister from Bedford-Stuyvesant to nearby Brownsville when he was seven years old. At the time, Bed-Stuy was in bad shape, but right away, the second-grader saw that he was in wilder territory. "You could totally feel the difference," he wrote in his memoir. "The people were louder [in Brownsville], more aggressive. . . . Everything was hostile. . . . Cops were always driving by with their sirens on, ambulances always coming to pick up somebody, guns going off, people getting stabbed, windows being broken." As for many of Brownsville's children then and today, Tyson's home life didn't offer much sustenance. His mother beat him regularly; one of his few encounters with the man he thought was his father took place during a several-minute ride in the man's Cadillac. When his mother was too drunk to walk him to school, evidently an unremarkable occurrence, he would be roughed up by neighborhood kids as he walked alone—if he was lucky. On unlucky days, he was robbed at gunpoint. Hunger was the only thing leading him to the building where he was supposed to be getting an education: "I'd go to school, eat breakfast, and leave. I'd walk around the block for a few hours. Then I'd go back for lunch and leave."

Within a few years, Tyson was already a veteran thief and gangbanger. His one edifying activity was raising pigeons. One day, a local boy stole one of the birds that he had just purchased from a pet store. Tyson demanded it back; the tyke/thief took the bird out from under his jacket and twisted its head until he had entirely decapitated the animal. When he threw the bloody stump in Tyson's face, the world-class boxer-to-be had his first memorable fight. He was eleven years old.[42]

The casualties of Brownsville's crime and the general air of brutality went beyond the lives lost, bodies injured, or children traumatized; the physical, institutional, and social entity evoked by the word "community" itself was shattered. Sick of vandalism and nonpaying tenants, landlords abandoned their buildings; some burned them down in order to recoup insurance money. Businesses, civic institutions, and schools shut their doors—at least when they could. Crime drove out most white store owners by the mid-1970s; few minority businesses took their place except for a smattering of small bodegas, according to Walter Thabit, author of *How East New York Became a Ghetto*. Entire blocks, Pete Hamill wrote, already in 1969, were "abandoned to the rats and the wind."[43]

Residents had to go outside the neighborhood to buy food for dinner or blood-pressure medication. Churches closed, and so did parochial schools. The 1990s remained equally grim. Gunmen took hostage the staff at the library on New Lots Avenue, threatening one of the few remaining civic institutions.[44] In 1992, in the most notorious incident of many at Thomas Jefferson High School, two fifteen-year-olds were shot at point-blank range by a classmate, several hours before Mayor David Dinkins was scheduled to give a motivational speech to the student body. After the event, the *New York Times* interviewed a teacher who said that in the previous five years, fifty of her students had died.[45] That's *fifty.*

LEAVING BROWNSVILLE

In some serious sense, 1970 marked the end of history in Brownsville. Crime—Brownsville frequently had the highest homicide rate in New York City—poverty, broken and chaotic families, and dismal schools remained the norm throughout the following decades. Yes, there have been some bright spots. In the 1980s, East Brooklyn congregations joined with the city to build 1,100 affordable single-family row houses where applicants are screened for income and criminal history. Known as the Nehemiah Houses, they continue to provide a small annex of tidy neighborliness near Van Dyke and the other towers. As in the rest of New York City and the nation as a whole, crime has plummeted in Brownsville over the past fifteen years. The relative safety has helped to revive Pitkin Avenue, now lively with new business, including moderate-priced chains like The Children's Place. Poverty rates have declined from 42 percent in 2000 to 38 percent in 2010.[46] As of the early 2000s, reading and math scores began to improve under the leadership of a new school superintendent, Kathleen Cashin. The numbers have held steady or even improved a bit since then.

But Brownsville's status as one of the most troubled neighborhoods in New York City is beyond dispute. Brownsville continues to have the highest per-capita murder rate in the city. In 2014, more people were shot in that two-square-mile area than in all of Manhattan.[47] One of the few oases in the community, the Brownsville Recreation Center, has an indoor pool, performance space, and gym, but because it sits between rival territories, many kids don't use it. They know the dangers when word gets out that they are trespassing.[48] The Van Dyke Houses remain among the worst projects in the city; in 2014, major crimes had risen to eighty-two, having jumped from fifty-five in 2009. It was the highest number of any NYCHA development.[49]

City, state, federal, and philanthropic money continues to support a plethora of programs to improve the area: jobs programs, juvenile-justice programs, juvenile-health programs, programs teaching leadership skills, entrepreneurial skills, civic—or social justice—engagement skills, and so on. Many of them are capably run and thoughtfully designed, far more than the experiments of the War on Poverty years, but one has to wonder whether they amount to little more than damage control.

One, in particular, a nonprofit parent-counseling program called "Power of Two," points to just how severely and early Brownsville's roughness embeds itself into the psyche of so many of the 1,300 children born in the area every year. The goal of Power of Two, narrowly targeted to Brownsville's young mothers in their teens and early twenties as well as to occasional fathers, is to increase parents' sensitivity to their babies and toddlers. Researchers have found that in comparison with middle-class parents, ghetto parents tend to be harsh with their young children: yelling, pulling, and intrusive, rough behaviors are commonplace in the homes that the counselors visit; cuddling, holding, or playing are rare. Erasma Monticciolo, the Power of Two's savvy vice president of programs and community engagement, argues that Brownsville parents raise children to expect that "you don't have control of your destiny" and to adapt to the conditions around them. "I was raised that the world was tough, you had to be independent," mothers—and grandmothers—sometimes say.

In one clarifying example described to me by Power of Two counselor Jazmine Dowtin, a Brownsville native and social worker, she watched a father spray water in his young child's face. The child flinched and then, seeing her father laugh, tentatively did the same. "Look, she's laughing," he told Dowtin—perhaps sensing her unease. So he did it again—until Dowtin gently suggested that the child was actually not enjoying this game. "The child may laugh and come back for more," Dowtin explained to me. "It's the only attention she's getting." For me, Power of Two's impressive protocol and thoughtful counselors were a marked contrast to the shocking necessity of their mission: to teach parents to notice their children's emotions.

You could argue that all parents raise their children to adapt to the world as they know it and that, after all, Brownsville is "violent, harsh, and unfair," in Monticciolo's words. But the roughness that children begin learning in their earliest months leaves them ill equipped to leave Brownsville. Therein lies the nub of the matter. Brownsville's social isolation, whatever its roots in racism, government fecklessness, bad ideas, and economic disruption, continues to entrap its residents. The best hope is not to "empower the community," as we've been trying to do since the 1960s, but to disrupt its isolation.

This may not be as unlikely as it seems. Knowledgeable observers speculate that the neighborhood, well serviced by subway lines and adjacent to the invasion of young apartment-hungry graphic designers in Bushwick, Crown Heights, and Bed-Stuy, is next in line for gentrification. The rezoning of next door's East New York, Brownsville's closest socioeconomic cousin, has provoked consternation among community leaders.

They're making a mistake. The difficult truth—and it is immensely difficult—is that gentrification would be about the best thing that could ever happen to Brownsville. NYU sociologist Patrick Sharkey, who has been studying neighborhood poverty in the United States, writes about the segregation of neighborhoods like Brownsville in his book *Stuck in Place: Urban Neighborhoods and the End of Progress Toward Racial Equality.* "The most common experience for black families since the 1970s, by a wide margin, has been to live in the poorest American neighborhoods over consecutive generations. Only 7 percent of white families have experienced similar poverty in their neighborhood environments for consecutive generations."[50] Sharkey is is not alone in viewing concentrated black poverty of this sort as one of the greatest barriers against upward mobility.[51] Diluting neighborhood poverty not only improves a specific geographic place; it boosts the fortunes of local kids. "There is strong evidence," as Sharkey writes, "that when neighborhood disadvantage declines, the economic fortunes of black youth improve and improve rather substantially."[52]

Anti-gentrification warriors, while reasonably concerned about the immediate hardship of people displaced by rising rents and unethical landlords, tend to ignore the long-term risks of being "stuck in place." Americans, members of an immigrant nation, have always moved to new places in search of better opportunities. That was once especially the case for the poor; Brownsville "measured all success by our skill in getting away from it," as Alfred Kazin wrote in the 1930s. For a long time, this was also true of African Americans, who were actually more mobile than whites. For reasons no one completely understands, blacks had stopped moving by 1970.

It's a fact that may well have intensified their disadvantage. An award-winning paper by University of Michigan's Eric Chyn compared the adult outcomes of children forced to move from their demolished Chicago housing projects with their peers who lived in nearby public housing that remained in place. The displaced children were significantly more likely to be employed and to have higher earnings than those who stayed put.[53] Malcolm Gladwell describes similar success among blacks forced out of New Orleans after Hurricane Katrina.[54]

Yet today's Brownsville seems to do everything it can to keep its residents in their place. As Brownsville parents prepare even their youngest children for ghetto life, those children bring their expectations to schools, which have done a poor job of offering an alternative vision. Meanwhile, as the sociologist Scott Winship notes, a morass of varied state rules for Medicaid, food stamps, and unemployment insurance discourage potential strivers; New York State's exceptionally generous Medicaid benefits are a particularly powerful disincentive. Single parenthood also makes moving a more daunting undertaking. Single parents are inevitably more dependent on family and friends than a couple who have each other and thus double the chance of creating new social networks. Public housing is perhaps the biggest barrier. NYCHA was supposed to be providing "springboard housing," Richard Price observes. Instead, it has turned into quicksand. Once people move in, they are slow to leave, especially with rental prices as high as they are;[55] the average tenure of a NYCHA resident has grown to twenty-two years. In many cases, they never leave. Worse, their children don't, either. NYCHA gives residents' children and grandchildren the right to stay in their parents' or grandparents' apartment as long as they have been living there before their death.[56] And so it is that an apartment at Van Dyke can remain a family home for generations.

It's been a perfect formula for keeping Brownsville gridlocked, watching from the sidelines while the New Brooklyn moves on.

Sunset Park

Chinese Immigrants in Blue Sky Brooklyn

*L*ike other prospering American cities, New York seems to many almost a fortress of inequality. It's Bill de Blasio's "tale of two cities"—white versus black and Hispanic, rich versus poor, pimped-up condominiums versus crime-plagued housing projects, or, in terms of Brooklyn's geography that I've described so far, Williamsburg versus Brownsville, Park Slope versus East New York.

It's a woefully incomplete picture, ignoring dozens of neighborhoods that have rarely come to the attention of a Condé Nast writer or social justice activist. In the south and west parts of the borough especially, Brooklyn remains the immigrant city, the Borough of Homes and Churches that it always was. Over 37 percent of Brooklyn's population is foreign born.[1] From Mexico, Bangladesh, Pakistan, Afghanistan, Ghana, Poland, Guatemala, and Russia, they find jobs as seamstresses, construction workers, and home health-care aides; thousands of others start their own businesses. The vast majority are penniless when they arrive; but like immigrants in the past, they're determined to find economic opportunity for themselves and their kids. Considering that many will succeed in finding what they're looking for, you'd have to conclude that Brooklyn is not just two cities, but many more.

Surprising as it seems to Brooklynites who grew up in the Jewish, Italian, and Irish period, the Chinese are now the largest and fastest-growing of the borough's immigrants.[2] Over the past several decades, hundreds of thousands of immigrants from the Fujian province of China, most poor, many undocumented, have been cramming into dormitories and SROs, working brutally long hours waiting tables, washing dishes, and cleaning hotel rooms, sending their Chinese-speaking children to public schools and on to public universities, if not more elite private ones. The Chinese are changing South Brooklyn's

ethnic landscape every bit as much as hipsters and trustafarians have revolution-
ized its northern neighborhoods. By turning an abandoned neighborhood into
a launching ground into the middle class, they perplex common assumptions
about poverty, opportunity, and mobility in an era of bankrupting college
tuitions and working-class decline.

HOW THE CHINESE CAME TO SUNSET PARK

The Chinese are hardly new ingredients in New York's melting pot. The
downtown Manhattan neighborhood area known as Chinatown has been an
ethnic enclave for well over a century. For much of that time, the number of
residents who shopped the crowded vegetable markets on Mott Street and
manned the restaurants near Chatham Square was limited by strict immigration
policies in the United States and equally harsh emigration rules in both China
and Taiwan. But after the immigration reform act of 1965, followed by the
political uncertainty facing Hong Kong and Taiwan in the 1980s, the Chinese
presence in New York City swelled dramatically. By 1990, the Chinese
were the second-largest immigrant group in Gotham, surpassed only by
Dominicans.[3]

Earlier Chinese immigrants to New York had settled in that obscure corner of downtown Manhattan long considered New York City's only "Chinatown." But that district's population doubled between 1965 and 1990.[4]
Especially as Wall Street traders and a club set enamored of the gritty downtown laid their own claim to the area, Manhattan's Chinatown was running
out of space. Its quasi-gentrification was ultimately Brooklyn's gain. Relatively
well-to-do Taiwanese flocked to Queens, where they built thriving communities in Elmhurst and Flushing, an area now called "Little Taipei." Other
Chinese—particularly, recent settlers from the mainland province of Fujian—
followed the D, N, and R subway lines from Chinatown to southwest Brooklyn, where apartments were cheaper.

The little-known area called Sunset Park—between southern Park Slope
(Bill de Blasio's home base) and leafy Bay Ridge—became Brooklyn's own
Chinatown; it is now the largest Chinatown in New York City. Situated in
the area that slopes from the southern Brooklyn waterfront with its hulking
Industry City Army Terminal and dead-on views of the Statue of Liberty up
past the numbered avenues to Fort Hamilton Parkway, over time Sunset Park's
modest blocks of two- and three-story brick homes have witnessed a microcosm of Brooklyn's immigrant churn. About 150 years ago, Irish and Polish
immigrants who worked at the docks and piers were the first to turn this part
of Brooklyn's farmland into something resembling an urban neighborhood. In
the late 1880s, a large influx of Scandinavian shipbuilders, cargo handlers, and

harbor pilots also settled in the area, which, depending on whom you ask, became known either as Finntown or Little Norway. The main shopping street, Eighth Avenue, became known as Lapskaus Boulevard, named for the stewlike dish that was a staple of the Norwegian diet and ubiquitous in the restaurants that lined the thoroughfare.

A few signs of this earlier immigrant history remain scattered around Sunset Park. The mammoth church Our Lady of Perpetual Help, whose stained-glass windows are engraved with the names of local Irishmen, can still be seen from blocks away. Not too far away on Fourth Avenue, the Irish Haven pub is an old-fashioned dive bar still popular among Guinness drinkers with no use for the gentrified mixologists of the New Brooklyn. The Finnish-built Alku houses were the first cooperative housing in the United States; the Lutheran Medical Center, founded in the 1880s by a Norwegian deaconess, remains a vital neighborhood institution.

By the mid-twentieth century, however, both the waterfront and the neighborhood that housed so many of its workers had fallen into steep decline. The Norwegians who stayed left for Bay Ridge and suburban destinations. After Norway discovered the North Sea oil deposits, Norwegian immigration came to a halt. Puerto Ricans moved in along the dreary Fourth and Fifth Avenues, which had been recently cut off from the piers by Robert Moses's much-hated Brooklyn-Queens Expressway. Today, much of the area is heavily Latino, mostly Central Americans who arrived in the later decades of the century. While still poor, it is far safer than it was in those high-crime decades. Fifth Avenue boasts many blocks bustling with Ecuadorean taco stands and Mexican bodegas. Latinos didn't bother with many of the boarded-up blocks along Eighth Avenue in the blocks above 50th Street. Perhaps the area seemed too hopeless. Instead, the newest Chinese arrivals, crowded out of Manhattan's famed Chinatown, staked their claim.

One reason for the Chinese attraction to Sunset Park was the potential commercial thoroughfare: Eighth Avenue. The Chinese are enamored of the number eight because in their native tongue, it sounds similar to the word for prosperity; people often try to change their telephone numbers to include as many eights as possible. (It would also come to seem fortuitous that 86th Street and Eighteenth Avenue are the main commercial streets in Bensonhurst, where many Chinese have settled more recently.) Another advantage was the subway station on Eighth Avenue; as the first aboveground stop on the N line in Brooklyn, newcomers who could neither speak nor read English could easily recognize it. Paul Mak, director of the Brooklyn Chinese-American Association, explains that the Chinese refer to it as the "blue sky" station, and yes, hokey as it sounds, they meant not only its outdoor platform but its symbolism for the hopes that they held for their new life in America.

In one respect, the Chinese arrival is just another example of Brooklyn's vertigo-inducing, plan-defying, and utterly unpredictable ethnic churn. From another vantage point, it is something new. The old Brooklyn's immigrants from abroad were mostly European—or from one-time European colonies. But the arrival of the Chinese points toward a fundamental shift in the nature of Brooklyn's—and the nation's—diversity. Today, immigrants are following their bliss from Pakistan, Bangladesh, India, Afghanistan, Africa, Ecuador, and Mexico, joining the Jamaicans and Haitians who arrived in the mid- to late twentieth century. Still, the Chinese are the largest and fastest-growing of the borough's proliferating non-European immigrant groups, 14 percent of all foreign-born, two times the number of the second-place Jamaicans.[5]

Walking along Eighth Avenue, you may not spot a single non-Asian face. The markets sell dried shrimp and scallops, a staggering variety of gnarly ginseng roots, medicinal herbs, oils, and powders. Though official city numbers are considerably lower, Paul Mak estimates that Sunset Park and adjoining blocks house at least 150,000 Chinese. Most of them are poor and barely schooled men and women from the mainland province of Fujian.

BECOMING A MODEL MINORITY

The Chinese in America are often, and to their occasional irritation, described as the "model minority": resourceful, college-going, entrepreneurial, and almost pathologically hardworking. Their success has been a vexing subject, especially for liberals who fear that it serves as an implicit rebuke against less successful minorities. If the Chinese, from a deeply alien culture, often speaking obscure dialects, can make it, why can't Hispanics or, more painfully, blacks?

It can't be said that the Chinese didn't suffer discrimination. Asian immigrants first came to the United States in significant numbers more than a century and a half ago as low-skilled male laborers who mined, farmed, and built the railroads. For that, they got little thanks. The Chinese Exclusion Act of 1882 barred all new immigration from China; the Immigration Act of 1917, and then the National Origins Act of 1924, extended the immigration ban to include virtually all of Asia. In the largest mass lynching in American history, seventeen Chinese men were hanged in Los Angeles by a mob of 500 people. In the 1870s and 1880s, there were no fewer than 153 anti-Chinese riots across the American West, including in Seattle, Tacoma, Denver, and Rock Springs, Wyoming. Later in the twentieth century, attitudes softened. Some scholars theorize that during the civil rights struggle, Americans, who, up until then, had never had much good to say about Chinese "coolies" and laundrymen, only softened their attitudes to prove their racial innocence.[6]

In many respects, more recently arrived Fujianese, some of whom live in Manhattan's Chinatown, Flushing, and throughout Brooklyn, but who are mostly concentrated in Sunset Park, won't do much to subdue model-minority resentment. The medieval horrors of life in China and sometimes of their journey to America make their success, though more tenuous and modest than that of the more highly educated and urban Hong Kong and Taiwanese, hugely impressive. Many of the Chinese immigrants who arrived in New York after the 1965 immigration act were graduate students in math and the sciences. It was easy to explain the achievements of their own children, Ivy-bound "whiz kids," as a *Time* cover article called them as early as 1987. "Tiger Mom" and Yale law professor Amy Chua was one of those whiz kids. Her father, an electrical engineer of Fujian descent, immigrated from the Philippines to study at Berkeley in 1961. As of 2010, the Asian American median household income was $83,500, the highest of any demographic group, according to a study by Pew Research Center.[7]

For the most part, however, the Fujianese belong in a different category. The Fujianese were farmers, fishermen, and laborers in the province's newish sweatshop factories. Most of them didn't graduate high school; their knowledge of the English language is basically nil. In China, they have almost no chance of improving their lives. Some have seen proof of America's possibilities when neighbors purchased refrigerators with money sent to them by relatives who had gone to America, or, in a few cases, built large homes with wooden floors. Others are gulled by boastful stories from returnees. In any case, for many families, there seems to be only one choice: get themselves—or at least, their children—to the United States.

Their ways of doing that are frequently at odds with their model-minority image. Visas are nearly impossible to come by, at least for those who do not have family already in the States. A growing number of Chinese apply for asylum visas, most of them based on trumped-up complaints; the Chinese have the largest number of asylum visas among New York immigrants.[8] Other Fujianese turn to smugglers, or "snakeheads," as they are known, to create fake visas and guide them through a nightmare journey that often involves long, dangerous weeks or months in the airless holds of barely seaworthy ships, long stretches in safe houses in Thailand or Guatemala, or treks across the Mexican desert, all at a mere cost of $50,000 or more. (Patrick Radden Keefe's 2009 book *The Snakehead* is a phantasmagoric but factual depiction of the multibillion-dollar Chinatown-based smuggling business.) A large number who come to New York these days arrive via Canada, using the passports of relatives; they rely on the fact that border guards are not especially adept at distinguishing Chinese faces.[9] It's impossible to get a precise number of undocumented Fujianese in New York City, but educated estimates run as high as half a million since 1980. Ken Guest, an anthropology professor at Baruch College, estimates that 50 percent of Fujians in the city are there illegally.[10]

Despite their reputation for self-sufficiency, the Fujianese don't hesitate to take advantage of any government benefits that they might be able to finesse. They are quick to sign their kids up for food stamps, Medicaid, and disability. Some undocumented adults even manage to get themselves on the rolls. "They find creative ways to beat the system," Mak says. He sees plenty of evidence of a failure of "accountability" in the current welfare regime.

But the fact is that the Fujian are poor—really poor, as in four-people-to-a-single-room, all-rice-diet, soda-can-collecting poor. All in all, about 20 percent of the Chinese in New York live below the poverty line;[11] Paul Mak says that the number in Sunset Park is closer to 90 percent. At the Sunset Park schools that are almost entirely Chinese, 80 percent to 100 percent of students qualify for free lunch. Many one- and two-family homes in the area are now housing six families or more, mostly couples with children, leading to a constant crisis of overcrowding in schools and not a few regretful thoughts of home. Adding injury to insult, their poor English skills and fear of bringing themselves to the attention of the police make them frequent targets of street crime.

Despite all the obstacles, the Fujianese work like dogs. In New York City, the Chinese are more likely to live in dual-earning households than any other ethnic group.[12] Until five or ten years ago, women typically sewed in garment-factory sweatshops; today, they are more likely to clean hotel rooms or take care of the elderly. The men wait tables and wash dishes in restaurants. Their hours are brutal: ten hours or more a day, six and often seven days a week. According to the official data (the numbers don't include the undocumented), they are less likely than unskilled native-born Americans to be unemployed even during the Great Recession.[13] If they can't find work in New York, they "commute" elsewhere. The Chinese-restaurant labor market is an interstate business, says Guest, who has studied the community closely; restaurant owners from all over the South and Midwest advertise in employment offices in Chinatown, promising a salary and dormitory accommodations. Local Chinese entrepreneurs have started bus companies that transport waiters and chefs to Tampa or Chicago and then back to their families in Brooklyn—for their rare day off.

For all that, the Fujianese don't tend to complain about their lot. According to Min Zhou, a UCLA sociologist and a leading expert on the nation's Chinatowns, in China they could expect a monthly income of only $30; the lucky ones working a factory job might make a bit more. In the United States, on the other hand, a busboy can earn a monthly $800; a chef, maybe $2,000.[14] Yes, they are often treated terribly: not speaking English, fearful of deportation, they can be fired on a whim, and their employers have been known to stall payments or deny them entirely.

What about their legendary Chinese family values? You won't find many immigrant parents munching microwave popcorn while watching *Toy Story* on the living-room flat screen with the kids. In fact, they don't *have* a family life, or at least not one that middle-class Americans would recognize as such. "I never saw my parents," Mandy Wong, a graduate of Brooklyn Tech High School and now a junior at Hamilton College, told me. Her parents "worked from 10 a.m. to 1 p.m." Her grandparents, who spoke no English and could neither read nor write their own dialect, took care of her. She had many chores, including, by the time she was in third grade, serving as primary caretaker for her younger brothers. She had few friends—not because she was an unlikable child but because friends were deemed an unnecessary waste of Chinese time.

Stephanie Yu, a Sunset Park–raised recent graduate of SUNY Binghamton, was also largely supervised by her grandmother, though she was luckier: her mother walked her to school every morning. But that was all she saw of her till nine or ten at night—seven days a week. Still, "I was considered one of the lucky ones because I had grandparents to take care of me and didn't have to spend all of my time in the sweatshop," referring to the many poor Fujianese children who had nowhere to go after school but their mothers' steaming workplaces. Stephanie remembers being at her mother's worksite one afternoon and noticing several children with glitter in their hair. They had been hiding from inspectors in a large box that happened to be filled with glitter-embellished dresses. Stephanie doesn't mention something noted by Ken Guest: sometimes children are, in fact, enlisted as reduced-fee, or even free, labor.

Few sweatshop factories remain in Manhattan or in Brooklyn Chinatown. But with smugglers to repay and families back home in dire need, mothers see no choice but to work ferocious hours. Some poor young couples are forced to put their kids in local "boarding schools" of uncertain quality. Others send their babies back to grandparents in China until they are old enough for school. Not unexpectedly, according to Ken Kwong, a professor at Hunter School of Social Work, who has studied what he calls this "reverse migration," the arrangement often leads to problems for children and parents; a five-year-old who remembers only Chinese village life with his grandparents is probably not going to run into the arms of his self-sacrificing mother or, for that matter, his English-speaking first-grade public school teacher when he arrives in Brooklyn.

Uneducated, poor, and absent parents who don't speak English: in most people's minds, it seems like a formula for troubled kids. The resource gap between low-income and affluent children is generally viewed as a major source of inequality and immobility, not to mention a deep injustice. Rich kids get trips to Europe, swimming classes, fancy schools, and valuable social connections, not to mention two doting parents; poor kids, at best, get a little unhealthy food on the table, a bed to share with siblings, and thirty distracted kids in a class with an inept teacher presiding. Of course, for those kids, the future looks dim.[15]

That may be true for some Fujianese kids. Mak says that about 15 percent of their preschool population are special-education, though almost all these are distressed children who have only recently come from China to be reunited with their parents in the United States. Boys who arrive in the United States only when they are nearing adolescence have a particularly hard time. Adapting to high school peer culture after fourteen years in China is immensely stressful, and young adolescent immigrants are at great risk of dropping out.[16]

But in general, the kids from Sunset Park look on track to achieve the sort of upward mobility that is supposed to be close to impossible in a "two cities" New York. A WYNC analysis showed that Sunset Park's zip code (and neighboring Borough Park's) had among the largest number of acceptances at the city's specialized high schools. "Most of the other admissions to the elite schools," the report noted, "came from middle- to upper-class neighborhoods like the Upper West Side and Fresh Meadows."[17] (In 2012, of the 14,415 students enrolled in the eight specialized high schools that require a test for admissions, 8,549 were Asian.)[18] The fortunate strivers like Mandy Wong get scholarships to a first- or second-tier college; others, like Stephanie Yu, go to one of New York's state campuses, or commute to Brooklyn College or Baruch. Several city public university professors I spoke with weren't ready to rave about their language skills. And their future in the labor market is still unfolding. But it's a safe bet that, unlike their fathers—and their gender studies–major peers—they will not be waiting tables.

THE CHINESE SUCCESS SEQUENCE

So what accounts for the poverty-defying trajectory of the Fujian kids? The answer seems to be fourfold. First is a cultural trait that, though a cliché, is undeniably powerful: a zealous focus on children's education. For Chinese immigrants, education for the next generation is close to a religion. It is the path to a good life, which, given the subsistence hardships of their past, understandably means financial comfort and stability. Many young Chinese have direct experience with their own personal Tiger Mothers; one recent college graduate, now a public school math teacher, told me that his mother used to keep him up late at night and wake him at five to go over math problems—when he was in first and second grade. Ruth Stanislaus, principal of P.S. 971 in Sunset Park, whose student population is now a little over half Chinese, was taken aback when one mother of a kindergartner—a five-year-old, mind you—announced in faltering English: "My son must go Harvard."

If, as sometimes appears to be the case, "Harvard" is the first English word learned by immigrant Chinese mothers, the second word is probably "Stuyvesant." Remember that Fujianese parents are generally young and poorly educated themselves; according to Paul Mak, some of the newer arrivals haven't yet figured out how important school is for their kids' future. It doesn't take long for them to learn. Gossiping with other parents living with their kids in the single room down the hall, and reading, if they can, the Chinese-language newspapers and watching TV with their ubiquitous ads for test-prep companies, they quickly get an education of their own in words like "Brooklyn Tech," "Bronx Science," and, of course, "Stuyvesant," the names of premier high schools that require a test for admission. Even the poor figure out a way to get their fourth- or fifth-graders into test-prep classes. The WNYC report found one Sunset Park family that put aside $5,000 for classes for their three sons out of a yearly household income of $26,000. Several years ago, the city began offering free prep classes for underrepresented black and Hispanic kids planning to take the admissions test. After a legal challenge, they were forced to include other minority ethnic groups. According to the *New York Times*, 43 percent of the students in the program are now Asian.[19]

The second reason for upward mobility is the Chinese immigrant belief in that sorely tested myth: the American dream. Chinese families are not Pollyanna-ish about America; they believe that they have been discriminated against, and they tell their kids to expect discrimination as well. A Pew study found that only about a fifth of respondents believe that Chinese Americans and whites get along very well. Even fewer say that Chinese Americans get along well with blacks or Hispanics.[20] Tales of being bullied at school are commonplace. And there are reports of some Recession-battered immigrants trying to return to China.

But most seem to maintain what is sometimes called "immigrant optimism." Sunset Park residents see no sign of a slowing of new Fujianese influx into their area. America remains Golden Mountain, the term that originated when the first Chinese arrived and sought gold in the California hills. They are not just looking for a job; they are looking to live the dream, which they see as owning a home, being their own boss—and sending their kids to an Ivy League school. For them, upward mobility is not a strictly personal story; it is familial and multigenerational. Which takes us to the third reason that Fujianese kids are doing pretty well.

The Chinese parents of Sunset Park may not have the time or inclination for family movie night or school-night dinners, but they have their own way of creating intense family ties and obligations. Couples frequently share living space with their children's grandmothers, aunties, uncles, and cousins. Children think of their destiny as their family's destiny. Chinese kids are not expected to follow their passions or find their individual talents. Their goals—material success and family name—are indistinguishable from their family's goals.[21] Parents work for their kids and extended kin; kids work—go to school, do their homework—for their parents and extended kin. Their parents' sacrifice, the twelve-hour days, the six or seven days a week, the money that could be spent on a dinner at a special restaurant set aside for relatives in Fujian, are instilled into them as proving an essential truth about the good life that looks only superficially like that imagined by most middle-class Americans. "You try to make up for their hardships," one successful Stuyvesant admittee explained to the *New York Times*.[22]

The Chinese view is reminiscent of Alfred Kazin's description of Brownsville parents we saw in chapter 7: "My father and mother worked in a rage to put us above their level; they had married to make *us* possible. We were the only conceivable end to all their striving; we were their America." As in the case of Kazin's generation of Jews, these qualities make Chinese immigrant marriages remarkably stable, which, in turn, adds to both children's family ties and upward mobility. Along with the smaller population of Russian immigrants, the Chinese have the highest proportion of married-couple households among immigrant groups. Unlike other immigrants and native-born Americans as well, poverty does not seem to lead to nonmarital births or divorce. Most poor households in New York City are headed by single mothers. That's not the case among the Chinese; 56 percent of Asian households in poverty in 2006 were led by married couples, more than twice as high as the 26 percent of all poor city households.[23] As recent research by Raj Chetty has suggested, communities with high proportions of married-couple families also have high rates of economic and social mobility.[24]

Not that all is well in the Chinese family. By American standards, Chinese immigrant couples look as though they could use some counseling. Phillip Kasinitz, who has studied second-generation immigrants, says that the Chinese respondents often told him that their parents barely talked to each other; many fathers had girlfriends.[25] But then, no one seems to expect anything remotely like the Harry-and-Sally, American companionate ideal. The family, including husband and wife, is a working partnership, bound together by mutual necessity and some deep, generationally transmitted sense of loyalty and duty. It's a good guess that there are few—and perhaps even no—soulmates in Brooklyn's Chinatown. But then, there are lots of kids graduating high school and college.

The final and least understood reason for Chinese upward mobility is the ethnic enclave—in this case, Sunset Park—itself. To spin a familiar phrase, it takes a Chinatown to raise an immigrant child.[26] On the most practical level, the Chinese hire their own and they work for their own. Newcomers who can't read the Eighth Avenue subway station sign or don't know the difference between a dime and a silver dollar are generally able to find jobs anyway. They may be pitifully low-paying jobs under exploitative bosses in faraway cities, but the way they view it, they are jobs nonetheless. The enclave also helps promote social ties. Mak says that there are many groups in Sunset Park organized around hometowns or family names; people with the last name Lee join the Lee association, for instance, where they can find tips on jobs, advice about the best tutoring centers, and fellow mah-jongg players, and where they can brag about their children's successes. Mak himself is representative of the Chinese gift for civic association. He founded the Brooklyn Chinese American Association in 1988 and has since turned it into a twenty-four-hour site provider of after-school programs, day care, senior centers, legal advice, and mediation with the police and other government officials.

Scholars often worry that ethnic enclaves lead to isolation and reduce assimilation. That may be the case among older immigrants. Sunset Park adults can generally manage without learning English. Few of them aspire to get their own college degree or certificate or to rise above their station by any other means than possibly owning their own restaurant or shop. Many stay poor. When it comes to children, however, Sunset Park's social isolation is a boon. It's no secret that mainstream American habits are not always leading kids to educational and life success. In Sunset Park, Chinese kids are part of a counterculture that is reinforced on a daily basis by family members, by other adults, by Chinese television shows, by local test-prep centers. Shopkeepers might ask whether they've done their homework. They don't ask what they want to be when they grow up because the correct answer is all but universally shared. The role models for poor Chinese kids, observers point out, are not basketball players and rap stars but successful businesspeople and professionals.

MOVING UP

While most eyes have been on the shifting demographics of places like Bushwick and Greenpoint, the Chinese have been redefining several of southwest Brooklyn's legendary white ethnic neighborhoods near Sunset Park. Their mobility is playing a big role in creating the New Brooklyn. Like the hipsters in North Brooklyn, they are changing the social character of historically Italian and Jewish areas, where they not infrequently confront racial hostility; they are also displacing some longtimers.

Yet you'd be hard-pressed to find any anti-gentrification protests or activists taking up the cause. There's an obvious, though unfortunate, reason for this indifference. The neighborhoods in question don't have any of the flashpoints of the gentrification debate that places like Bushwick or Williamsburg have: there are few or no brownstones or nineteenth-century industrial buildings suitable for lofts and condos; and few artists, rap stars, movie directors, journalists, blacks, or Hispanics live there. These nondescript, old lower-middle-class neighborhoods stretching through many miles of southern and western Brooklyn have no hope of ever being cool.

The most dramatic change has taken place in Bensonhurst, a neighborhood of one- and two-family attached and unattached houses and small apartment buildings to the southwest of Sunset Park. Bensonhurst, known for much of the twentieth century as Brooklyn's Little Italy, was filled with *salumerias*, social clubs, pool halls, and, as the tabloids were fond of reporting, Mafioso. Today, Bensonhurst natives like Sammy "the Bull" Gravano, a well-known Gambino syndicate hitman, and his daughter Karen, who chose a somewhat more legitimate career as a star of the VH-1 reality show *Mob Wives*, would hardly recognize the joint. Bensonhurst is now the largest Chinese district in New York City; more than 36,000, or about 36 percent of its population, is of Chinese origin, an increase of 57 percent between 2000 and 2010.[27] To the despair of Italian small-business owners—the Chinese, it appears, don't eat a lot of pizza—only 7.8 percent of the population is Italian, and most of the latter are getting on in years. CUNY sociologist Phillip Kasinitz puts it this way: "If you work in a senior center, you'd think Bensonhurst was Italian. If you're a public school teacher, it looks Chinese."

A lot of Bensonhurst's Chinese are the grown and successful children of the poor Sunset Park immigrants we've already read about. They completed their education, got their white-collar jobs, and are ready to move to a less crowded district with nicer accommodations than the one where they grew up, yet hopefully close enough to take advantage of the Chinese supermarkets on Eighth Avenue. Generally, their parents come with them to help raise their children while they pursue Chinese-American success. From there, they frequently move yet again to Chinese neighborhoods in the Long Island suburbs, thereby becoming what Peter Kwong calls "uptown Chinese."

Chinese immigrants have become a significant presence in other formerly white ethnic neighborhoods contiguous with Bensonhurst as well. Borough Park, once an Irish and Italian precinct, which now has the largest concentration of Hasidic and Orthodox Jews in the United States, has become 15 percent Chinese in a mere decade's time. Dyker Heights, best known to outsiders for the Disneyland of lights displayed each Christmas by the mostly Italian residents, is now close to 30 percent Chinese. (The neighborhood earned brief prominence in 2015, when one of its Chinese residents, a police officer named Wenjein Liu, was executed while he and his partner sat in their parked patrol car in Bedford-Stuyvesant.) Once-Italian Bay Ridge, the *Saturday Night Fever* setting that sits in the shadow of the Verrazano Bridge, now has a large Chinese population; yet another district, the polyglot area around Avenue U between Coney Island and Ocean Avenue, has earned the title of the latest "satellite Chinatown."

As a neighborhood, Chinese Sunset Park will likely thrive as long as large swaths of China's population look for ways to escape grinding poverty and as long as American immigration policy remains as it is. As a group, however, the Chinese look on track to dissolve into America's great multicultural stew. American upward mobility has always been double-edged: achievers gain material comforts, freedom to marry whom they want and to prefer pizza and roast turkey over sea cucumber. They also lose touch with the particular identity that defined and sustained their ancestors and the community that it created. About 28 percent of Asian-Americans marry non-Asians; that's higher than other minorities except American Indians.[28] Those couples usually don't move to Sunset Park or even Bensonhurst. Their mixed-race children grow up with second- and third-generation Americans who know nothing of the Chinese language or the Lunar New Year. Will the coming generation of Chinese mothers working at Cravath Swaine or Goldman Sachs leave their jobs, move in with their grown children, and raise their grandchildren to know Chinese ways, the way their own grandmothers did?

The question hangs in the air of any successful immigrant community.

·9·

Canarsie

West Indians in the Promised Borough

$\mathcal{C}$onsider the hipster shambling onto the L train at Union Square after a 180-minute "happy hour" on the Lower East Side, and falling into a well-deserved sleep. He misses his stop in Williamsburg; he's in a deep REM state when the train pushes out of the Myrtle-Wyckoff stop in Bushwick. Continuing eastward, there's still little sign of life at Broadway Junction near Bedford-Stuyvesant and East New York, or along the elevated track into Brownsville. After forty-five minutes, a conductor shakes him awake. It's the end of the line, and he is in a place whose name he dimly remembers hearing maybe once in his three long years in Brooklyn: Canarsie.

Rubbing his eyes, he might well conclude that this place "Canarsie" is not actually in Brooklyn. The split-level and ranch houses, the blocks of small attached brick homes with vinyl or metal awnings and white curlicue painted iron railings and window bars suggest something more like Bruce Springsteen's New Jersey. Each home, no matter how humble, has a garage or a driveway with a recently washed car. Eavesdropping on some locals, he might be puzzled to hear that when they need to do some shopping, they often drive to one of the neighborhood's strip malls or the much larger Gateway Mall to the east, or Kings Plaza to the southwest. He stumbles across a few gas stations and car washes (for a big choice of muffler, tire, and body shops, look to any one of the streets merging into the neighborhood), but Starbucks—or any indie "flat white" kind of place, for that matter—are conspicuously absent. Dunkin' Donuts, IHOP, or one of the dozens of the area's minimarts are the only places to get a caffeine fix and sober up.

Canarsie's un-Brooklyn-like aesthetic and car- and mall-centric lifestyle limit its appeal for the brewpub and bike-lane crowd. Brooklyn's aspiring first- and second-generation immigrants, however, have long loved this place: its

Jamaica Bay–side location, relative safety, trees, abundant parkland, and, most of all, its modestly priced houses. "The greatest thing about Canarsie is that it's always been the perfect place for middle-income, first-time homebuyers who want to live the American dream," Frank Seddio, the ebullient Brooklyn Democratic chairman and native son with a loving, encyclopedic knowledge of the area, tells me when I meet him at his office on Flatlands Avenue.

The latest arrivals to live the dream in Canarsie are black immigrants from the West Indies. Just as Seddio describes, they are middle-income—median household earnings for the area are high (by Brooklyn standards): $64,000.[1] They are house-proud families with children. Like the Chinese of Sunset Park, they are loaded with immigrant grit and confidence in their children's future in America. Alas, for a variety of reasons, they are not as likely as the Chinese to see that immigrant mission accomplished.

CANARSIE: FROM VAUDEVILLE JOKE
TO RACE CAULDRON

Flat, marshy, and sparsely settled with truck farms, fishermen's shacks, summer cottages, and a cluster of pretty turn-of-the-century country churches, Canarsie was Brooklyn's literal backwater until well after World War II. True, New York City's transit system stretched as far as this little village way to the southeast—but barely. Almost an hour-long haul from midtown Manhattan, for a long time the neighborhood didn't appeal to commuters—or hardly anyone else, for that matter. In the 1950s television series *The Honeymooners*, Jackie Gleason would aim his fist at his dimwitted neighbor Ed Norton, played by the scarecrow-thin Art Carney: "Norton!" he would bellow, "I'm going to kick you all the way from here to Canarsie!" Even a bus driver and sewer worker barely scraping by in a bare-bones Bensonhurst walkup thought of Canarsie as a punch line.

In the 1950s, developers spied potential in those marshes. They weren't thinking of the dual-earner, college-educated upper-middle-class couples of the sort that drive much of today's urban development; such folks were as rare as penguins in those parts. They had their eye on another group. These were the Italian and Jewish children of the crowded, Depression-era Brownsville and East New York, who had become solidly employed blue-collar workers. Among the first buyers in postwar Canarsie, fewer than 25 percent of men had graduated from high school, but they mixed with a smattering of white-collar workers like teachers, clerical workers, salespeople, and civil servants.[2]

Equipped with GI loans and growing families, these young adults were drawn to the modest single-family homes sprouting up in the famous Levittown and other developments on Long Island and in New Jersey. Canarsie was the urban version of this suburban sprawl, promising the same open space, safety, decent schools, modern cleanliness, and conveniences. It was a Disneyland setting for people who had known only aging tenements and dismal walk-ups. So sought after was the life that Canarsie offered that between 1950 and 1980, the population swelled from 30,000 to 80,000 contented souls.

Not that postwar Canarsie was Mayberry. Mafia wiseguys like Henry Hill, immortalized in the movie *Goodfellas*, hung out at the Bamboo Lounge, a local bar and restaurant. Still, Canarsie's Jews and Italians, who had not historically always been the best of Brooklyn friends, shared a determination to put the worst of history and poverty behind them and create a snug community centered on family, church, synagogue, and the modest pleasures of diners, Saturday matinee movies, and Sunday at the Canarsie pier. To this day, Canarsie nostalgia is thriving on Facebook and YouTube as middle-aged adults shout out to their former classmates and neighbors and find comfort in memories of stickball games, hanging-out corners, and the purple fluorescent lights that decorate the ceiling of Original Pizza on Avenue L, a Canarsie golden-age joint still popular today.

Yet Canarsie, despite its quasi-suburban demeanor, was still *of* Brooklyn. As we've already seen, by the mid-1960s crime in the borough was beginning a steady rise into record-breaking territory. Canarsians may have been able to put Brownsville tenement life behind them, but the actual fraying district was less than two miles away. Those who worked in or visited the old neighborhood were shocked by the changes in their childhood home: the iron gates protecting every storefront, pairs of policemen (to avoid walking the beat alone), and men on street corners drinking beer or smoking strange-smelling cigarettes. Canarsie itself had several NYCHA housing projects. Except for the eternally troubled Breukelen Houses, those developments were at first integrated and middle-income. (Howard Schultz, future founder and CEO of Starbucks, grew up with his parents, a cabdriver and an office receptionist, in the Bayview Houses, near Jamaica Bay.) That changed when NYCHA altered the residency rules and, as they had in Brownsville, nonworking welfare mothers and their children began to replace the lower middle class. Reports of muggings and robberies and even a drive-by shooting led white Canarsians to fear that blacks were bringing crime and poverty into their haven.

Tensions became most acute in local schools. As soon as it opened in the 1960s, Canarsie High School saw scattered fights between Italian and black kids from Breukelen Houses. During the 1970s, as the school's black population grew to about 27 percent, turf struggles over stairways, hallways, and bathrooms were commonplace. When it opened in September 1970, violence erupted almost immediately at South Shore High School. The new building was lauded by the New York City Board of Education as the "most sophisti-cated school ever built in the city."[3] It was also one of the biggest. After five years, its student population ballooned to 6,800, making it the second-largest high school in the United States. Administrators kept the lid on the huge, multiracial, and multi-neighborhood student body by imposing a kind of un-official segregation: whites and blacks were often scheduled for separate classes and different lunch hours.

A 1971 Board of Education plan to bus children from Brownsville's Til-den projects to Canarsie's Wilson Junior High intensified tensions and drew even liberal Jewish residents into the area's race hostilities. Some people com-pared the parents' protest to 1950s Little Rock, Arkansas.[4] That's overstated. According to Jonathan Reider, author of an indispensable history of these years, the Wilson student body had been 50 percent black—mostly children from the Breukelen projects—*before* the new busing plan was introduced. It wasn't just white parents who were opposed to upsetting the school's balance and community identity; the school's black parents weren't happy with the plan, either. Adding to the resentments of local white parents was a fresh mem-ory of Ocean Hill–Brownsville. In that instance, they noticed, much of the political establishment had embraced the idea of "community control." In their case, community control was damned as racist.

To the community's great shame, Canarsians turned some legitimate objections to the busing plan into a display of racial cruelty that almost lived up to the Little Rock comparison. A mob of local whites, some of them the children of socialist Brownsville, who had grown up reciting the injustices against Eugene Debs and the Scottsboro Boys, whose garment-worker parents had waxed about the brotherhood of man, screamed, "Niggers go home!" at the black children who tremblingly held on to teachers as they entered the building. Locals held banners declaring "Canarsie Schools for Canarsie Chil-dren!" Some 90 percent of parents at Wilson Junior High kept their children home rather than send them to school with the thirty-one new black and Puerto Rican Tilden children, while classes were canceled at other district schools after mass absences and threats of violence.

The school boycott was not the immediate cause of Canarsie's eventual racial turnover. Over the next decade and a half, occasional racial flare-ups coincided with erosion in the white population from 90 percent to 75 percent of Canarsie. But most of the leavers appeared to be older pioneer couples heading to retirement rather than whites fleeing black neighbors.[5]

That all changed in 1991. Brooklyn's growing West Indian population had found in Canarsie exactly the same safety, good schools, and affordable homes that had enticed Italians and Jews to the area decades earlier. Real estate agents were reluctant to take black customers to the mostly white enclave, but after being threatened by the courts for civil rights violations, they relented. A Pakistani grocery store was repeatedly threatened, robbed, and finally burned down. The Fillmore Real Estate office on Flatlands Avenue was firebombed. The episodes brought Al Sharpton and a large group of protesters to the local streets. One of them held a banner proclaiming, "The white man is the devil!" while local residents shook watermelons at the passing black marchers. The awful publicity following the march helped "blockbusting" real estate agents panic homeowners into selling en masse; if they waited to find a buyer until every other white person had sold, they asked, what would happen to their life's investment?

Canarsie's name, said the *Times*, had become "synonymous with bigotry."[6] Like many stereotypes, this one was based on extremes. A number of middle-class blacks had been living peaceably in Canarsie next to friendly white neighbors since the 1970s. To this day, white veterans like Frank Seddio remain happily settled among black neighbors. But white flight from Canarsie was so dramatic as to make the history books. Never before had a New York City neighborhood flipped so quickly. In 1990, Canarsie was 75 percent white and 10 percent black. A mere decade later, it was 60 percent black. By 2010, the number had climbed to 85 percent, where, more or less, it remains today.[7]

AFRO-CARIBBEAN CANARSIE AND THE BLACK-BLACK DIVIDE

Americans tend to think of race in black and white terms, but whites and blacks are a diverse group. Nowhere is this more the case than in Brooklyn. In the 1920s, before the height of black migration from the Jim Crow South, almost a quarter of the black population in Brooklyn were immigrants from the islands of the Caribbean. They hailed primarily from Jamaica, but Trinidad and Barbados also sent large numbers of American dreamers. In the earliest days, Afro-Caribbeans started off in Harlem, but they soon discovered the A train and the appeal of the houses of Bedford-Stuyvesant and Crown Heights.[8]

After the 1965 restrictions loosened on non-European immigrants, the West Indian population swelled. The number of black immigrants to the United States quadrupled between 1980 and 2013; the New York City metropolitan area was the destination for nearly 30 percent of them.[9] The metro area is now home to roughly 250,000 black Jamaican immigrants, 40 percent of the nation's total Jamaican population. Haitians, Guyanese, and Africans from Nigeria and the Ivory Coast now add to the mix.[10] Those who earned enough money or had relatives with an available room moved to the small homes of Canarsie.

Canarsie's street life might seem mildly exotic not just to Canarsie's original Jews and Italians but to the denizens of black neighborhoods in American cities like Chicago or Atlanta, where Caribbean blacks are rare. Though still far less dense than the majority of New York City neighborhoods, large extended families and boarders make the streets seem more urban than the old days. Black Canarsians work at many of the same jobs as the whites they replaced—as police officers, bus drivers, and secretaries—though now the neighborhood's soundtrack from passing cars and crowded shops has evolved from Sinatra to Metallica to reggae. At produce markets, residents might not be able to find arugula, but they're sure to see plenty of coconuts and plantains. Once, little-league baseball teams marched in Memorial Day parades to Canarsie Park; today, it's cricket and soccer that excite locals. Dozens of Jamaican, Haitian, and other Caribbean restaurants spread down Flatlands Avenue, Rockaway Parkway, and Avenue L, serving familiar island specialties like oxtail stew or, in a nice bit of culinary fusion, Rasta Pasta, a penne made with Jamaican ingredients like coconut milk and jerk spices.

But the differences between American-born blacks and Canarsie's Caribbean-born blacks reach far deeper than collard greens and curried goat, deep enough to create tensions between the two groups and lead to divergent life prospects. This doesn't mean that Brooklyn's West Indians haven't continued to feel the sting of racial prejudice. West Indian kids complain about being followed around in stores by security people. Boys, in particular, notice white women holding tight to their bags when they walk by.

Black immigrants were also the victims of a number of horrific race crimes in Brooklyn in the 1980s and 1990s. In 1986, Trinidad-born Bed-Stuy resident Michael Griffith was chased by a white mob onto a highway in Howard Beach, Queens, where he died after being hit by a car. In 1997, police officers in Brooklyn's 70th precinct sodomized the Haitian-born Abner Louima with a broom handle, leaving him with severe colon and bladder injuries. Black immigrants are known for viewing African Americans as overly touchy about perceived racial slights, but a 1991 riot in the largely West Indian section of Crown Heights exposed a similar penchant among the former islanders. After an Orthodox Jewish driver in a funeral procession for a renowned local rabbi hit and killed a Guyanese seven-year-old named Gavin Cato and severely wounded his young cousin, a furious crowd screaming, "Let's get the Jew!" beat and stabbed to death an Australian rabbinical student, though he had no connection to the accident.[11] No one can be sure how many of the Crown Heights rioters were West Indian, but we do know that Lemrick Nelson, the sixteen-year-old who eventually confessed to the stabbing, was the son of Trinidadian parents.[12]

Especially given this painful history, black middle-class Canarsie presents a difficult truth: on a number of significant measures, West Indians, particularly

Jamaicans, have more in common with Brooklyn's Chinese than they do with the borough's African Americans. Employment rates for Caribbean women and men are considerably higher than for American-born blacks. Seventy-seven percent of West Indian men and 73 percent of the women are in the labor force; those numbers surpass American black men and both U.S.-born black and white women. West Indian single mothers are much more likely to be working than native black women are; as a result, far fewer are on welfare.[13] In 1978, the economist Thomas Sowell became the first to notice that West Indian immigrants were outearning native-born blacks.[14] That remains the case. Nationwide, 18 percent of Caribbean immigrants are poor, compared with 28 percent of African Americans. Their median household income is $43,000; for their native black counterparts, the number sits at $33,500.[15]

The West Indians in New York City were able to save enough money so that by 1990, they had turned Queens into something almost unique in the United States: a large county where blacks were earning more than whites. In 2005, black households in Queens had a median income of over $51,836, compared with $50,960 among white households.[16] Tufts sociologist Orly Clerge, who is working on a book about black "ethnoburbs," finds that Canarsie is mostly a way station for upwardly mobile immigrant blacks in New York—much like Bensonhurst for the Chinese—between the poverty of Harlem or East New York to the middle-class comfort of southeastern Queens and, for the best-off, the Long Island suburbs.

One reason West Indians have fared relatively well is their ability to expand into occupations into which few other immigrants or American-born blacks had made inroads. Domestic service was one of the most common lines of work, especially for early female migrants, but there were others. Former secretary of state Colin Powell's parents, who both grew up in large poor families in Jamaica, were able to tap into a small Jamaican niche in Manhattan's garment sector in the 1940s.[17] Luther Powell, Colin's father, got a job in a company stockroom, where he must have impressed his bosses; the uneducated country boy worked his way up to a job as foreman of the shipping office. He and his seamstress wife were able to raise Colin and his older sister in the Hunts Point area of the Bronx—at the time, a polyglot, working-class community with plenty of striving, working families like themselves and some Powell relatives.[18] The rest is U.S. history.

Though entrepreneurialism is not a West Indian marker—they are less inclined to start their own businesses than, say, Chinese or Koreans—West Indians are still two times as likely to be self-employed as African Americans.[19] Public transportation on the Caribbean islands ranks somewhere between bad and abysmal; enterprising locals there created private van companies. Immigrants noticed a similar need in the far reaches of Flatbush and Canarsie and, to the annoyance of public officials worried both about public transit ridership and orderly streets, began their own services, popularly known as "dollar vans."

West Indians have been most successful in occupations where their English-speaking ability has given them an edge over other immigrants and their strong social networks keep them in a dynamic employment feedback loop. They have been overrepresented in construction work relative to both their population and to African Americans (and Asians). Decades ago, as early as 1970, according to the sociologist Roger Waldinger—West Indian women had begun clustering into what would soon become New York's largest service sector: health and hospitals. By 1990, 22 percent of Caribbean New Yorkers were working in hospitals, nursing homes, or health services; 41 percent of those workers were in professional, technical, or managerial positions.[20] As of the mid-2000s, one-fifth of the city's health-care technicians, nurses, and administrators were West Indian immigrants.[21] Recent immigrants, in particular, get on the nanny track, caring for Park Slope and Dumbo children while their upper-middle-class parents plug away at the office.

So how do we explain Canarsie in light of Brownsville? How do we make sense of West Indian successes when America continues its long struggle with racial inequality? Academic research, a good deal of it done by the West Indians, who dominate many university African studies departments, return to a few dominant ideas. One is simply that white American employers prefer West Indian workers. New York employers have sometimes admitted as much. West Indians have a reputation, deserved or not, as more conscientious and reliable—less likely to show up late or not at all—than native-born blacks. Some analysts have speculated that immigrants, more desperate to make a new life, are easier to exploit.[22] Others note that West Indians—having grown up in places where it's unremarkable for blacks to run companies, lead governments, and perform surgery—have more self-confidence than their American counterparts.

Another theory has it that West Indians, like all voluntary immigrants— and tragically, unlike American blacks—are "self-selected." People who choose to pick up and leave their native country behind are often different from the stayers. A higher percentage of New York City's Jamaicans, for instance, have a high school degree than Jamaican stayers and, for that matter, other immigrant groups. A remarkable 68.7 percent of Jamaican immigrants have graduated from high school; that's the case for only 54.6 percent of Chinese immigrants. Jamaica doesn't have enough jobs for its skilled citizens: to this day, estimates of the percentage of Jamaicans with tertiary education who leave their country mostly for the United States, Britain, and Canada, fall between 35 percent and 60 percent. Jamaica's brain drain may bias any conclusions that Americans draw about "West Indians."[23]

There is also probably something hard to measure—some inexplicable drive, some well of congenital adventurous energy—that leads people like Colin Powell's parents to risk leaving everything they knew and loved behind to create a life in a strange (and race-challenged) city. The United States has always drawn people who not only envisioned a better life but were hell-bent on achieving it. The immigrant drive took a particular form in the West Indian case: buying a house. The novelist Paule Marshall, who lived in Bedford-Stuyvesant around the time Colin Powell was growing up in the Bronx, wrote about the "fierce idolatry" that her West Indian neighbors felt for the houses of their neighborhood. Traveling to Flatbush and Sheepshead Bay to clean middle-class homes, the women did their best to ignore the white children who taunted them. "Their only thought was of the 'few raw-mout' pennies at the end of the day that would eventually 'buy house.' "[24] West Indians' tradition of rotating credit associations, which they call "partners," continues to help them put together the funds for a down payment. Today, though the neighborhood was hit hard by the foreclosure crisis in 2008 and Hurricane Sandy in 2012, Canarsie has the highest ownership rates of any neighborhood in Brooklyn.[25]

Like the Chinese, West Indians import with them traditional notions of discipline and familial obligations that also separate them from African Americans. Their old-fashioned style can seem harsh. Sociologists Mary Waters and Jennifer Sykes began "in-depth interviews" with thirty Caribbean parents living in New York by asking what they found most surprising about the United States. They expected to hear "racial discrimination" or maybe "winter weather," which comes as a shock to those whose idea of a chill is a tropical breeze. Instead, they heard: laws against beating your children. "I didn't know about child abuse until I came here," one parent tells the researchers, meaning, of course, that she thought that taking a switch to her child's bottom was just ordinary discipline.[26] A teacher in a Canarsie high school told me that she has gotten used to hearing, "I'll whoop his ass!" when she tells a parent that his or her child is causing trouble in class. The familiar tropes of middle-class American parenting—reassuring heart-to-heart interventions, time-outs, respecting a child's privacy—strike newcomers as absurd. In their view, children are not reasoning individuals; they are dependent, bendable creatures. "A twelve-year-old at home and a twelve-year-old here is [sic] two very different things," one mother sums it up for the interviewers. "A twelve-year-old child at home is a child. A twelve-year-old child here is a man."[27]

The tension between Old World strictness and modern American permissiveness is a familiar story in urban America. Early-twentieth-century social workers tried to temper the harsh ways of Italian and Irish parents and assimilate them to middle-class American norms. They weren't always successful. Permissive middle-class child-rearing may not be well adapted to urban street life. Poor, contemporary immigrants don't see themselves as simply disciplining their children; they are defending them from dangerous streets and peers. Like the Chinese, West Indian parents frown on dating, parties, sleepover dates with friends, or hanging out on the street corner. West Indians kids are "kept inside," writes Van C. Tran, a Columbia University sociologist; that's one "strategy of economic mobility" in Brooklyn neighborhoods where temptations call from every corner deli and playground.[28]

The cultural differences between West Indians and African Americans strained relations between the two groups once they came to live side by side. Since the early days of black Harlem, locals have mocked the "black Jews" for their alien, frugal ways as well as their tropical dress and food. West Indians would describe American blacks as lazy and low class—West Indian kids still sometimes accuse their friends who don't keep up with their schoolwork of being "African American"—while the latter saw the immigrants as smug and superior. The music critic Nelson George, who spent part of his childhood in the Tilden Houses in Brownsville before moving to Flatbush with his mother and younger sister, remembers visiting the "neat little homes" of Caribbean schoolmates. "I felt the odd condescending tone in adult voices. I sensed that they felt it was a shame I lived in the projects and my parents were from 'down South.' . . . We resented their presence and didn't understand their words, their food, or their attitude."[29]

AFRO-CARIBBEANS AND THE
BLACK-WHITE DIVIDE

Valerie Stevens (not her real name), the twenty-seven-year-old daughter of Haitian immigrants, grew up in Canarsie but barely knows the place. Her mother, a secretary, and father, a high school teacher, purchased their house in the neighborhood in 1994, amid Canarsie's troubled turnover. Haiti is not known for its stellar education system, and, on average, Haitian immigrants haven't had the same economic success in the United States that, say, Jamaicans have had.[30] But back home, Valerie's father had gone to Catholic schools and had become an agronomist. His experience made him determined to send his daughter to Saint Jude, a Catholic institution in Canarsie. "I never considered public school," he told me, since "even in Haiti, there's less discipline in public schools than Catholic." As a teenager, Valerie commuted more than an hour to Marymount School on the Upper East Side of Manhattan. When I asked her to talk about Canarsie, she explained that she didn't actually know much, despite having lived there since she was six years old. "I didn't hang out in the neighborhood. I had a few friends, but I was very sheltered." Her father's guardedness did not extend to his hopes for his daughter: he reminded her regularly that "no place has more opportunity than America." She lived up to his ambitions, going on to get her BA from Princeton. She is now a program evaluator at CUNY while she works on her dissertation in sociology at the Graduate Center there.

Valerie's story highlights some of the characteristics of a successful Brooklyn immigrant upbringing, Chinese and black and others: the intense focus on education, a wary distance from street and peer culture, reminders of parental sacrifice and the possibilities of life in New York. We've already seen how those characteristics can pay off for second-generation Chinese kids; they often seem to do the trick for West Indians as well, as Harvard Law School professor Lani Guinier and Henry Louis Gates Jr., chair of the university's African American studies department, inadvertently showed in a 2003 talk at a university black student reunion. Guinier and Gates observed that only a third of Harvard's black students were from families in which all four grandparents were born in the United States. Affirmative action, they concluded, was helping black immigrants get into Harvard instead of the American blacks that the policy was designed to benefit. The education expert Anthony Carnevale (commenting on the controversy ignited by Guinier and Gates) put it this way: "These immigrants represent Horatio Alger, not *Brown v. Board of Education*."[31]

The skewed ratios were not just Harvard's problem. A few years after Guinier and Gates's talk, a group of Princeton sociologists crunched the numbers in a national survey of college freshmen. Their findings were discomfiting. In twenty-eight of the nation's top colleges, immigrants were overrepresented among black students. Though black immigrants and children of immigrants were only 13 percent of all black eighteen- and nineteen-year-olds, they were 27 percent of the entering freshmen. Digging deeper, the researchers unearthed more disturbing news: the more selective the institution, the greater the percentage of black immigrants. Among the Ivy League institutions in the sample, for instance, first- and second-generation immigrants made up 41 percent of the black population.[32]

Part of the gap might be ascribed to selection bias. Parental education is about the biggest predictor of children's achievement, and, as it happens, immigrant fathers in the Princeton study were significantly more likely to be college-educated than native fathers. But some of it was historical and cultural. West Indians often pride themselves on their education system. Colin Powell notes that under the British, Jamaica established good schools with mandatory attendance, something not all that common in other poor countries. Shirley Chisholm, a Brooklynite who was born and educated in the West Indies and who became the first black woman to serve in the U.S. Congress, attributed her own success to the "early education in the strict, traditional, British-style schools of Barbados."[33] Their observation conforms to what we know about immigrant kids' performance. Compared with kids whose parents came from the Dominican Republic and Mexico, for example, Caribbean kids do better in school.

Or, at least, some do. Canarsie's story suggests that though West Indian immigrants work long hours and share a sense of newcomer optimism, their children are actually moving along two separate tracks. On the first track are people like Valerie Stevens, well on their way to making good on their parents' bet on their future. More than likely, they went to private or parochial school—the case for more than a third of Canarsie's K–12 kids (but only 13 percent of the city as a whole)[34]—and grew up with their mother and father in the house. On the second track are the faltering kids who, though generally respectful of teachers and parents and planning for college, will graduate high school without the skills to carry through. Taken as a whole, second-generation West Indian kids are more successful than their African American peers but less so than native-born and immigrant whites[35] and even than their better-educated parents.[36] One survey of twenty-four- to thirty-two-year-olds who grew up in New York revealed that 64 percent of second-generation Chinese and 54 percent of native whites had completed college. That was true for only 28 percent of West Indians and, worse, 15 percent for African Americans.

The primary blame for Canarsie's faltering West Indian kids has to be laid at the schoolhouse door. Just one example: at P.S. 115, considered one of the area's better elementary schools, only 32 percent of fifth-graders met New York state standards in math; in reading, the number was a dismal 26 percent. Only 4.4 percent of West Indian students go to one of the city's magnet high schools, compared with almost 20 percent of Chinese.[37] The local high schools are a poor substitute. The graduation rate at Canarsie High School plunged from an unimpressive 57 percent in 2003 to 42 percent in 2007—well below the citywide average of 58 percent.[38] In 2011, city officials closed it down and reorganized it into four smaller schools that so far are graduating the large majority of kids but for reasons that may not reflect their actual skills. South Shore's class of 2006 graduation rate, however, was also only 42 percent, and, according to the DOE, the school was "unsalvageable."[39] It, too, has been divided into four smaller schools whose performance remains uncertain.

What happened to Canarsie's schools, once a source of pride for residents and quick sales for real estate agents? Residents pointed to a variety of culprits. Canarsie high schools had become a dumping ground for the leftovers from other Brooklyn school closures. Budget cutbacks had made classes too big and counselors too few. Parents complained that teachers weren't disciplining their kids. The schools became segregated.

The fact that New York City public schools don't always do a great job at preparing kids for college would not surprise many Gothamites. But for understandable reasons, most immigrant parents have yet to figure that out. Immigrants often assume that "school is school," says Tufts University's Orly Clerge. In Canarsie, "parents assume it's a nice neighborhood; the schools will do the job." In Sunset Park, Chinese immigrants quickly learn from their more experienced compatriots the reality of a second-rate (at best) system and the things that they'll have to do to compensate for it. Canarsie, on the other hand, does not provide a community echo chamber reverberating with the names "Stuyvesant" and "Harvard." While the neighborhood is crammed with day-care centers for young children, test-prep and language schools for school-aged children of the sort that are omnipresent in Chinatown are hard to find. Given the reality of the schools' performance, District 18's high parental satisfaction attests to either parents' low engagement or indifference, neither of them hopeful signs for the future of Canarsie's kids.[40]

A District 18 high school math teacher, whom I'll call Michael—he asked to remain anonymous for reasons that will become obvious—spells out the problem. "If I leave a voicemail at five students' homes, I'll [speak to] maybe three [parents]. Half of them say that they'll deal with their kids, but the other half brush it off and say, 'You deal with this.'" Only about twenty of his 120 students have parents who show up for conferences. "A large number are working or taking care of younger kids. A lot just don't care."

The mostly Jamaican, Haitian, Trinidadian, and West African parents of Michael's students haven't failed to convey expectations, but neither they nor the schools have translated those expectations into actual achievement. Michael continues: "They all seem to think that they're going to go to college and then become a doctor. But some of the students are reading at sixth-grade level, and most of their math skills are bad." Since 94 percent graduate, "a good number will be accepted to college, but they're not prepared and they don't finish. They end up in debt." When an AP biology class was first introduced at his school in 2006, some kids were getting a four or five (out of a possible score of five) on the exam. In 2015, not a one managed to do so. Michael, who has been teaching for only a few years, is clearly fond of his students and has every intention of staying at his job—even as he hears his veteran colleagues muttering to one another: "It gets worse every year." It's worth mentioning that Canada and the UK, countries with large West Indian populations, aren't doing any better for their immigrant kids.[41] In the UK, even boys of higher-income Jamaican parents are falling behind.

Another worrying pattern separates West Indians from other successful immigrant groups. Black immigrant children are the least likely of all immigrant kids (and only half as likely as U.S. children overall) to be living with their two parents.[42] Unlike Hispanic immigrants, who become more prone to single motherhood over generations in the United States, Caribbeans bring a long tradition of young, nonmarital childbearing and multiple-partner fertility (having children by a succession of partners) with them from the islands. The authors of *Inheriting the City*, a survey of second-generation immigrant kids in New York, write that, like native blacks, "West Indians do not expect childbearing to be tied to marriage."[43]

West Indians have been able to avoid some of the downsides of early single parenthood. Since they live with extended families that include grandparents, aunts, uncles, cousins, and perhaps the child's father or the mother's new partner, they are less likely to be poor than native-born black single mothers. The large households mean more earners and higher household income. Among immigrant groups, they are second only to the Chinese in the percentage of households with two workers; those numbers are also considerably higher than those of native blacks.[44] Extended family members also help with child care, giving mothers the chance to stay in the labor force and keeping West Indian welfare rates relatively low.

But extended families—and, for that matter, homeownership and hard work—can help West Indians only so much. West Indians usually have their children young; it's timing that can easily interfere with education. About 30 percent of West Indian immigrant women in college already had at least one child.[45] In the general population, boys growing up without their fathers in the house are at greater risk of poor education outcomes; that holds for West Indian boys as well. We know that children growing up in communities with a higher proportion of married-couple households have a better chance of upward mobility than those growing up with large numbers of single-parent households. Those communities also have a better chance of becoming affluent. Demographers studying Queens attribute the borough's higher-than-white black household income to the number of black immigrants in married-couple households.

Some of the children of Canarsie's West Indians like Valerie Stevens are going to make it out of southeast Brooklyn to the ethnoburbs of Queens or Long Island. But unlike the kids of Sunset Park, she may be more the exception than the rule.

Conclusion

Recovering Cities

*T*hings were bad for American cities forty years ago—so bad that just about anyone who could manage it got out of town. Older northern, industrial metro areas were hemorrhaging jobs, businesses, and people; infrastructure was rotting away—in the early 1980s, one wit told me that she was convinced that tehe aging Manhattan Bridge between Brooklyn and Manhattan was held together by chewing gum and paper clips. Working-class neighborhoods were sinking into poverty; poor neighborhoods were swamped by a drug and crime pandemic.

Detroit's unraveling was about the saddest of the lot, an example of the "abject collapse of an industrial city," in journalist Scott Martelle words. "Massive iconic factories stand silent and cold. Blocks of commercial district are vacant and open to the elements, burned by fires that seemed to spread like a virus." It reached a point where it was "cheaper to buy a home in Detroit than a new car."*

New York lost 10 percent of its population between 1970 and 1980; poorer neighborhoods like Bedford-Stuyvesant and Bushwick lost upward of 30 percent.[1] St. Louis, Philadelphia, Washington, D.C., Cleveland, and Buffalo, as well as smaller American cities like Dayton, Syracuse, and Milwaukee all watched helplessly as neighborhoods, schools, shops, and community organizations emptied. Let's not forget Western European cities like London, Birmingham, Amsterdam, and Hamburg; they were also in the same sinking, rusty boat.[2]

None of these cities recovered in its former guise. Not a one. Smokestack factories and the union-benefited working class never came back, at least not in numbers that made a big difference. The businesses serving that working class shuttered; few entrepreneurs were interested in taking their place. Why would anyone want to invest in a zombie metropolis?

Except that by the turn of the millennium, some of these cities did come back to life: Seattle, San Francisco, Boston, and New York, to name just a few of the most blessed ones. There are also signs of life in Chicago, Philadelphia, and even riot-torn Baltimore. My home base of Brooklyn may have been the most surprising of the urban phoenixes. The onetime Borough of Homes and Churches, the home turf of "dem Bums," became, in the words of GQ magazine, "The Coolest City on the Planet."

Aspiring entrepreneurs abound across the borough—especially female ones. After a whopping 77 percent increase over the past decade in the number of women entrepreneurs, Brooklyn now has the highest female start-up rate in the country.[3] Given all that energy, it's no wonder that if you ask a group of ambitious college seniors where they'd like to live after they graduate, chances are that "Brooklyn" will rank high on their lists.

Their preference is crucial, since battered industrial cities need high-earning residents whose taxes can pay for replanting parks and shoring up collapsing subway-station ceilings and bridges, not to mention helping support housing, homeless shelters, school programs, legal representation, and the like for a large population of poor people. Still, the decline of factories and the invasion of those higher-earning—or future high-earning—residents has, like a powerful chemotherapy, cured the disease by producing some painful and seemingly chronic side effects.

"Creative destruction" is one way to describe what's happened. The urban postindustrial economy taketh away the kiln operator at the sugar refinery, the machine setter at the box factory, and the affordable townhouse while it giveth web designers, start-up entrepreneurs, farm-to-table celebrity restaurateurs, crowd-sourced craft-brew masters, and diminutive million-dollar condos.

Sometimes lost in the bitter debates over this double-edged transformation is the fact that no matter what their challenges, expensive, gentrifying cities like Brooklyn are far better off than their cheap-rent counterparts. Cities like Dayton, Fresno, Louisville, and Milwaukee that have struggled unsuccessfully to attract a large professional and creative middle class would like nothing better than for such people to beat a path to their forlorn neighborhoods and open their oh-too-precious cafés. True, those places have lower rates of inequality than glamour-pusses like Los Angeles and New York. They also have more concentrated poverty.

Creative destruction necessitates a city's careful handling of two broad interconnected goals that might be thought of this way: nurture the creative force and mitigate the destructive one. The latter is understandably the one that preoccupies urban experts and government officials, particularly involving housing. Housing shortages, high costs, dodgy landlords, callous developers, and evictions are a cold fact of life in postindustrial cities from San Francisco to Washington, D.C., to Berlin.

For those lower-income urbanites who are stably housed in public projects or subsidized apartments, as many Brownsville residents are, the expanding educated middle class brings ambiguous gains. Yes, recovering neighborhoods are generally safer, cleaner, and better serviced than those that stay low income, but those improvements haven't done much to relieve joblessness and underemployment, especially among racial minorities. American cities failed to integrate the poor and unskilled minorities pouring into their precincts before and after World War II; to this day, far too many of their children and grandchildren are entrenched in poverty no matter what neighborhood they live in. Displacement, while not as widespread as commonly thought, can add to their disadvantage. It is often (though not always) a misery for the individuals being forced to move; it can also disrupt social networks and intensify the fragmentation of contemporary life.

As the educated class has moved from suburbs to cities, inequality has become jarringly visible, aggravating unease and resentment. In gentrifying cities from Toronto to Sydney to Brooklyn, luxury high-rises, with their swimming pools and roof decks, shadow blocks cramped with aging projects, walk-ups, and row houses. Lower-income residents who do work frequently end up servicing the well-to-do: chopping their onions and avocados in restaurant kitchens, minding their children, cleaning the locker rooms of their gyms, riding bikes through traffic and rain to deliver burritos for their dinner, dry-cleaning their clothes, painting their nails, and waxing their eyebrows.

The inequality between toiling service provider and gym-toned customer is more complicated in Brooklyn and many other North American cities than it might seem at first. More likely than not, the people performing these tasks are immigrants. In recent decades, immigrants have revived decaying urban neighborhoods every bit as much as bike-lane enthusiasts have, though the media tends to give short shrift to their contributions to urban resurgence. As an immigrant city, Brooklyn was, for much of its history, a way station between Old World no-exit poverty and middle-class comfort. More than many people realize, it still is.

In ungentrified parts of the borough, people live in Brooklyn not to sip pour-over coffee and go to tech meet-ups but to escape countries with static economies that offer no hope for people wanting to make something of themselves. Cleaning the toenails of an event planner while she discusses her client's wedding on her cell phone may not look like anyone's picture of upward mobility, but it buys rice and chicken and shoes for the kids going to schools that immigrant parents assume—sometimes, too optimistically—are educating their young to create their own destinies.

So what does Brooklyn's transformation teach us about reviving an aging industrial city? And, since its resurgence is so very far from perfect, what are Brooklyn's cautionary tales? How can cities create the conditions ripe for innovation and growth as well as more opportunity for the striving poor and working class? None of the policies I'm about to recommend will stop the presses, but the previous chapters should make it easier to see why social scientists and policymakers keep returning to them.

First, though, it's necessary to concede that Brooklyn and the other phoenix cities enjoy notable history and geography; you could say that they were blessed with good genes. San Francisco and Seattle, in particular, had regional natural beauty, almost all the revived urban districts have architectural charm, a lot of them have well-planned—if not well-maintained—transportation infrastructure, and reputable hospitals and universities. Brooklyn was lucky to have good DNA as well, but most of all, it had a mother ship: Manhattan, a world capital of finance, media, the arts, and philanthropy.

Still, any city can maximize whatever physical assets it has. St. Louis will never be San Francisco, but cities like it can create some of the conditions that attract strivers, both educated and not. Let's begin with the former.

Today, the smart set is either working in tech-related fields or providing high-end services and entertainment—legal advice, back surgery, music events, artisanal cuisine, media—for those working in tech-related fields. "Today's growth is driven by the 'creative economy,'" says Adam Friedman of the Pratt Center for Community Development, "from film and television production to architecture and advertising, and tech sectors such as the design and operation of computer systems to Internet publishing and broadcasting."[4]

The good news for cities other than San Francisco is that they don't need to host a Google complex in order to ride the tech train. Digital is no longer limited to a bounded technology sector. It is transforming all industries and blurring the lines between them as well: education, health, retail, manufacturing, and public policy. That means that existing companies and institutions are crucial in enticing educated workers.

Brooklyn's experience is useful here. Noticing a nascent start-up community in the Dumbo area of Brooklyn in the early 2000s, business and educational institutions got to work. New York mayor Michael Bloomberg and local business leaders had already established the Downtown Brooklyn Partnership, a development corporation to coordinate local Business Improvement Districts and think about the big picture for downtown. The partnership brought together some of the start-up people to discuss their companies' needs and to show them available commercial space and amenities.

Brooklyn's educational institutions have also been crucial players in the borough's business growth. The Brooklyn Law Incubator and Policy Clinic, launched in 2008, advises aspiring entrepreneurs about everything from intellectual-property law to contract agreements—and simultaneously trains young lawyers in this growing field. Under the guidance of Jon Askin, a law professor and tech enthusiast, the clinic organized meet-ups for companies sharing a particular focus. "You don't know what the next great idea is going to be when you have brilliant freaks of different perspectives living and working on top of each other," Askin says. Brooklyn Law School has also begun partnering with B. Amsterdam, a Netherlands incubator, since "a lot of European start-ups want space in Brooklyn." (An incubator is for entrepreneurs at the very early, experimental stage; an accelerator offers more explicit business mentoring for those further along.)

Askin's outfit is only one of a number of schools boosting young local businesses. Pratt Institute has an accelerator for fashion businesses and an incubator for aspiring designers. Brooklyn College has started a film school at the Steiner Studios in the Navy Yard. City Tech, part of the City University of New York, is coordinating with the Navy Yard to arrange internships and organize curriculums. Kings County Hospital has an Advanced Biotech Incubator for nurturing early-stage biotech companies; maturing companies can move to space at Biobat, a science and technology center at the huge Brooklyn Army Terminal, owned by New York City. Biobat connects companies to academic and financial institutions.

Brooklyn also offers plenty of "what not to dos" when it comes to attracting fledgling businesses. For one thing, don't, like Brooklyn does, greet potential new businesses with excessive, multiagency, confusing, and sometimes Orwellian-seeming regulations. In New York City, new business owners need a staff of lawyers and expediters to negotiate a permit process that, on average, takes over seven months. A 2016 report from the city comptroller discovered "6,000 rules and regulations, 250 business-related licenses and permits, and fifteen separate agencies" governing small businesses.[5]

A *Crain's* cover article told the story of a Bed-Stuy bakery owner fined $10,000 because a grease trap needed replacing. His co-owner described running a small company in Brooklyn as like "operating in a business hospice." Artisanal food entrepreneurs like these can often find customers; what they can't do is untie the knot of regulations. Meanwhile, scaling up is an exercise in frustration. Brooklyn doesn't have enough production facilities smaller than 10,000 square feet that a growing business needs.[6] Brooklyn's loss could be another city's gain: there are reports that frustrated entrepreneurs are eyeing Detroit and Baltimore.[7]

Nurturing the educated, "creative" workforce is one thing that it takes to bring a city back. What about lower-skilled people, the ones so well served by the former industrial economy and now struggling in a postindustrial one? How can a digitalized economy benefit them? Asked another way, how do we make contemporary cities an accelerator, as it were, for a hopeful middle class?

The answer has to begin with education in the broadest possible sense. When we think about education, of course, we generally mean schools. Neighborhoods of aspirational poor, such as Canarsie and Sunset Park, need schools that will fuel the second generation's launch. If Canarsie is in any way typical—and sadly, it is—that's not happening. Over the past decades, urban schools have been notoriously bad at teaching children the most basic skills. Even as city officials have boasted higher high school graduation rates, fewer than half of those graduates were college-ready in 2015.[8] Judging from the stunning 80 percent of freshmen at CUNY who need one or more remedial classes, that figure seems, if anything, modest.[9]

The literature on school reform is too vast to review here, but charter schools have had some success in educating the disadvantaged kids that the public schools so often leave behind. A few first-rate charter schools could do wonders for a place like Canarsie, where parents are education-minded and eager for more traditional school discipline. A good charter school might help engage parents unused to giving their kids the kind of supervision that appears to be an essential part of the formula of success. It should be added that in addition to failing lower-income kids, mediocre (and worse) city schools motivate educated young adults to move to the suburbs. Once they look at the local schools, young parents understandably lose their enthusiasm for city living.[10] That's a big loss to cities.

Just as important to the future of the striving poor is a sober reexamination of the college-for-all mantra that still infects the public discourse. For a variety of reasons—unsupportive or absent parents, indifferent peer groups, individual ability, or preference—some kids are not going to master AP calculus or the comparative philosophies of Hobbes and Locke. And sadly, too many of those who make their way into college will only manage to do so through soft-hearted teachers and social promotion. These poorly prepared kids are at serious risk of dropping out of college, with only student debt to show for their efforts.

If you were to believe much of the policy and education establishment, you'd conclude that those without a college degree are doomed to a life of stocking shelves or selling drugs. Not so. Old manufacturing jobs have certainly faded away, but a new generation of "middle-skill" jobs are coming on line in the postindustrial economy,[11] many of them in the fast-growing health and tech sectors.[12] Usually earning between $40,000 and $60,000 annually, nurses, health technicians, aviation mechanics, construction tradespeople, manufacturing process technicians, and software developers don't earn as much as Ivy League consultants, of course, but their incomes may come close to a marketing manager from a lower-tier public university and will well surpass a dropout or high school grad with no extra training.

Meanwhile, employers say that they can't find enough workers capable of doing the jobs that are available. Governments can do a number of things to encourage more middle-skilled training and positions. First and foremost, they can bring back what Old Brooklyn (and elsewhere) called vocational education but what has now been rechristened "Career and Technical Training" (CTE). Starting during the Bloomberg administration, New York greatly expanded CTE. The programs emphasize partnering with local businesses and work-based learning and are beginning to show signs of success.[13]

Admittedly, the challenges for introducing good CTE programs are daunting. Businesses often balk at offering apprenticeships, up-to-date teaching staff is hard to find, and state education credentialing procedures are often perversely bureaucratic. To address the first two problems, cities might offer tax incentives to companies to hire apprentices and for recent CTE grads to teach a course or two to younger students. CTE is probably the best hope we have for placing the less skilled in decently paying careers. It should be a top policy priority.

Education—again, speaking in the broadest sense—also happens at home, which takes us to another crucial ingredient for bringing a city back: stronger families. There is little question that children growing up in stable two-parent families have a better shot at moving up the income ladder.[14] That is especially true in a postindustrial economy where the rewards go to the skilled. We saw how this played out in chapters 7 and 8. On the one hand, Chinese parents, though poor as proverbial church mice and unavailable for helicoptering, provide predictability and double-strength, laser-beam focus on their children's education. On the other hand, West Indian children are far more likely to grow up in volatile households, with fathers and stepfathers, half-siblings and stepsiblings coming and going. It's a domestic scene that can easily distract both parents and children from the regular routines and concentration necessary for understanding 11th-grade chemistry homework. (It goes without saying that a dual-income family is also in a much better position to finesse the expense of living in a city like Brooklyn.)

No one knows precisely what to do about this kind of gap between family cultures, but it's a sure thing that as long as it continues, so will the gap between poor and rich, and between black or Hispanic and white.

Some policy areas afflict every city dweller, no matter how educated or rich. First up, crime. Violent crime has plummeted in many parts of the United

States since the 1990s, but nowhere more than in New York. Brooklyn bene-fited enormously from the proactive policing that was introduced in the 1990s during the Giuliani administration and that continued in a similar form through the following two administrations. It's possible that a city in which thieves, thugs, and panhandlers see outdoor-café patrons as fair game could somehow attract and retain a middle class. But it hasn't worked that way before. Businesses owners need a degree of certainty that their offices and stores won't be ransacked and that their employees won't be subject to assault. Exhibit A: Brownsville after the 1960s, when crime shuttered shops up and down the once-lively Pitkin Avenue. Needless to say, effective crime-fighting depends on good relations with local communities; every police department needs consistent outreach. This is far harder than it sounds; police hear as many complaints about drug dealing and turf battles as they do aggressive policing from local citizens. Police brass who can speak to both sets of critics while keeping crime rates down are essential for any city's revival.

Not unrelated to crime control, and also essential to thriving cities, are strong transportation and infrastructure. Cities can flourish only when they can safely and efficiently move people and goods around. Brooklyn grew and prospered because New York City and local businesses invested in modern transportation technologies as they were discovered in the late nineteenth and early twentieth centuries. It's no exaggeration to say that trolleys, buses, and subways made Brooklyn what it is, allowing people to find space, air, and housing ever farther south and east and still get to Manhattan offices and other worksites in half an hour.

Today, that transit system lags way behind technology and growth, both commercial and residential. As things stand now, a person who lives and works in Brooklyn (or Queens) often must commute through Manhattan, an absurdly inefficient detour. Bus routes within and between Brooklyn and Queens are either interminable or inconvenient.

Tucker Reed, who until mid-2106 headed the Downtown Brooklyn Partnership, says that transportation is one of the first problems that comes up when he speaks to employers, especially for those in hard-to-reach Dumbo and the Navy Yard. Mayor Bill de Blasio's administration is mulling a new streetcar along the Brooklyn waterfront from Red Hook to Queens. It might alleviate some of the problem and would certainly be a crowd-pleasing, color-ful addition to Brooklyn's transportation network.

Since the Giuliani years, city hall has put considerable funds into another Brooklyn infrastructure project: refurbishing the Navy Yard. It's money that appears to be well spent, not only helping to create jobs but building Brook-lyn's identity as a center for new, small manufacturing. Unfortunately, city leaders tend to take an if-it-ain't-broke-don't-fix-it approach to those unseen pipes and tunnels and wires underground, preferring to spend limited money on projects with more visible and short-term payoffs. Especially in older cities, that's a fool's game.

A good example: New York City had two tunnels (one built in 1917, the other in 1936) to bring water into the boroughs. In 1970, officials decided that it was time to replace them—which, indeed, it was. Unfortunately, the civic will was weak. For over thirty years, the construction, subject to delays, lawsuits, and financial shortfalls, lay half-finished and useless. In 2002, after Mayor Bloomberg was informed that if the aging tunnels were forced to stop operating, it would "close down the city," he put the project on the fast track.

However, in April 2016, Mayor de Blasio returned to the familiar hope-and-a-prayer strategy and pulled the funds—leaving half of the city's total population dependent on a single ancient passage for water for at least another decade. His administration's announcement came on the heels of news about Flint, Michigan's lead-contaminated water supply. The public balked. The mayor changed course and agreed to put money into one of the most essential services that city government can provide.

Finally, housing—the policy problem that is on city dwellers' minds everywhere. The United States produces about 1.6 million new college graduates yearly, up from 840,000 in 1970 and one million in 1990. Many of those graduates will want to U-Haul their gear to places like Brooklyn, San Francisco, and other cities with a good supply of high-wage jobs. The Sustainable DC Plan, endorsed by the D.C. City Council, expects 250,000 new residents over the next twenty years.[15] Officials project another 260,000 people moving to Portland before 2035.[16] Seattle has been growing by 14,000 to 18,000 residents a year for a while.[17] Planners predict that New York City's population will grow by a million by 2030.[18] The same dynamic—growing numbers of college-educated young people crowding into knowledge-work cities—is overwhelming the capitals and hot spots of Western Europe. It's possible that for unforeseeable reasons, affluent people will stop trying to make a home in the city. For now, that seems unlikely. And if there's any lesson to be learned from the 1970s, it's that such a turn would be really bad news.

An influx of educated newcomers into urban areas means fast-rising housing costs; if there are any exceptions to that fact on any continent, I haven't found them. Consider two of Brooklyn's formerly working-class areas, now among the most sought-after neighborhoods in New York City: Williamsburg and Greenpoint. Their share of residents with college degrees rose 43.7 percent between 2000 and 2014; likewise, median household income increased 41 percent. Median rents have followed the same dizzying rise—close to 58 percent over the same period.[19] Those neighborhoods become educated-class enclaves. In general, the issue is less that the new residents displace the old; it's that poorer residents can no long afford to move in.

Headlines tell us that the solution is more "affordable housing," by which people usually mean housing for the poor and working class. Actually, "affordable," in this context, means below market rate, which, given the heights that the market has reached in recent years, would still be unaffordable for large swaths of the population. Considering the ever-growing demand, it would be more accurate to say that in Brooklyn and other gentrifying cities, there is simply not enough housing. Period.

In Brooklyn—given Mayor Bloomberg's rezoning, the cranes crowding the skylines and scaffolding lining the sidewalks, and the number of glossy ads for new amenity-rich condos—that may seem absurd. It's not. Only 14 percent of the rezoned lots in NYC between 2003 and 2007 were upzoned. Some 23 percent were downzoned, meaning that they couldn't be built to allow more density. The total effect was to increase residential capacity by a piddling 1.7 percent.[20] Compare the decade between 1960 to 1970, when New York increased its number of dwellings by 13.4 percent.[21]

Meanwhile, a nearly impenetrable encyclopedia of zoning restrictions keeps large swaths of Brooklyn and New York City off-limits to new housing. In spring 2016, the *New York Times* plotted the buildings that would never have been built if current zoning regulations had been in effect. The paper estimated that a full 40 percent of Manhattan's buildings would have been deemed too tall, or contained too many apartments or businesses.[22] San Francisco's antidevelopment regulations are even worse;[23] the city decided in the 1960s not to build *anything* but affordable housing. Fast-forward to the rise of the tech industry in Silicon Valley and within San Francisco itself, and you have the tightest, least penetrable housing market in the United States.

The subject of housing leads to my final observation about what it takes to bring a city back, one probably immune to public policy: temper your nostalgia. People have powerful images in their minds of the way their neighborhood or city is meant to be. The image is generally from a not-too-distant past, based on their own memories or on the descriptions of others—a writer or an artist or a relative. *That*, they insist, is the real Brooklyn—or San Francisco, or Houston, or Philadelphia.

The longing to hold on to the landscapes, streetscapes, and people of our youth is as human as mourning the dead. Cities need ties to their past. The great lesson of Robert Moses's reign, so memorably evoked by Jane Jacobs, was that cities bulldoze communities deemed undesirable or unproductive at their own peril. Dislocation is happening in many cities so fast and so dramatically that it unsettles social relations and overwhelms all sense of continuity. All people, except perhaps for a luxury developer, feel a twinge of anxiety when they see the field of cranes cluttering the skylines of New York and London. Preserved neighborhoods like Brooklyn Heights and Park Slope—and similar townhouse neighborhoods in other cities—don't just provide places for people to live. They providing solace and grounding to city dwellers, preventing us from spinning off into a rootless, alien future.

But it's worth remembering that people grieved the disappearance of fields and farmland when Brooklyn developers built the now-beloved, landmarked blocks of brownstones in the nineteenth century.[24] They shuddered when the factories replaced the fields along the waterfront—factories that people now fight to preserve. They fought when neighborhoods were cleared to build the treasured Brooklyn Bridge. Williamsburg's working class scowled when the artists arrived in the 1990s, while the artists cried foul when the Wall Streeters arrived in the new millennium. Just about everyone living in a gentrifying city—Washington, D.C., Chicago, Portland—hankers for the days before the first Starbucks arrived, the days when, they just know, the city was "authentic."

Brooklyn's history is rich with examples of communities that spawned the civic organizations vital to civil society: the charities of early Brownsville, the block associations of Bed-Stuy, the "Lee" and "Chung" associations of Sunset Park, the Park Slope Civic Council. But Brooklyn and its proud residents have to understand the tension between their affection for their local history and both the needs of future city dwellers and the ephemerality of all things human. Brush gets cleared and trees get cut down to make farmland, which, over time, erupts into streets and houses and neighborhoods. Neighborhoods get denser, and locals die or they take off for better opportunities, starting over; groups assimilate or move on. Bedford-Stuyvesant, to take just one example, goes from rural village to German bourgeois suburb to Jewish enclave to black ghetto to whatever comes next.

Even Jane Jacobs wasn't born in the place she held up as a citified ideal. Nor, for that matter, did she die there. Like all of us, she was just passing through.

Notes

INTRODUCTION

1. http://www.census.gov/quickfacts/table/RHI105210/36047.
2. County and City Data Books, Census Bureau 1944–1984 editions.
3. https://www.osc.state.ny.us/osdc/rpt4-2015.pdf.
4. Just one of many examples can be found here: http://www.vogue.com/865218/bonjour-brooklyn-models-writers-actors-and-artists-have-been-flocking-to-this-new-york-city.
5. Roger David Waldinger, *Still the Promised City: African Americans and New Immigrants in Postindustrial New York* (Cambridge, MA: Harvard University Press, 1996), 33.
6. Peter Maskell, "Redistribution of Denmark's Manufacturing Industries, 1972–1982: Causes and Consequences," *Scandinavian Housing and Planning Research*, 1985.
7. Patrick McGeehan, "New York Area Is Magnet for College Graduates," *New York Times*, August 16, 2006. http://www.nytimes.com/2006/08/16/nyregion/16degrees.html.
8. http://www.census.gov/quickfacts/table/PST045215/00.
9. http://www.techinsider.io/the-most-exciting-innovations-of-the-year-2015–10.
10. https://www.osc.state.ny.us/osdc/rpt4-2015.pdf.
11. http://www1.nyc.gov/assets/hra/downloads/pdf/facts/drs/..District%20Resource%20Statement%20Vol.%2009%20for%20HRA.pdf.
12. http://www.pewsocialtrends.org/2016/05/11/are-you-in-the-american-middle-class/.
13. http://www.urban.org/research/publication/growing-size-and-incomes-upper-middle-class
14. http://www.cccnewyork.org/wp-content/publications/CCCReport.ConcentratedPoverty.April-2012.pdf.

CHAPTER 1

1. "Colonial Highways of Greater New York," Report of the Comptroller, City of New York, Bureau for the Examination of Claims, Department of Finance, 1908. https://archive.org/stream/colonialhighways00newys/colonialhighways00newys_djvu.txt.

2. Russell Shorto, *The Island at the Center of the World* (New York: Vintage, 2004), Kindle edition.

3. http://www.brooklynhistory.org/exhibitions/lefferts/slavery-in-brooklyn.

4. Eric Foner, *Gateway to Freedom: The Hidden History of the Underground Railroad* (New York: Norton, 2016). Excerpted in https://blog.longreads.com/2015/04/30/slavery-and-freedom-new-york-city.

5. Bob Furman, "Brooklyn Heights History: Slavery and Abolition," Brooklyn Heights blog, http://brooklynheightsblog.com/archives/29828.

6. Joseph Alexiou, *Gowanus: Brooklyn's Curious Canal* (New York: New York University Press, 2015), Kindle edition.

7. Suzanne Spellen, "Walkabout: Brooklyn and the Erie Canal," Brownstoner blog, October 2, 2012. http://www.brownstoner.com/history/walkabout-brooklyn-and-the-erie-canal.

8. William Berkson, "Government Investment and 'Opportunity for All,'" *Washington Monthly*, June 24, 2016. http://washingtonmonthly.com/government-investment-opportunity-for-all.

9. Marc Linder and Lawrence S. Zacharias, *Of Cabbages and Kings County: Agriculture and the Formation of Modern Brooklyn* (Iowa City: Iowa University Press, 1999), 301.

10. Ellen M. Snyder-Grenier, *Brooklyn: An Illustrated History* (Philadelphia: Temple University Press, 2004), 112.

11. New York City Landmarks Preservation Committee, "Fulton Ferry Historic District Designation Report," 1977. http://www.nyc.gov/html/lpc/downloads/pdf/reports/FULTON_FERRY_HISTORIC_DISTRICT.pdf.

12. David McCullough, *The Great Bridge: The Epic Story of the Building of the Brooklyn Bridge* (New York: Simon & Schuster, 2001).

13. Alexiou, *Gowanus*.

14. http://www.demographia.com/dm-nyc.htm.

15. James T. Fisher, *On the Irish Waterfront: The Crusader, the Movie, and the Soul of the Port of New York* (Ithaca, NY: Cornell University Press, 2009), 1.

16. Tyler Anbinder, *City of Dreams: The 400 Year Epic History of Immigrant New York* (New York: Houghton Mifflin Harcourt, 2016).

17. Hasia R. Diner, "The Most Irish City in the Union: The Era of the Great Migration," in *The New York Irish*, ed. Ronald H. Bayer and Timothy J. Meagher (Baltimore: Johns Hopkins University Press, 1996), 96.

18. https://artofneed.wordpress.com/2013/11/04/the-brooklyn-irish.

19. https://artofneed.wordpress.com/2013/03/30/brooklyns-irishtown.

20. https://artofneed.wordpress.com/2014/02/18/gangs-of-brooklyn.

21. Rebecca Dalzell, "The Whiskey Wars That Left Brooklyn in Ruins" *Smithsonian Magazine,* November 18, 2014. http://www.smithsonianmag.com/history/whiskey-wars-left-brooklyn-ruins-180953352/?no-ist.

22. Quoted in http://brooklynology.brooklynpubliclibrary.org/post/2011/08/05/Peter-Coopers-Glue-Works.aspx.

23. Will Anderson, *The Breweries of Brooklyn: An Informal History of a Great Industry in a Great City* (New York: Will Anderson, 1976).

24. http://www.oldcoffeeroasters.com/arbuckle.htm.

25. Suzanne Spellen, "The Arbuckle Coffee Company: Brooklyn's Other Great Brew,

Part Two," Brownstoner blog, October 8, 2015. http://www.brownstoner.com/history/dumbo-clinton-hill-brooklyn-john-arbuckle-coffee-history.

26. Landmarks Preservation Committee, "Havemeyer and Elder Filter, Pan and Finishing House," September 25, 2007, pp. 8–9. http://www.nyc.gov/html/lpc/downloads/pdf/reports/domino.pdf.

27. Francis Morrone, "The Waterfront That Sugar Built," *New York Sun*, August 16, 2007. http://www.nysun.com/arts/waterfront-that-sugar-built/60690.

28. Christopher Gray, "Architectural Wealth, Built for the Poor," *New York Times*, October 10, 2008, p. RE7. http://www.nytimes.com/2008/10/12/realestate/12scap.html?_r = 1.

29. Jacob August Riis, *How the Other Half Lives* (New York: Charles Scribner's Sons, 1890), 294.

30. New York City Landmarks Preservation Commission, "Clinton Hill Historic District Designation Report," 1981. http://www.nyc.gov/html/lpc/downloads/pdf/reports/CLINTON_HILL_HISTORIC_DISTRICT.pdf.

CHAPTER 2

1. Quoted in Marc Linder and Lawrence S. Zacharias, *Of Cabbages and Kings County: Agriculture and the Formation of Modern Brooklyn* (Iowa City: University of Iowa Press, 1999), 131.

2. http://www.thirteen.org/brooklyn/history/history3.html.

3. Robert L. Fishman, "American Suburbs/English Suburbs: A Transatlantic Comparison," *Journal of Urban History*, May 1987. http://www.mangeogsoc.org.uk/pdfs/centenaryedition/Cent_17_Rodgers.pdf.

4. Kenneth Jackson, *Crabgrass Frontier: The Suburbanization of the United States* (New York: Oxford University Press, 1985), 71.

5. Linder and Zacharias, *Of Cabbages.*

6. Wilhelmena Rhodes Kelly, *Bedford Stuyvesant* (New York: Arcadia, 2007). http://www.nyc.gov/html/lpc/downloads/pdf/reports/2496.pdf.

7. http://www.nyc.gov/html/lpc/downloads/pdf/reports/FULTON_FER RY_HISTORIC_DISTRICT.pdf.

8. McCullough, *The Great Bridge.*

9. Ibid.

10. Ibid., 400.

11. Terry Clifford, "Notes from the Underground," *New York* magazine, July 10, 1978, p. 88.

12. http://www.nytimes.com/2005/11/27/nyregion/thecity/for-you-half-price.html.

13. John Tierney, "Brooklyn Could Have Been a Contender," reprinted in Kenneth T. Jackson and David S. Dunbar, *Empire City: New York Through the Centuries* (New York: Columbia University Press, 2005). Also, David Hammack, *Power and Society in Greater New York* (New York: Russell Sage Foundation, 1982).

14. http://www.bklynlibrary.org/brooklyn-collection/history-brooklyn-daily-eagle.

15. New York City Landmarks Preservation Committee, Clinton Hill Historic District,

City of New York, 1981. http://www.nyc.gov/html/lpc/downloads/pdf/reports/CLINTON_HILL_HISTORIC_DISTRICT.pdf.

16. Albert Fried, *The Rise and Fall of the Jewish Gangster in America* (New York: Columbia University Press, 1980).

17. Craig Steven Wilder, *A Covenant with Color: Race and Social Power in Brooklyn* (New York: Columbia University Press, 2000).

18. Suzanne Spellen, "A Mixed Race Wedding in 1907 Bed Stuy Attracts Unwanted Attention." http://www.brownstoner.com/history/bed-stuy-brooklyn-racism-20th-century-173-putnam-ave.

19. Wilder, *A Covenant with Color*.

20. Joshua B. Freeman, *Working Class New York: Life and Labor Since World War II* (New York: New Press, 2001), 33.

21. http://www.newyorker.com/magazine/1935/06/15/only-the-dead-know-brooklyn.

22. Pete Hamill, "Brooklyn: The Sane Alternative," *New York* magazine, July 14, 1969. http://nymag.com/news/features/46992.

23. Freeman, *Working Class New York*, 38.

24. Tierney, "Brooklyn Could Have Been a Contender," 2005.

25. Robert Caro, *The Power Broker: Robert Moses and the Fall of New York* (New York: Vintage, 1975), 329.

26. Ibid., 523.

27. Robert Fitch, in *The Assassination of New York* (New York: Verso, 1993), is one of a number of writers arguing that the city's deindustrialization was planned by financial and real estate elites to rid the city of the poor and working class. This explanation holds up only if those elites had control over cities throughout the Western world where similar changes were happening.

28. Amy Mittelman, *Brewing Battles: A History of American Beer* (New York: Algora, 2008).

29. Martin L. Schneider, "When Brooklyn Controlled the Nation's Sugar," *Brooklyn Eagle*, May 23, 2012. http://www.brooklyneagle.com/articles/when-brooklyn-controlled-nations-sugar.

30. Joseph Alexiou, *Gowanus: Brooklyn's Curious Canal* (New York: New York University Press, 2015), Kindle edition.

31. Freeman, *Working Class New York*, 163.

32. Jan Morris, *The Great Port: A Passage Through New York* (New York: Faber and Faber, 2009).

33. Quoted in Andy McCue, *Mover and Shaker: Walter O'Malley, the Brooklyn Dodgers and Baseball's Westward Expansion* (Lincoln: University of Nebraska Press, 2014), 124.

34. Sam Anderson, "Exorcising the Dodgers," *New York* magazine, September 16, 2007. http://nymag.com/nymag/features/37643.

CHAPTER 3

1. APA, "Park Slope, Brooklyn: New York Great Neighborhoods of America," https://www.planning.org/greatplaces/neighborhoods/2007/parkslope.htm.

2. Nate Silver, "The Most Livable Neighborhoods in New York," *New York* magazine, April 11, 2010, http://nymag.com/realestate/neighborhoods/2010/65374.

3. Charles Lockwood, *Bricks and Brownstone: The New York Row House: 1790–1929* (New York: Rizzoli, 2003).

4. Edith Wharton, *A Backward Glance: An Autobiography* (New York: Simon & Schuster, 1933).

5. Suleiman Osman, *The Invention of Brownstone Brooklyn: Gentrification and the Search for Authenticity in Postwar New York* (Chicago: University of Chicago Press, 2011), Kindle edition.

6. Loretta Lees, Tom Slater, and Elvin Wyly, *Gentrification* (New York: Routledge, 2008).

7. Kenneth T. Jackson, "Race, Ethnicity, and Real Estate Appraisal," *Journal of Urban History*, August 1980, 419–52.

8. Emily S. Rueb, "Park Slope Plane Crash: The Neighborhood in 1960," *New York Times*, December 13, 2010.

9. Robert Hanley, "Five Youths Shot in Park Slope Riot," *New York Times*, June 28, 1973.

10. Wendell Jamieson, "The Crime of His Childhood," *New York Times*, March 2, 2013. http://www.nytimes.com/2013/03/03/nyregion/40-years-after-an-acid-attack-a-life-well-lived.html?pagewanted=all&_r=1.

11. Phillip Benjamin, "Rise in Crime Laid to a '600' School," *New York Times*, May 29, 1960.

12. Osman, *The Invention of Brownstone Brooklyn*.

13. Ruth Glass, "London; Aspects of Change," reprinted in Japonica Brown-Saracino, *The Gentrification Debates: A Reader* (London: Routledge, 2010), 19–27.

14. Philliana Patterson, "Looking Back: How Yuppies Discovered Park Slope," *The Real Deal*, October 18, 2007. http://therealdeal.com/issues_articles/looking-back-how-yuppies-discovered-park-slope.

15. Dennis Hevesi, "Everett Ortner, Leader in Brooklyn's Brownstone Revival Dies at 92," *New York Times*, May 26, 2012. http://www.nytimes.com/2012/05/27/nyregion/everett-ortner-a-leader-in-the-restoration-of-brooklyn-brownstones-dies-at-92.html; and John Casson, "A Cinderella Story on Berkeley Place," Park Slope Civic Council websites, September 25, 2010. http://parkslopeciviccouncil.org/a-cinderella-story-on-berkeley-place.

16. Quoted in Rueb, "Park Slope Plane Crash."

17. "Remembering Everett Ortner," Park Slope Civic Council website, July 13, 2012. http://parkslopeciviccouncil.org/remembering-everett-ortner.

18. Osman, *The Invention of Brownstone Brooklyn*.

19. http://www.nyc.gov/html/lpc/downloads/pdf/reports/parkslope_hd.pdf.

20. http://www.nyc.gov/html/lpc/downloads/pdf/reports/2443.pdf.

21. Tamara Rothenberg, "And She Told Two Friends: Lesbians Creating Urban Social Space," in *Mapping Desire: Geographies of Sexuality*, ed. David Bell and Gill Valentine (New York: Routledge, 1995), 150–65.

22. Furman Center for Real Estate and Public Policy, "Trends in New York City Housing Price Appreciation," Furman Center at NYU, 2008.

23. Franklin E. Zimring, *The City That Became Safe: New York's Lessons for Urban Crime and Its Control* (New York: Oxford University Press, 2011). Also Heather Mac Donald, *The War Against Cops* (New York: Encounter, 2016).

24. Amy Ellen Schwartz, "Has Falling Crime Driven New York's Real Estate Boom?" *Journal of Housing Research*, January 2003, 101–35.

25. Peter Grant, "Home Sales Go Thru the Roof," *NY Daily News*, October 19, 1997. http://www.nydailynews.com/archives/news/home-sales-roof-city-boom-droves-boro-ing-digs-pricier-roof-home-sales-article-1.780647.

26. Osman, *The Invention of Brownstone Brooklyn*.

27. Loretta Lees, "Super-Gentrification: The Case of Brooklyn Heights, New York City," *Journal of Urban Studies*, November 2013, 2487–509.

28. Diane Cardwell, "Highs and Lows in Park Slope Rezoning Plan," *New York Times*, April 2, 2003. http://www.nytimes.com/2003/04/02/nyregion/highs-and-lows-in-park-slope-rezoning-plan.html.

29. Robbie Whelan, "Brooklyn's Burden: Fourth Avenue," *Wall Street Journal*, July 17, 2012. http://www.wsj.com/news/articles/SB10001424052702303703004577472753921529304.

30. https://www.6sqft.com/brownstone-of-park-slopes-original-gentrifiers-sells-for-3-million.

31. Marlene A. Lee and Mark Mather, "U.S. Labor Force Trends," Population Reference Bureau, June 2008. http://www.prb.org/pdf08/63.2uslabor.pdf.

32. Lena Edlund, Cecilia Machado, and Maria Micaela Sviatschi, "Bright Minds, Big Rent: Gentrification and the Rising Return to Skill," NBER Working Paper 21720, November 2015.

33. Ibid.

34. Sean Reardon, "The Widening Academic Achievement Gap Between Rich and Poor," in *Whither Opportunity, Rising Inequality and the Uncertain Chances of Lower Income Children*, ed. Richard Murnane and Greg Duncan (New York: Russell Sage, 2011).

35. Gretchen Livingston, "The Links Between Education, Marriage, and Parenting," Pew Research Center, November 2013.

36. http://www.cdc.gov/minorityhealth/chdireport.html.

37. https://www.census.gov/hhes/socdemo/education/data/cps/previous/index.html.

38. http://www.city-data.com/neighborhood/Park-Slope-Brooklyn-NY.html. See also http://www1.nyc.gov/assets/planning/download/pdf/data-maps/nyc-population/acs/puma_socio_10to12_acs.pdf#bk06.

40. Quoted in Osman, *The Invention of Brownstone Brooklyn*.

41. Cecilia D'Anastasio, "John Scioli, Brooklyn's Most Eccentric Book-Seller Explains Why He's Cashing Out," Gothamist, August 14, 2015. http://gothamist.com/2015/08/14/cobble_hill_community_books.php.

42. Pete Hamill, "Brooklyn Revisited," *New York* magazine, September 28, 2008.

43. Osman, *The Invention of Brownstone Brooklyn*.

44. Garth Johnston, "Nosy Neighbors Can't Handle Carroll Gardens Coffee Smell," Gothamist, February 24, 2012. http://gothamist.com/2012/02/24/nosy_newcomers_cant_handle_carroll.php.

45. Chris Arnade, "In Brooklyn, Gentrification Wipes Out Pigeons and Chickens to Make Room for Cats and Dogs," *US Guardian*, September 28, 2014. https://www.theguardian.com/money/2014/sep/28/new-york-gentrification-brooklyn-wealth-poverty-drive-change.

46. Osman, *The Invention of Brownstone Brooklyn*.

47. Lees et al., *Gentrification*.

48. Paul Moses, "Poor Excuse," *Village Voice*, June 28, 2005. http://www.villagevoice.com/news/poor-excuse-6403196.

49. Lance Freeman and Frank Barconi, "Gentrification and Displacement, New York in the 1990's," *Journal of the American Planning Association*, Winter 2004, 39–52.

50. Ingrid Gould Ellen and Katherine O'Regan, "How Low Income Neighborhoods Change," Furman Center for Real Estate and Public Policy 2010, in *Regional Science and Urban Economics*, March 2011.

51. Kathe Newman and Elvin K. Wyly, "The Right to Stay Put Revisited: Gentrification and the Resistance to Displacement in New York City," *Urban Studies*, January 2006, 23–57.

52. Lei Ding, Jackelyn Hwang, and Eileen Dvringi, "Gentrification and Residential Mobility in Philadelphia," December 2015. Federal Reserve Bank of Philadelphia.

53. Joe Cortright, "The Perils of Conflating Gentrification and Displacement," City Observatory website, February 20, 2015. http://cityobservatory.org/longer-governing-response.

CHAPTER 4

1. http://www.vogue.com/1067755/marlow-goods-wythe-hotel-store.

2. Dena Kleiman, "Brooklyn Terror: Youth Gang Takes Over an Apartment House," *New York Times*, October 26, 1977. http://www.nytimes.com/1977/10/26/archives/long-island-opinion-brooklyn-terror-youth-gang-takes-over-apartment.html.

3. Kay S. Hymowitz, *Manning Up: How the Rise of Women Is Turning Men into Boys* (New York: Basic Books, 2012).

4. Margrit Kiminsky et al., "Health Profile of Cancer, Asthma and Childhood Lead Poisoning in Greenpoint/Williamsburg," Department of Health, City of New York, December 1992. http://www.hunter.cuny.edu/shp/centers/coeh/publications/coehGW1.pdf.

5. For a useful memoir of the time, see Robert Anasi, *The Last Bohemia: Scenes from the Life of Williamsburg Brooklyn* (New York: Macmillan, 2012).

6. Ethan Pettit, "Immersionism in Williamsburg, 1989–98." https://www.facebook.com/ethan.pettit/media_set?set=a.10151773005512362.655962361&type=3.

7. James Kalm, "The Brooklyn Canon: Airbrushed Out of History," Loren Munk, website, http://www.lorenmunk.com/writing/the_brooklyn_canon.html; and Ebon Fisher, "The Sex Salon and the Web Jam," *Utne Reader*, January–February 1995. http://www.nervepool.net/ebUtne.html.

8. "Where Do We Go After the Rave?" *Newsweek*, July 25, 1993. http://www.newsweek.com/where-do-we-go-after-rave-194814.

9. Mark Rose, "Brooklyn Unbound," *New York Press*, 1991. http://www.nervepool.net/ebintro2.html.

10. Robin Rogers-Dillon, "Zoning Out: The Politics of North Brooklyn," *Brooklyn Rail*, October 1, 2001. http://www.brooklynrail.org/2001/10/local/zoning-out-the-politics-of-north-brooklyn.

11. Virginia Postrel, *The Substance of Style: How the Rise of Aesthetic Value Is Remaking Commerce, Culture, and Consciousness* (New York: Harper Perennial, 2004). Also my "Portrait of the Artist as a Young Businesswoman," *City Journal*, Spring 2009.

12. Richard Florida, "Bohemia and Economic Geography," *Journal of Economic Geography*, 2002, 55–71. https://www.creativeclass.com/rfcgdb/articles/Bohemia%20and%20Economic%20Geography.pdf.

13. Sam Dean, "Q and A with Andrew Tarlow, the Restaurateur Who Invented Brooklyn (Sorta)," *Bon Appetit*, January 5, 2014. http://www.bonappetit.com/people/out-of-the-kitchen/article/andrew-tarlow-interview; and Leslie Pariseau, "Talking Shop with Andrew Tarlow of Marlow Sons and the Wythe Hotel," *GQ*, May 2, 2012. http://www.gq.com/story/talking-shop-with-andrew-tarlow-of-marlow-sons-and-the-wythe-hotel.

14. Sarah Chandler, "A Brand Grows in Brooklyn: NYC's Most Happening Borough," CNBC website, October 17, 2014. http://www.cnbc.com/2014/10/17/brooklyn-the-billion-dollar-brand.html.

15. "Meet Lexy Funk," Brooklyn Industries website. https://www.brooklynindustries.com/index.cfm/fuseaction/content.page/nodeID/21917c51-d4e2-4952-a75f-f22556d4ce91 and Fred A. Bernstein, "A Business Grows and a Family Follows, Under the Same Roof," *New York Times*, March 25, 2007. http://www.nytimes.com/2007/03/25/realestate/25HAbi.html.

16. Sharon Zukin traces the shift back to the artists of Soho in *Loft Living: Culture and Capital in Urban Change* (Baltimore: Johns Hopkins University Press, 1982).

17. Ibid.

18. Richard Lloyd, *Neo-Bohemia: Art and Commerce in the Postindustrial City* (New York: Routledge, 2010).

19. David Brooks, *Bobos in Paradise: The New Upper Class and How They Got There* (New York: Simon & Schuster, 2001).

20. Ann Fensterstock, *Art on the Block: Tracking the New York Art World from Soho to the Bowery, Bushwick and Beyond* (New York: Macmillan, 2013), 163.

21. "New York's Design Economy," Center for an Urban Future, May 2014. https://nycfuture.org/data/info/new-yorks-design-economy.

22. Thomas DiNapoli, "An Economic Snapshot of Brooklyn," Office of the State Comptroller, May 2014. https://www.osc.state.ny.us/osdc/rpt4-2015.pdf.

23. Justin Moyer, "Our Band Could Be Your Band," *Washington City Paper*, May 14, 2012. http://www.washingtoncitypaper.com/news/article/13043064/our-band-could-be-your-band-how-the-brooklynization-of.

24. Lloyd, *Neo-Bohemia*.

25. Florida, "Bohemia and Economic Geography."

26. Max Chafkin, "Can Rob Kalin Scale Etsy?" *Inc. Magazine*, April 2011. http://www.inc.com/magazine/20110401/can-rob-kalin-scale-etsy.html.

27. Mark Mauer, "Who's Winning the Brooklyn Office Battle?" *The Real Deal*, January 2016. http://therealdeal.com/issues_articles/whos-winning-the-brooklyn-office-battle.

28. Daniel Geiger, "Once on the Fringes, This Brooklyn Neighborhood Is Now in with the Tech Crowd," *Crain's*, November 30, 2015. http://www.crainsnewyork.com/article/20151130/REAL_ESTATE/15112 9916/once-on-the-fringes-this-brooklyn-neighborhood-is-now-in-with-the-tech-crowd.

29. Matt A. V. Chaban, "Tech Tenants Filling a Slice of Brooklyn Called Dumbo Heights," *New York Times*, August 26, 2014. http://www.nytimes.com/2014/08/27/realestate/commercial/tech-tenants-filling-a-slice-of-brooklyn-nicknamed-dumbo-heights.html.

30. CPEX, "Brooklyn Retail Report, 2016." http://cpexre.com/system/research_items/documents/000/000/093/original/2016_Brooklyn_Retail_Report.pdf?145493 6733.

31. Justin Rocket Silverman, "Williamsburg's Wythe Avenue Soars as Global Mecca for Entertainment and Nightlife," *NY Daily News*, April 11, 2014. http://www.nydailynews.com/life-style/real-estate/wythe-ave-hits-prime-time-entertainment-mecca-article-1.1749819.

32. Mark Scott, "Stockholm's Housing Shortage Threatens to Stifle Fast-Growing Start-Ups," *New York Times*, December 14, 2014. http://www.nytimes.com/2014/12/15/technology/stockholms-housing-shortage-threatens-to-stifle-start-ups.html.

33. Eliot Brown, "Berlin's Housing Problems Boil Over," *Wall Street Journal*, October 6, 2015. http://www.wsj.com/articles/berlins-housing-problems-boil-over-1444123804.

34. Moises Mendoza, "Neukölln Nasties: Foreigners Feel Accused in Berlin Gentrification Row," *Der Speigel*, March 11, 2011. http://www.spiegel.de/international/germany/neukoelln-nasties-foreigners-feel-accused-in-berlin-gentrification-row-a-750297.html.

35. http://gis.nyc.gov/doitt/nycitymap/template?z = 6&p = 997656,199861&a = ZOLA&c = ZOLA&f = ZONING.

36. Nicole P. Marwell, *Bargaining for Brooklyn: Community Organizations in the Entrepreneurial City* (Chicago: University of Chicago Press, 2007); and Jen Chung, "Rezoning Williamsburg and Greenpoint," *Gothamist*, April 1, 2005. http://gothamist.com/2005/04/01/rezoning_greenpoint_and_williamsburg.php.

37. Norm Oder, "Affordable Housing the Focus at the New Domino Hearing," Atlantic Yards/Pacific Park Report, August 1, 2007. http://atlanticyardsreport.blogspot.com/2007/08/affordable-housing-focus-at-new-domino.html.

38. Jessica Dailey, "Mapping the Top Best-Selling Buildings of 2012," *Curbed New York*, January 29, 2013. http://ny.curbed.com/maps/mapping-the-10-best-selling-buildings-of-2012.

39. "Community District Needs: Brooklyn," New York City Department of Planning, 2012. http://www1.nyc.gov/assets/planning/download/pdf/about/publications/bkneeds_2012.pdf.

40. Stephen Smith, "Brooklyn's Affordability Crisis Is No Accident," *CityLab*, January

16, 2013. http://www.citylab.com/tech/2013/01/brooklyns-affordabilty-crisis-no-accident/4401. See also Amanda Waldroupe, "Q and A: Stephen Smith of Market Urbanism," *Bklynr*, May 14, 2015. http://bklynr.com/qa-stephen-smith-of-market-urbanism.

41. Furman Center for Real Estate and Public Policy, "How Have Recent Rezonings Affected the City's Ability to Grow?" March 2010. http://furmancenter.org/files/publications/Rezonings_Furman_Center_Policy_Brief_March_2010.pdf.

42. Robert Frank, *The Conquest of Cool Business Culture, Counterculture and the Rise of Hip Consumerism* (Chicago: University of Chicago Press, 1997).

43. Jack Conte, "Pamplemouse 2014 Tour Profits (or Lack Thereof," Medium.com, November 24, 2014. https://medium.com/@jackconte/pomplamoose-2014-tour-profits-674 35851ba37#.j267lc368.

44. The phrase comes from Peter Jon Lindberg, "The Brooklynization of the World," *Condé Nast Traveler*, August 19, 2015. http://www.cntraveler.com/stories/2015-08-19/the-brooklynization-of-the-world.

CHAPTER 5

1. Brooklyn Navy Yard Development Corporation website, "History." http://brooklynnavyyard.org/the-navy-yard/history.

2. Charles V. Bagli, "De Niro and Miramax Plan a Studio at the Brooklyn Navy Yard," *New York Times*, April 29, 1999. http://www.nytimes.com/1999/04/29/nyregion/de-niro-and-miramax-plan-a-film-studio-at-the-brooklyn-navy-yard.html.

3. Terry Pristin,"De Niro Group Replaced as Developers in Brooklyn," *New York Times*, October 4, 1999. http://www.nytimes.com/1999/10/14/nyregion/de-niro-group-replaced-as-developers-in-brooklyn.html.

4. Nina Rappaport, *Vertical Urban Factory* (New York: Actar, 2016). Interview with the author, winter 2015.

5. Pratt Center for Community Development, "Brooklyn Navy Yard: An Analysis of Its Economic Impact and Opportunities for Replication," February 2013.

6. http://kingscountydistillery.com/about.

7. Lore Croghan, "Techies Coming to Brooklyn Navy Yard with Futuristic New Inventions, New Jobs," *NY Daily News*, March 24, 2013. http://www.nydailynews.com/new-york/brooklyn/techies-coming-brooklyn-navy-yard-futuristic-new-inventions-new-jobs-article-1.1295443.

8. Christian, "Air Force Special Tactics Goes for Crye Armour—Because Delta Has 'Em," *Kit Up* February 28, 2011. http://kitup.military.com/2011/02/air-force-special-tactics-goes-for-crye-armor-because-delta-has-em.html.

9. "After Cooper: Crye Precision," March 6, 2013, Cooper Union website. http://www.cooper.edu/about/news/after-cooper-crye-precision.

10. Jonathan Bowles, "Manufacturing in NYC: A Snapshot," Center for the Urban

Future, November 2015. https://nycfuture.org/data/info/manufacturing-in-nyc-a-snapshot.

11. John Surico, "Q and A with David Ehlenberg, of the Brooklyn Navy Yard Corporation," *Bklynr*, December 11, 2014. http://bklynr.com/qa-david-ehrenberg-of-the-brooklyn-navy-yard-development-corporation.

12. Andy Newman, "Pfizer's Birthplace, Soon Without Pfizer," *New York Times*, January 28, 2007. http://www.nytimes.com/2007/01/28/nyregion/28pfizer.html?_r = 0.

13. Aaron Chatterji et al., "Clusters of Entrepreneurship and Innovation," NBER Working Paper 09013, 2013. http://www.nber.org/papers/w19013.

14. Amy Cortese, "Entrepreneurial Incubators: Brooklyn's Smartest Start-Ups Cook Cheek-by-Jowl in Unconventional Kitchens," *Brooklyn Edible*, Summer 2012. http://www.ediblebrooklyn.com/2012/entrepreneurial-incubators.

15. Greenpoint Manufacturing and Design Center website. http://www.gmdconline.org/about-us.

16. Mayara Guimaraes and Reuven Blau, "New Report Shows Booming Manufacturing Sector—and Rapid Gentrification—in Gowanus Canal Zone," *NY Daily News*, September 24, 2013, http://www.nydailynews.com/new-york/brooklyn/gentrification-manufactur ing-side-side-gowanus-article-1.1466523.

17. Danielle Schlanger, "Industry City Unveils 1 Billion Dollar Plan," *Commercial Observer*, March 9, 2015. https://commercialobserver.com/2015/03/industry-city-unveils-1-billion-plan.

18. Daniel Geiger,"Brooklyn Industrial Center Is Being Turned into a Major Retail Hub," *Crain's New York*, June 23, 2016. http://www.crainsnewyork.com/article/20160623/REAL_ESTATE/160629918.

19. Liam la Guerre, "The Plan: Inside Time Inc.'s Brooklyn Offices at Industry City," *Commercial Observer*, March 9, 2016. https://commercialobserver.com/2016/03/the-plan-inside-time-inc-s-brooklyn-offices-at-industry-city.

20. Keiko Morris, "A New Office Building for the Brooklyn Navy Yard," *Wall Street Journal*, July 6, 2015. http://www.wsj.com/articles/a-new-office-building-for-brooklyn-navy-yard-1436230346.

21. Thomas Di Napoli, "An Economic Snapshot of Brooklyn," May 2014. http://osc.state.ny.us/osdc/rpt4-2015.pdf#search = %20brooklyn%20manufacturing.

22. Corinne Ramey, "Sweet 'N Low Closes Factory in Brooklyn," *Wall Street Journal*, January 8, 2016. http://www.wsj.com/articles/sweetn-low-closes-factory-in-brooklyn-1452285662.

23. Sophie Quinton, "In Manufacturing, Blue Collar Jobs Need White Collar Training," *National Journal*, February 27, 2102, reprinted in Yahoo News. https://www.yahoo.com/news/manufacturing-blue-collar-jobs-white-collar-training-055935953.html.

24. Rosa Goldensohn, "Manufacturers See Good Jobs Go Unfilled as Brooklyn Residents Lack Work Experience," *Crain's*, June 22, 2016. http://www.crainsnewyork.com/article/20160622/SMALLBIZ/160629945.

25. Center for the Urban Future, "Making It Here: The Future of Manufacturing in New York City," July 2016. https://nycfuture.org/pdf/Making_It_Here_Report.pdf.

CHAPTER 6

1. Joseph Coscarelli, "Spike Lee's Amazing Rant Against Gentrification: We've Been Here!" *New York* magazine, February 25, 2014.

2. Much of the following history relies on Craig Steven Wilder, *A Covenant with Color: Race and Social Power in Brooklyn 1636–1990* (New York: Columbia University Press, 2000). See also Brian Purnell, *Fighting Jim Crow in the County of Kings: The Congress of Racial Equality in Brooklyn* (Louisville: University of Kentucky Press, 2013).

3. Craig Wilder and Harold X. Connolly, *A Ghetto Grows in Brooklyn* (New York: New York University Press, 1977).

4. Kenneth T. Jackson first wrote about the subject in "Race, Ethnicity, and Real Estate Appraisal," *Journal of Urban History*, August 1980, 419–52, and expanded on it in his well-known book *Crabgrass Frontier: The Suburbanization of the United States* (New York: Oxford University Press, 1985). Also see Amy Hiller, "Redlining and the Homeowner's Loan Corporation," *Journal of Urban History*, 2003, 394–420.

5. Beryl Satter, *Family Properties: How the Struggle over Race and Real Estate Transformed Chicago and Urban America* (London: Picador, 2010).

6. Connolly, *A Ghetto Grows in Brooklyn*, 206.

7. Matias Echanove, "Bed-Stuy on the Move: Demographic Trends and Economic Development in the Heart of Brooklyn," master's thesis, Columbia University, 2003, poster at http://urbanology.org/bedstuy.

8. Joshua B. Freeman, *Working Class New York: Life and Labor Since World War II* (New York: New Press, 2001), 187.

9. James T. Fisher, *On the Irish Waterfront: The Crusader, the Movie, and the Soul of the Port of New York* (Ithaca, NY: Cornell University Press, 2009), 9.

10. Suzanne Spellen, "The Great Milk Wars Part 4," Brownstoner website, November 17, 2011. http://www.brownstoner.com/history/walkabout-the-great-milk-wars-conclusion.

11. Echanove, "Bed-Stuy on the Move."

12. Walter C. Rucker and James N. Upton, *Encyclopedia of America's Race Riots*. Greenwood, 2011 vol. 1.

13. Jack Newfield, *Robert Kennedy: A Memoir* (New York: Plume, 1969), 87.

14. Ibid., p. 92.

15. Jeff Coplon, "The Tipping of Jefferson Avenue, *New York* magazine, April 15, 2005. http://nymag.com/nymag/features/11775.

16. "This Is the Story of One Block in Bed-Stuy," *New York* magazine, November 17, 2015. http://nymag.com/oneblock.

17. Wilder and Connoly/Connolly, *A Ghetto Grows in Brooklyn*, 125.

18. Clarence Taylor, *The Black Churches of Brooklyn* (New York: Columbia University Press, 1994), 104, 132.

19. Purnell, *Fighting Jim Crow in the County of Kings*, 21.

20. Taylor, *The Black Churches of Brooklyn*.

21. Alison Gregor, "Bedford Stuyvesant: Diverse and Changing," *New York Times*, July 9, 2014. http://www.nytimes.com/2014/07/13/realestate/bedford-stuyvesant-diverse-and-changing.html.

22. Ibid.

23. "Tract 1237," All-City New York website. http://walk.allcitynewyork.com/2011/08/tract-1237.html. Census Tract 1237 Google maps: https://www.google.com/maps/d/u/0/viewer?ll=40.688969%2C-.73.950176&spn=0.045557%2C0.072956&msa=0&z=13&source=embed&ie=UTF8&mid=1wzTCekQ052NRG0VgQWDIl80Myos.

24. Lance Freeman, *There Goes the 'Hood: Views of Gentrification from the Ground Up* (Philadelphia: Temple University Press, 2011), 56.

25. Echanove, "Bed-Stuy on the Move."

26. Tracy E. Hopkins, "In Her Neighborhood," *University of Chicago Magazine*, September–October 2009. http://magazine.uchicago.edu/0910/arts_sciences/neighborhood.shtml.

27. CPEX, 2014 Brooklyn Retail Report, http://cpexre.com/system/research_items/documents/000/000/093/original/2016_Brooklyn_Retail_Report.pdf?1454936733.

28. Furman Center for Real Estate and Urban Policy, "State of New York City's Housing and Neighborhoods: 2015 Report," 72.

29. Citizens' Committee for Children, "Concentrated Poverty in New York City," April, 2012. http://www.cccnewyork.org/wp-content/publications/CCCReport.ConcentratedPoverty.April-2012.pdf.

30. "Brooklyn Community District 3: Bedford Stuyvesant," Community Health Profiles 2015, New York City Department of Health. https://www1.nyc.gov/assets/doh/downloads/pdf/data/2015chp-bk3.pdf.

31. Citizens' Committee for Children, "Keeping Track Online: Reading Test Scores," 2015. http://data.cccnewyork.org/data/map/148/reading-test-scores-common-core-3rd-grade#148/a/5/240/21/a.

32. Inside Schools, "Boys and Girls High School," InsideSchools.org, Center of New City Affairs at the New School. http://insideschools.org/component/schools/school/720.

33. Rachel Monahan and Meredith Kolodner, "Number of Homeless Students Jumps 100%," *NY Daily News*, January 17, 2010. http://www.nydailynews.com/new-york/education/number-homeless-students-jumps-100-19-20-schools-shutdown-list-article-1.460919.

34. William Julius Wilson, "Afterword: Second Edition," *The Truly Disadvantaged: The Inner City, the Underclass and Public Policy* (Chicago: University of Chicago Press, 2012), 255.

35. Mary Patillo-McCoy, *Black on the Block: The Politics of Race and Class in the City* (Chicago: University of Chicago Press, 2008).

36. Monique Taylor, *Harlem Between Heaven and Hell* (St. Paul: University of Minnesota Press, 2002).

37. Coscarelli, "Spike Lee's Amazing Rant Against Gentrification."

38. Gregor, "Bedford Stuyvesant: Diverse and Changing."

CHAPTER 7

1. NYU Furman Center, "State of New York City's Housing and Neighborhoods 2014." 103. http://furmancenter.org/files/

sotc.NYUFurmanCenter_SOC2014_HighRes.pdf; and New York City Community Health Provider Partners, "Brooklyn Community Needs Assessment," October 13, 2014. http://www.health.ny.gov/health_care/medicaid/redesign/dsrip/pps_applications/docs/maimonides_medical_center/3.8_maimonides_cna.pdf.

2. Joe Cortright and Dillon Mahmoudi, "Lost in Place: Why the Persistence and Spread of Poverty—Not Gentrification—Is Our Biggest Urban Challenge," *City Observatory*, December 2014. http://cityobservatory.org/wp-content/uploads/2014/12/LostinPlace_12.4.pdf.

3. Alfred Kazin, *A Walker in the City* (New York: Houghton Mifflin Harcourt, 1969), 10.

4. Wendell E. Pritchett, *Brownsville, Brooklyn: Blacks, Jews, and the Changing Face of the Ghetto* (Chicago: University of Chicago Press, 2003), 10.

5. Stone Avenue Library, Brooklyn Public Library website. http://www.bklynlibrary.org/locations/stone-avenue/photos.

6. "Brownsville Clinic Open 99 Years Ago," Margaret Sanger Papers Project website, posted October 15, 2016. https://sangerpapers.wordpress.com/tag/brownsville-clinic.

7. Carole Bell Ford, *Girls: The Jewish Women of Brownsville, Brooklyn* (Albany: State University of New York Press, 1999).

8. Kazin, *A Walker in the City*. 56.

9. Nathan Glazer and Daniel Patrick Moynihan, *Beyond the Melting Pot: Negroes, Puerto Ricans, Jews, Italians, and Irish of New York City* (Cambridge, MA: MIT Press, 1970).

10. Roger Waldinger, *Still the Promised City* (Cambridge, MA: Harvard University Press, 1996).

11. Gerald Sorin, *Nurturing Neighborhood: Brownsville Boys' Club and Jewish Community in Urban America* (New York: NYU Press, 1990).

12. Joel Schwartz, *The New York Approach: Robert Moses, Urban Liberals, and Redevelopment of the Inner City* (Columbus: Ohio State University Press, 1993).

13. Pritchett, *Brownsville, Brooklyn*.

14. Ibid.

15. Ibid., 206.

16. Nicholas Dagen Bloom, *Public Housing That Worked: New York in the Twentieth Century* (Philadelphia: University of Pennsylvania Press, 2014), 208–9.

17. Fred Siegel, *The Future Once Happened Here: New York, D.C., LA, and the Fate of America's Big Cities* (New York: Encounter, 1997).

18. Charles Hirschman, "Minorities in the Labor Market," in *Divided Opportunities: Minorities, Poverty and Public Policy*, ed. Gary Sandefur and Marta Tienda (New York: Springer, 1988), 66.

19. Vincent Cannato, *The Ungovernable City* (New York: Basic Books, 2009), 549.

20. Harold X. Connolly, *A Ghetto Grows in Brooklyn* (New York: New York University Press, 1977).

21. Steven and Abigail Thernstrom, *America in Black and White: One Nation Indivisible* (New York: Simon & Schuster, 1997).

22. Edward L. Glaeser and Matthew Kahn, "From Lindsay to Giuliani: The Decline of the Local Safety Net?" *Federal Reserve Bank of New York Economic Policy Review* 5, no. 2 (1999): 117–32.

23. Quoted in Benjamin Schwartz, "Building an Underclass: How Urban Planners Helped Demolish Britain's Working Families," American Conservative website, March 15, 2015. http://www.theamericanconservative.com/articles/building-an-underclass.

24. Walter Thabit, *How East New York Became a Ghetto* (New York: New York University Press, 2003).

25. Wendy Wang, "The Link Between a College Education and a Lasting Marriage," Pew Research Center, December 4, 2015. http://www.pewresearch.org/fact-tank/2015/12/04/education-and-marriage.

26. Kay S. Hymowitz, *Marriage and Caste in America: Separate and Unequal Families in a Post-Marital Age* (Chicago: Ivan R. Dee, 2007).

27. Pritchett, *Brownsville, Brooklyn*, 157.

28. Richard Price, "The Rise and Fall of Public Housing in NYC: A Subjective Overview," *Guernica*, October 1, 2014. https://www.guernicamag.com/features/the-rise-and-fall-of-public-housing-in-nyc.

29. Bloom, *Public Housing That Worked*, 222.

30. Dana Goldstein, *The Teacher Wars: A History of America's Most Embattled Profession* (New York: Knopf Doubleday, 2014).

31. Much of the following history comes from Jerald E. Podair, *The Strike That Changed New York: Blacks, Whites, and the Ocean Hill Brownsville Crisis* (New Haven, CT: Yale University Press, 2008).

32. Quoted in Daniel Hiram Perlman, *Justice, Justice: School Politics and the End of Liberalism* (City: Peter Lang, 2008), 138.

33. Podair, *The Strike That Changed New York*, 65.

34. Ibid., 62.

35. Ibid., 124.

36. Ibid., 208. ʼ

37. Oscar Newman, *Defensible Space: Crime Prevention Through Urban Design* (New York: Macmillan, 1973).

38. Thabit, *How East New York Became a Ghetto*.

39. Ginia Bellafonte, "A Housing Solution Gone Awry," *New York Times*, June 1, 2013. http://www.nytimes.com/2013/06/02/nyregion/in-marcus-garvey-village-a-housing-solution-gone-awry.html.

40. Kym Leibman, Lauren Tenney, and Susan Segert, "Good Design Alone Can't Change Society," *Progressive Planning Magazine*, Summer 2005.

41. Jack Newfield, "Rev vs. Rev," *New York* magazine, January 7, 2002. http://nymag.com/nymag/features/5570.

42. Mike Tyson, *The Undisputed Truth* (New York: Blue Rider, 2013), Kindle edition.

43. Pete Hamill, "Brooklyn: The Sane Alternative," *New York* magazine, July 14, 1969. http://nymag.com/nymag/features/46992/index7.html.

44. Greg Donaldson, *The Ville: Cops and Kids in Urban America* (Oxford: Oxford University Press, 1993).

45. Alison Mitchell, "2 Teenagers Shot to Death in Brooklyn School," *New York Times*, February 27, 1992. http://www.nytimes.com/1992/02/27/nyregion/2-teen-agers-shot-to-death-in-a-brooklyn-school.html?pagewanted=all.

46. Furman Center, State of New York City's Housing and Neighborhoods, 2015 edition. http://furmancenter.org/research/sonychan.

47. https://www.dnainfo.com/new-york/crime-safety-report/brooklyn/brownsville.

48. Mosi Secret, "On the Brink in Brownsville," *New York Times*, May 1, 2014. http://www.nytimes.com/2014/05/04/magazine/on-the-brink-in-brownsville.html.

49. Sarah Ryley et al., "NYCHA Units See Spike in Crime," *NY Daily News*, April 6, 2014. http://www.nydailynews.com/new-york/nyc-crime/nycha-residents-live-fear-major-crimes-public-housing-soar-article-1.1747195.

50. Patrick Sharkey, *Stuck in Place: Urban Neighborhoods and the End of Progress Toward Racial Equality* (Chicago: University of Chicago Press, 2013), 40.

51. See also Cortright and Mahmoudi, "Lost in Place"; Robert J. Sampson, "Moving to Inequality: Neighborhood Effects and Experiments Meet Structure," *American Journal of Sociology*, July 2008, 189–231. http://www.ncbi.nlm.nih.gov/pmc/articles/PMC4211272; and Scott Winship, "When Moving Matters: Residential and Economic Mobility Trends in America, 1880–2010," Manhattan Institute, November 10, 2015. https://www.manhattan-institute.org/html/when-moving-matters-residential-and-economic-mobility-trends-america-1880-2010-8048.html.

52. Sharkey, *Stuck in Place*, 162.

53. Eric Chyn, "Moved to Opportunity: The Long-Run Effect of Housing Demolition on Labor Market Outcomes for Children," Job Market Paper, University of Michigan Economics Department, July 2016. http://www-personal.umich.edu/~ericchyn/Chyn_Moved_to_Opportunity.pdf.

54. Malcolm Gladwell, "Starting Over," *The New Yorker*, August 24, 2015. http://www.newyorker.com/magazine/2015/08/24/starting-over-dept-of-social-studies-malcolm-gladwell.

55. Mireya Navarro, "As New York Rents Soar, Public Housing Becomes a Lifelong Refuge," *New York Times*, August 3, 2015.

56. "Resident Policies and Procedures," New York City Housing Authority. https://www1.nyc.gov/assets/nycha/downloads/pdf/RESIDENTS.POLICIESPROCEDURES.OCCUPANCYSUCCESSION.pdf.

CHAPTER 8

1. http://www.census.gov/quickfacts/table/RHI105210/36047.

2. New York City Department of City Planning, "The Newest New Yorkers," 2013. http://www1.nyc.gov/assets/planning/download/pdf/data-maps/nyc-population/nny2013/nny_2013.pdf.

3. Ibid., 2.

4. David M. Remeirs, *Still the Golden Door: The Third World Comes to America* (New York: Columbia University Press, 1992), 104.

5. "The Newest New Yorkers," 36.

6. Ellen D. Wu, *Asian Americans and the Origins of the Model Minority* (Princeton, NJ: Princeton University Press, 2013).

7. Pew Research Center, "The Rise of Asian-Americans," April 4, 2013. http://www.pewsocialtrends.org/2012/06/19/the-rise-of-asian-americans.

8. Kate Hooper and Jeanne Batalova, "Chinese Immigrants in the United States," Migration Policy Institute, 2015. http://www.migrationpolicy.org/article/chinese-immigrants-united-states. and Kirk Semple, Joseph Goldstein, and Jeffrey E. Singer, "Asylum Fraud in Chinatown," *New York Times*, February 22, 2014. http://www.nytimes.com/2014/02/23/nyregion/asylum-fraud-in-chinatown-industry-of-lies.html.

9. Patrick Radden Keefe, "Snakeheads and Smuggling: The Dynamics of Illegal Chinese Immigration," *World Policy Journal*, Spring 2009, 33–44. Idem *The Snakehead: An Epic Tale of the Chinatown Underworld and the American Dream* (New York: Doubleday, 2009).

10. Conversation with the author, April 2014.

11. Asian American Federation, "Profile of New York City's Chinese Americans," 2013. http://www.aafny.org/cic/briefs/chinese2013.pdf.

12. "The Newest New Yorkers," 104.

13. Marlene Kim, "Unfairly Disadvantaged?" Economic Policy Institute, April 5, 2012. http://www.epi.org/publication/ib323-asian-american-unemployment/Figure B.

14. Min Zhou, "Chinatown: The Socioeconomic Potential of an Urban Enclave" (Philadelphia: Temple University Press, 1992), 99; idem *Contemporary Chinese America* (Philadelphia: Temple University Press, 2009), 118.

15. See, for instance, Sean F. Reardon, "The Widening Academic Achievement Gap Between Rich and Poor: New Evidence and Possible Explanations," in R. Murnane and G. Duncan, eds., *Whither Opportunity? Rising Inequality, Schools and Children's Life Chances* (New York: Russell Sage Foundation, 2011), 91–116.

16. Richard Fry, "The Higher Dropout Rate of Foreign Born Teens," Pew Research Center, 2005, p. 1.

17. Beth Fertig, "Around Sunset Park, Tutoring Is Key to Top High Schools," WNYC, March 12, 2013. http://www.wnyc.org/story/301916-around-sunset-park-tutoring-is-key-to-top-high-schools.

18. Kyle Spencer, "For Asians, School Tests Are Vital Steppingstones," *New York Times*, October 26, 2012, A18. http://www.nytimes.com/2012/10/27/education/a-grueling-admissions-test-highlights-a-racial-divide.html.

19. Ibid.

20. Pew Research Center, "The Rise of Asian-Americans."

21. Zhou, *Contemporary Chinese America*, 112, 194–95.

22. Spencer, "For Asians, School Tests Are Vital Steppingstones," 2012, note 18.

23. National Center for Children in Poverty, "New York Demographics of Low-Income Children." http://nccp.org/profiles/NY_profile_6.html; and "The Newest New Yorkers," 98.

24. Raj Chetty et al., "Where Is the Land of Opportunity?" June 2014. http://www.rajchetty.com/chettyfiles/mobility_geo.pdf.

25. Conversation with the author, April 2014.

26. Min Zhou writes about this extensively in her work. See n. 14 above.

27. Katie Nelson, "Asian Boom in Brooklyn," *The Daily News*, September 15, 2011.

http://www.nydailynews.com/new-york/brooklyn/asian-boom-brooklyn-n-lline-neighborhoods-brooklyn-census-data-shows-article-1.955293; and Gabby Warshawer, "Signs Denote Changing Times in Bensonhurst," *Wall Street Journal*, June 27, 2014. http://www.wsj.com/articles/signs-denote-changing-times-in-bensonhurst-1403916 852.

28. Wendy Wang, "Interracial Marriage: Who Is 'Marrying Out'?" Pew Research Center, June 12, 2015. http://www.pewresearch.org/fact-tank/2015/06/12/interracial-marriage-who-is-marrying-out.

CHAPTER 9

1. http://datausa.io/profile/geo/canarsie-%26-flatlands-puma-ny.

2. Much of this history is taken from Jonathan Rieder, *Canarsie: The Jews and Italians of Brooklyn Against Liberalism* (Cambridge, MA: Harvard University Press, 1985), Kindle edition.

3. Neil S. Friedman, "South Shore H.S. to Close by 2010," *Canarsie Courier*. http://www.canarsiecourier.com/news/2006-12-14/Front_Page/001.html?print = 1.

4. Ronald Smothers, "29 Junior High School Students from Brownsville Learn a Harsh Lesson on a Bus," *New York Times*, October 19, 1972. http://www.nytimes.com/1972/10/19/archives/29-juniorhigh-students-from-brownsville-learn-a-harsh-lesson-on-a.html.

5. E. R. Shipp, "Canarsie's Long-Held Racial Anxieties Resurface," *New York Times*, August 4, 1991. http://www.nytimes.com/1991/08/04/nyregion/canarsie-s-long-held-racial-anxieties-resurface.html?pagewanted = all.

6. Ibid.

7. "New York City Demographic Shifts: 2000–2010," Center for Urban Research. http://www.urbanresearchmaps.org/plurality; and http://www.city-data.com/neighborhood/Canarsie-Brooklyn-NY.html.

8. Craig Steven Wilder, *A Covenant with Color: Race and Social Power in Brooklyn* (New York: Columbia University Press, 2000).

9. Monica Anderson, "A Rising Share of the U.S. Black Population Is Foreign-Born," Pew Research Center, April 9, 2015. http://www.pewsocialtrends.org/2015/04/09/a-rising-share-of-the-u-s-black-population-is-foreign-born.

10. http://www1.nyc.gov/assets/planning/download/pdf/data-maps/nyc-population/census2010/pgrhc.pdf.

11. Jerome Krase and Judith N. DeSena, *Race, Class, and Gentrification: A View from the Street* (New York: Lexington, 2016), 39.

12. Alison Mitchell, "Bitterness for One Family and Relief for Another," *New York Times,* October 30, 1992. http://www.nytimes.com/1992/10/30/nyregion/bitterness-for-one-family-and-relief-for-the-other.html.

13. Suzanne Model, *West Indian Immigrants: A Black Success Story?* (New York: Russell Sage Foundation, 2008), 20.

14. Thomas Sowell, *Ethnic America* (New York: Basic Books, 1981).

15. Monica Anderson, "A Statistical Portrait of the Black Immigrant Population," Pew Research Center, April 2015.

16. Sam Roberts, "Black Incomes Surpass White in Queens," *New York Times*, October 1, 2006. http://www.nytimes.com/2006/10/01/nyregion/01census.html?_r = 0.

17. Roger David Waldinger, *Still the Promised City* (Cambridge, MA: Harvard University Press, 1996), 119.

18. Colin Powell, *My American Journey: An Autobiography* (New York: Random House, 1995), Kindle edition.

19. Model, *West Indian Immigrants*, 19.

20. Waldinger, *Still the Promised City*, 121.

21. M. Kohil, "Health Care Industries and the New York City Labor Market," *Monthly Labor Review*, September 2009.

22. Roger David Waldinger and Michael I. Licter, *How the Other Half Works: Immigration and the Social Organization of Labor* (Berkeley: University of California Press, 2003).

23. "Migration in Jamaica: A Country Profile," Organization of Migration, 2010.

24. Paule Marshall, *Brown Girl, Brownstones* (New York: Chatham, 1971), 4, 11.

25. Furman Center, "Brooklyn Community District Profiles," State of New York City's Housing and Neighborhoods, 2011.

26. Mary C. Waters and Jennifer E. Sykes, "Spare the Rod, Ruin the Child?" in ed., Nancy Foner, *Across Generations: Immigrant Families in America* (New York: New York University Press, 2009), 72–97.

27. Ibid., 81.

28. Van C. Tran, "More than Just Black: Cultural Perils and Opportunities in Inner-City Neighborhoods," in *The Cultural Matrix: Understanding Black Youth*, ed. Orlando Patterson (Cambridge, MA: Harvard University Press, 2005), 252–80.

29. Nelson George, *City Kid: A Writer's of Ghetto Life and Post-Soul* (New York: Viking, 2009), Kindle edition.

30. Anderson, "A Statistical Portrait of the Black Immigrant Population."

31. Sara Rimer and Karen Anderson, "Top Colleges Take More Blacks, but Which Ones?" *New York Times,* June 24, 2004. http://www.nytimes.com/2004/06/24/us/top-colleges-take-more-blacks-but-which-ones.html?_r = 0%20former.

32. Douglas S. Massey et al., "Black Immigrants and Black Natives Attending Selective Colleges and Universities in the United States," *American Journal of Education*, February 2007, 243–71.

33. "The Shirley Chisholm Project." http://shirleychisholmproject.tumblr.com/page/4.

34. http://www.city-data.com/neighborhood/Canarsie-Brooklyn-NY.html.

35. Philip Kasinitz et al., *Inheriting the City: The Children of Immigrants Come of Age* (Cambridge, MA: Harvard University Press, 2009).

36. Model, *West Indian Immigrants*.

37. Kasinitz et al., *Inheriting the City*, 139.

38. Meredith Kolodner, "Study Shows Larger City High Schools Posting Declining Graduation Rates," *NY Daily News*, June 17, 2009. http://www.nydailynews.com/new-york/education/study-shows-larger-city-high-schools-posting-declining-graduation-rates-article-1.375166.

39. Friedman, "South Shore H.S. to Close by 2010."

40. District 18 Survey Results, New York City Department of Education, 2014–15.

http://schools.nyc.gov/NR/rdonlyres/49BA6337-2339-43FD-A860-6E054B470A6A/0/
Survey_2015_District_18.pdf.

41. Richard Alba and Nancy Foner, *Strangers No More: Immigration and the Challenges of Assimilation in North America and Western Europe* (Princeton, NJ: Princeton University Press, 2015).

42. Ajay Chaudry and Karina Fortuny, "Children of Immigrants: Family and Parental Characteristics," Urban Institute, May 2010.

43. Kasinitz, *Inheriting the City*, 221.

44. Ibid.

45. Ibid., 165.

CONCLUSION

★ Scott Martelle, *Detroit: A Biography* (Chicago, Chicago Review Press, 2014) p. 74.

1. "Focus on Gentrification," in "State of New York City's Housing and Neighborhoods 2015," Furman Center for Real Estate and Policy, May 2016.

2. Robert Beauregard, *When America Became Suburban* (Minneapolis: University of Minnesota, 2006), 19.

3. Susan Price, "This Is the City with the Largest Number of Woman-Led Start-Ups," *Fortune*, June 1, 2015. http://fortune.com/2015/06/01/this-is-the-city-with-the-largest-percentage-of-women-led-startups.

4. Adam Friedman, "Letter to the Editor," *Crain's*, June 29, 2016. http://www.crainsnewyork.com/article/20160629/OPINION/160629844/growth-of-nycs-creative-class-threatens-to-worsen-inequality.

5. Red Tape Commission, "60 Ways to Cut Red Tape and Help Small Businesses Grow," Office of the Comptroller, March 2016. http://comptroller.nyc.gov/wp-content/uploads/documents/RedTapeReport.pdf.

6. Cara Eisenpress, "Brooklyn's Fancy Artisanal Food Businesses Are Getting Chewed Up," *Crain's*, May 29, 2016. http://www.crainsnewyork.com/article/20160529/SMALLBIZ/160529854/brooklyns-fancy-artisanal-food-businesses-are-getting-chewed-up.

7. Jennifer Conlin, "Last Stop on the L-Train: Detroit," *New York Times*, July 10, 2015. http://www.nytimes.com/2015/07/12/fashion/last-stop-on-the-l-train-detroit.html.

8. Elizabeth A. Harris, "New York City's High School Graduation Rate Tops 70%," *New York Times*, January 11, 2016. http://www.nytimes.com/2016/01/12/nyregion/new-york-citys-high-school-graduation-rate-tops-70.html.

9. "CUNY Master Plan 2016–2020," draft. http://www1.cuny.edu/sites/6/wp-content/uploads/sites/6/media-assets/CUNY-Master-plan_DRAFT_20160507.pdf.

10. Walter Sander and William A. Tesla, "Children and Cities," New Geography website, August 23, 2013. http://www.newgeography.com/content/003889-children-and-cities.

11. Council of State Governments, "Middle Skills to the Middle Class," May/June 2016. http://www.csg.org/pubs/capitolideas/2014_nov_dec/MiddleSkills.aspx.

12. Ann Norris, "Stuck in the Middle: Job Market Polarization," *Monthly Labor Review,* Bureau of Labor Statistics, July 2015. http://www.bls.gov/opub/mlr/2015/beyond-bls/stuck-in-the-middle-job-market-polarization.htm.

13. Tamar Jacoby and Shawn M. Dougherty, "The New CTE: New York City as Laboratory for America," Manhattan Institute for Policy Research, March 2016. http://www.manhattan-institute.org/html/new-cte-new-york-city-laboratory-america-8688.htm.

14. W. Bradford Wilcox, Robert Lerman, and Joseph Price, "Mobility and Money in U.S. States: The Marriage Effect," Brookings Institution, December 7, 2015. https://www.brookings.edu/2015/12/07/mobility-and-money-in-u-s-states-the-marriage-effect.

15. http://www.sustainabledc.org/wp-content/uploads/2012/10/SDC-Summary-Document-2-19_0.pdf.

16. Luke Hammill, "Portland Approves a Major Twenty Year Growth Plan, Looking to 2035. *The Oregonian,* June 15, 2016. http://www.oregonlive.com/portland/index.ssf/2016/06/portland_approves_major_20-yea.html.

17. https://nextcity.org/daily/entry/seattle-driving-downtown-cut-cars-traffic.

18. http://www1.nyc.gov/assets/planning/download/pdf/data-maps/nyc-population/projections_briefing_booklet_2010_2040.pdf.

19. Furman Center, "How Have Recent Rezonings Affected the City's Ability to Grow." Furman Center, "How Have Recent Rezonings Affected the City's Ability to Grow?," Policy Brief, March 2010. http://furmancenter.org/files/publications/Rezonings_Furman_Center_Policy_Brief_March_2010.pdf.

20. Ibid.

21. Peter D. Salins, "De Blasio's Misguided Housing Plan," *City Journal,* September 1, 2015. http://www.city-journal.org/html/de-blasio's-misguided-housing-plan-11655.html.

22. Quoctrung Bui, Matt A. V. Chaban, and Jeremy White, "40 Percent of Buildings in Manhattan Could Not Be Built Today," *New York Times,* May 20, 2106. http://www.nytimes.com/interactive/2016/05/19/upshot/forty-percent-of-manhattans-buildings-could-not-be-built-today.html?action = click&contentCollection = Opinion& module = Trending&version = Full&region = Marginalia&pgtype = article& _r = 0.

23. Urban Land Institute, "Priced Out: Persistence of the Workforce Housing Gap in the San Francisco Area," June 2012. http://uli.org/wp-content/uploads/ULI-Documents/Priced-Out-San-Francisco-FINAL.pdf.

24. Marc Linder and Lawrence S. Zacharias, *Of Cabbages and Kings County* (Iowa City: University of Iowa Press, 1999).

Index

About the Author

Kay S. Hymowitz is the William E. Simon Fellow at the Manhattan Institute and a contributing editor of *City Journal*. She is the author of four books including *Marriage and Caste in America: Separate and Unequal Families in a Post-Marital Age*, *Liberation's Children: Parents and Kids in a Postmodern Age*, and *Manning Up: How the Rise of Women Has Turned Men Into Boys*. She resides in Brooklyn, New York.

—